TITLES AVAILABLE IN THE BILL OF RIGHTS SERIES

THE FIRST AMENDMENT

The Establishment of Religion Clause: Its Constitutional History and the Contemporary Debate
    Edited by Alan Brownstein

The Free Exercise of Religion Clause: Its Constitutional History and the Contemporary Debate
    Edited by Thomas C. Berg

Freedom of Speech: Its Constitutional History and the Contemporary Debate
    Edited by Vikram David Amar

Freedom of the Press: Its Constitutional History and the Contemporary Debate
    Edited by Garrett Epps

BILL OF RIGHTS SERIES

Series Editor:
David B. Oppenheimer, *Associate Dean,*
Golden Gate University School of Law

Advisory Committee

Erwin Chemerinsky
Dean and Professor of Law,
University of California, Irvine,
School of Law

Jesse Choper
Earl Warren Professor of Public Law,
University of California, Berkeley,
School of Law (Boalt Hall)

Sheila Rose Foster
Associate Dean for Academic Affairs and
Albert A. Walsh Professor of Law,
Fordham Law School

Cheryl Harris
Professor of Law,
University of California, Los Angeles,
School of Law

Marjorie Heins
Founder and Director,
Free Expression Policy Project (FEPP)

Kevin R. Johnson
Dean and Mabie-Apallas Professor of
Public Interest Law and Chicana/o Studies,
University of California, Davis,
School of Law (King Hall)

Carrie J. Menkel-Meadow
Professor of Law; A.B. Chettle, Jr., Chair in
Dispute Resolution and Civil Procedure,
Georgetown University Law Center

Robert C. Post
David Boies Professor of Law,
Yale Law School

john powell
Professor of Law, Gregory H. Williams Chair
in Civil Rights and Civil Liberties;
Executive Director, Kirwan Institute for the
Study of Race and Ethnicity,
Ohio State University,
Michael E. Moritz College of Law

Deborah L. Rhode
Ernest W. McFarland Professor of Law,
Stanford Law School

Stephanie M. Wildman
Professor of Law and Director for the Center
for Social Justice & Public Service,
Santa Clara University School of Law

Eric Ken Yamamoto
Professor of Law,
University of Hawaii, William S. Richardson
School of Law

THE FIRST AMENDMENT
FREEDOM OF SPEECH

THE FIRST AMENDMENT
FREEDOM OF SPEECH

Its Constitutional History and the Contemporary Debate

EDITED BY VIKRAM DAVID AMAR

Prometheus Books

59 John Glenn Drive
Amherst, New York 14228-2119

Published 2009 by Prometheus Books

Freedom of Speech (The First Amendment): Its Constitutional History and the Contemporary Debate.
Copyright © 2009 by Vikram David Amar. All rights reserved. No part of this publication may
be reproduced, stored in a retrieval system, or transmitted in any form or by any means, dig-
ital, electronic, mechanical, photocopying, recording, or otherwise, or conveyed via the Internet
or a Web site without prior written permission of the publisher, except in the case of brief quotations embodied in critical articles and reviews.

Inquiries should be addressed to
Prometheus Books
59 John Glenn Drive
Amherst, New York 14228–2119
VOICE: 716–691–0133, ext. 210
FAX: 716–691–0137
WWW.PROMETHEUSBOOKS.COM

13 12 11 10 09   5 4 3 2 1

Library of Congress Cataloging-in-Publication Data

Amar, Vikram David.
    The First Amendment, freedom of speech : its constitutional history and the
contemporary debate / edited by Vikram David Amar.
        p. cm. — (Bill of Rights series)
    Includes bibliographical references.
    ISBN 978–1–59102– 632–7 (pbk. : alk. paper)
    1. United States. Constitution. 1st Amendment 2. Freedom of speech—United States—
History. 3. Constitutional history—United States. I. Amar, Vikram.

KF4772.F5677 2009
342.7308'53—dc22

                                                                        2009009445

Printed in the United States of America on acid-free paper

CONTENTS

5

APPENDIXES

BILL OF RIGHTS
SERIES EDITOR'S PREFACE

Abortion; the death penalty; school prayer; the pledge of allegiance; torture; surveillance; tort reform; jury trials; preventative detention; firearm registration; censorship; privacy; police misconduct; birth control; school vouchers; prison crowding; taking property by public domain—these issues, torn from the headlines, cover many, if not most, of the major public disputes arising today, in the dawn of the twenty-first century. Yet they are resolved by our courts based on a document fewer than five hundred words long, drafted in the eighteenth century, and regarded by many at the time of its drafting as unnecessary. The Bill of Rights, the name we give the first ten amendments to the United States Constitution, is our basic source of law for resolving these issues. This series of books, of which this is volume 4, is intended to help us improve our understanding of the debates that gave rise to these rights, and of the continuing controversy about their meaning today.

When our Constitution was drafted, the framers were concerned with defining the structure and powers of our new federal government, and balancing its three branches. They didn't initially focus on the question of individual rights. The drafters organized the Constitution into seven sections, termed "Articles," each concerned with a specific area of federal authority. Article I sets forth the legislative powers of the Congress; Article II the executive powers of the president; Article III the judicial power of the federal courts. Article V governs the process for amending the Constitution. Article VI declares the supremacy of federal law on those subjects under federal jurisdiction, while Article VII provides the process for ratification. Only Article IV is concerned with individual rights, and only in a single sentence requiring states to give citizens of other states the same rights they provide to their own citizens. (Article IV also provides for the return of runaway slaves, a provision repealed in 1865 by the Thirteenth Amendment.)

When the Constitutional Convention completed its work, in 1787, it sent the Constitution to the states for adoption. The opponents of ratification, known as the "Anti-Federalists" because they opposed the strong federal government envisioned in the Constitution, argued that without a Bill of Rights the federal government would be a danger to liberty. The "Federalists," principally Alexander Hamilton, James Madison, and John Jay, responded in a series of anonymous newspaper articles now known as the "Federalist Papers." The Federalists initially argued that there was no need for a federal Bill of Rights, because most states (seven) had a state Bill of Rights, and because the proposed Constitution limited the power of the federal government to only those areas specifically enumerated, leaving all remaining powers to the states or the people. But in time, Madison would become the great proponent and drafter of the Bill of Rights.

The proposed Constitution was sent to the states for ratification on September 17, 1787. Delaware was the first state to assent, followed rapidly by Pennsylvania, New Jersey, Georgia, and Connecticut. But when the Massachusetts Legislature met in January 1788 to debate ratification, several vocal members took up the objection that without a Bill of Rights the proposed Constitution endangered individual liberty. A compromise was brokered, with the Federalists agreeing to support amending the Constitution to add a Bill of Rights following ratification. The Anti-Federalists, led by John Adams and John Hancock, agreed, and Massachusetts ratified. When Maryland, South Carolina, and New Hampshire followed, the requisite nine states had signed on. Virginia and New York quickly followed, with North Carolina ratifying in 1789, and Rhode Island in 1790. In addition to Massachusetts, New Hampshire's, Virginia's, and New York's ratifying conventions conditioned their acceptance on the understanding that a Bill of Rights would be added.

The first Congress met in New York in March 1789, and among its first acts began debating and drafting the Bill of Rights. Federalist Congressman

James Madison took responsibility for drafting the bill, having by then concluded that it would strengthen the legitimacy of the new government. He relied heavily on the state constitutions, especially the Virginia Declaration of Rights, in setting out those individual rights that should be protected from federal interference.

Madison steered seventeen proposed amendments through the House, of which the Senate agreed to twelve. On September 2, 1789, President Washington sent them to the states for ratification. Of the twelve, two, concerning congressional representation and congressional pay, failed to achieve ratification by over three-quarters of the states (the congressional pay amendment was finally ratified in 1992). The remaining ten were ratified and, with the vote of Virginia, on December 15, 1791, became the first ten amendments to the Constitution, or the "Bill of Rights."

The Bill of Rights as originally adopted only applied to the federal government. Its purpose was to restrict Congress from interfering with rights reserved to the people. Thus, under the First Amendment the Congress could not establish a national religion, but the states could establish state support for selected religions, as seven states to some extent did (Connecticut, Georgia, Maryland, Massachusetts, New Hampshire, South Carolina, and Vermont). Madison had proposed that the states also be bound by the Bill of Rights, and the House agreed, but the Senate rejected the proposal.

Although the Declaration of Independence provided that "We hold these truths to be self-evident, that all men are created equal," the Constitution and Bill of Rights are conspicuously silent on the question of equality, because the agreement that made the Constitution possible was the North/South compromise permitting the continuation of slavery. Thus, today's issues like affirmative action, race and sex discrimination, school segregation, and same-sex marriage cannot be resolved through application of the Bill of Rights. This omission of a guarantee of equality led to the Civil War, and in turn to the post-Civil War Fourteenth Amendment that made the newly freed slaves US and state citizens, and prohibited the states from denying equal protection of the laws or due process of law to any citizen. In light of this amendment, the Supreme Court began developing the "incorporation doctrine," holding that the Fourteenth Amendment extended the Bill of Rights so that it applied to all government action. By applying the Bill of Rights so expansively, the legal and social landscape of America was fundamentally changed.

In the aftermath of the Civil War, as the Supreme Court slowly began applying the Bill of Rights to state and local governments through the Fourteenth Amendment, the debates of 1787–91 became more and more important to modern life. Could a high school principal begin a graduation ceremony by asking a minister (or a student leader) to say a prayer? Could a state require a girl under sixteen to secure her parent's permission to have an abortion? Could a prison warden deny a pain medication to a prisoner between midnight and 7:00 a.m.? Could a college president censor an article in a student newspaper? These questions required the courts to examine the debates of the eighteenth century to determine what the framers intended when they drafted the Bill of Rights (and raised the related question, hotly disputed, of whether the intent of the framers was even relevant, or whether a "living" Constitution required solely contemporary, not historical, analysis).

Hence this series. Our intent is to select the very best essays from law and history and the most important judicial opinions, and to edit them so that the leading views of what the framers intended, and of how we should interpret the Bill of Rights today, are made accessible to today's reader. If you find yourself passionately agreeing with some of the views expressed, angrily disagreeing with others, and appreciating how the essays selected have examined these questions with depth and lucidity, we will have succeeded.

David B. Oppenheimer
Professor of Law & Associate Dean for Faculty Development
Golden Gate University School of Law
San Francisco

INTRODUCTION
Guided Tour

Free speech in America, while enshrined in the First Amendment and often described as occupying a "preferred position" in the Constitution's constellation of rights, has not always been respected in practice. At the nation's founding, some read the First Amendment quite narrowly, arguing that it prohibited before-the-fact injunctions against speech—so-called prior restraints—but no more. Just a few years after the Constitution was ratified, Congress enacted the self-dealing Sedition Act of 1798, which allowed congressional incumbents to criticize their challengers but prohibited challengers from criticizing incumbents. (Because the act sought to punish the government's critics after the fact of speech rather than silence them before they spoke, its supporters argued that the statute didn't run afoul of the First Amendment.)

Remarkably, this act was never judicially invalidated (and indeed was enforced by Supreme Court justices riding circuit as lower court judges) but was, as Justice William Brennan observed in the famous *New York Times v. Sullivan*, 376 U.S. 254 (1964), ultimately repudiated by the "court of history." But this repudiation was late in coming and did not prevent broad suppression of the most vital political speech imaginable throughout the nineteenth century and first half of the twentieth century.

For example, antebellum states aggressively attempted to silence slavery critics in the mid 1800s, just as Congress had tried to silence its critics fifty years earlier. As Yale law professor Akhil Amar has observed:

13

[a]cross the South, mere criticism of slavery became a crime, and the Republican Party was in effect outlawed via the threat of after-the-fact punishment rather than prior restraint. In response, Republicans insisted on broad protections of expression. Their 1856 party slogan was "Free Speech, Free Press, Free Men, Free Labor, Free Territory, and Fremont." Fremont lost in 1856, but four years later Lincoln won. And the war came. In its wake, Reconstruction Republicans insisted that the South end its regime of antirepublican (and anti-Republican) censorship of opposition speech. Free folk— black and white, male and female, Republican and Democrat, Northern and Southern—must all be guaranteed the right to speak their minds about interlinked issues of law, politics, religion, morality, and even literature. (Reconstruction Republicans viscerally understood the importance of protecting a literary work like Uncle Tom's Cabin.) The Fourteenth Amendment thus commanded that all states observe citizens' fundamental rights and freedoms, with a broad right of free expression, ranging far beyond freedom from prior restraint, at the Amendment's very core.[1]

Even with this reconstruction revolution, federal courts were slow to respond favorably to speech claimants. After having stood by while Southern states effectively criminalized the antebellum Republican Party, federal courts for more than half a century after the Civil War refused to implement the "incorporation" of the First Amendment against the states that the Fourteenth Amendment clearly commanded. And when in 1907 the Supreme Court assumed for the sake of argument that incorporation existed, it did so only to insist that freedom of expression was limited to freedom from prior restraint and thus permitted state judges to fine a newspaper publisher who politically satirized the very judges in question. A dozen years later, in *Debs v. United States*, 249 U.S. 111 (1919), the Court upheld the imprisonment of prominent and somewhat popular government critic and repeated presidential candidate Eugene Debs because Debs had criticized federal war policy in a peaceful speech. Indeed, before the 1930s, a free speech claimant had never won in the Supreme Court, and it wasn't until 1965 that the Court struck down a federal enactment on free expression grounds.

Things are very different today. Over the past two decades alone, the Court has struck down close to two dozen federal statutes or regulations on free speech grounds. And this is to say nothing of the innumerable state laws that have been invalidated under the First Amendment over the last two generations. Indeed, most analysts think that the commitment to robust free speech protection will persist on the Supreme Court notwithstanding the recent important changes in Court personnel that have moved the Court, in general, to the right. So-called judicial conservatives, as much if not more so than "liberal" jurists, have seen the value of broad free speech protections. The most speech-protective of the justices on the current Court tend to be Justices Kennedy and Scalia, justices who otherwise are more associated with the more conservative end of the judicial ideological spectrum.

But some wonder whether this recent extension and cementing of First Amendment protections has arisen because of a (perhaps problematic) change in the focus of First Amendment doctrine. From the early 1900s through the 1980s, liberal individuals and groups were the ones who viewed freedom of speech as distinctively valuable. The roster of litigants in the major free speech cases during that period—that is, the people who were invoking the First Amendment's free speech clause to challenge government restrictions on expression—comprised a veritable Who's Who of the left side of the political spectrum.

They included, for instance, socialists, antiwar activists, civil rights advocates, and avant-garde artists. Consider the speakers in the era's famous cases: *Debs v. United States* (socialist leader Eugene Debs), *Dennis v. United States*, 341 U.S. 494 (1951) (communist leaders), *New York Times v. Sullivan* (critics of Southern racists), *Thornhill v. Alabama*, 310 U.S. 88 (1940) (labor picketers), *Cohen v. California*, 403 U.S. 15 (1971) (draft protester), *Tinker v. Des Moines Independent Community School Dist.*, 393 U.S. 503 (critic of the Vietnam war), *United States v. O'Brien*, 319 U.S. 367 (1968) (draft card–burning protester), *Texas v. Johnson*, 491 U.S. 397 (1989) (flag-burning protester), and *Miller v. California*, 413 U.S. 373 (1973) (purveyor of alleged obscenity).

Granted, some free speech litigants—such as Jehovah's Witnesses—could not reasonably be described as left wing. Yet even they typically espoused dissident beliefs and opposed conventional manifestations of patriotism or other accepted ideals. For instance, in *West Virginia State Board of Education v. Barnette*, 319 U.S. 624 (1943), plaintiffs attacked mandatory recitation of the Pledge of Allegiance.

Moreover, a summary list of headline cases like these actually *understates* the utility of free speech doctrine to progressive groups. The Supreme Court, not to mention the lower federal courts, decided numerous other cases relating to the freedom of speech and association rights of unions, civil rights activists, and antiwar protesters—more than could possibly be cited in any contemporary casebook or treatise (let alone here).

There are also exceptions that help prove the rule, so to speak. *Near v.*

Minnesota, 283 U.S. 697 (1931), a famous prior restraint case, protected an anti-Semitic publisher, and *Brandenburg v. Ohio*, 395 U.S. 444 (1969), used the First Amendment to protect a Ku Klux Klan rally. But these counterexamples are memorable in part because they stick out. Overwhelmingly, leftist speech was the meat and potatoes of the judicial free speech menu for the sixty years following World War I.

During this period, conservatives understandably came to view free speech protections and doctrines as unnecessary, unreasonably burdensome, and downright dangerous. Conservatives of this era thus generally supported the use of government power to restrict or punish speech that threatened established interests or traditional values.

Typically, the speech the government sought to suppress risked consequences conservatives wanted to avoid. In addition, a vigorously enforced free speech doctrine offered conservatives comparatively little in return; after all, they rarely found themselves invoking the First Amendment themselves. No wonder, then, that they tended to be satisfied with free speech cases and doctrines that were relatively weak, providing little protection to speakers.

But over the last two decades, that constitutional calculus has changed dramatically. Beginning in the early 1980s, there are, I believe, at least five substantive areas in which free speech doctrine has proven to be of significant value to conservative interests.

Take, for example, pro-life protesters—who may seek to engage in demonstrations and "sidewalk counseling" in front of clinics providing abortion services and to picket in the residential neighborhoods of abortion providers. Especially since the 1980s, these pro-life advocates have argued their activities deserve free speech protection in a number of cases.

One example is *Frisby v. Schultz*, 487 U.S. 474 (1988), involving residential picketing. Another is *Madsen v. Women's Health Center Inc.*, 512 U.S. 753 (1994), in which protesters challenged a judicially created "buffer zone" around an abortion clinic, within which they could not operate. Whether challenging municipal regulations or court injunctions, pro-life protesters began to increasingly rely on free speech arguments.

Not all of these challenges have been successful, of course. But many liberal speakers in the 1920s through the 1950s lost their free speech cases too. The key point is that abortion protesters have won enough victories (at least in part) in major free speech cases that they and their supporters recognize the value of free speech doctrine to their efforts.

Free speech doctrine also has proven to be a useful tool for attacking the constitutionality of "hate crime" statutes and many hate speech codes promulgated by colleges and universities. Consider a case such as *R.A.V. v. St. Paul*, 505 U.S. 377 (1992), which struck down a statute punishing speech and symbols intended to arouse fear and anger in ethnic minorities as unconstitutional content-based discrimination. In this and other cases, conservative groups have used the free speech clause to invalidate regulations that they believe impermissibly target conservative or reactionary speech and association.

In the last few decades, moreover, invocation of the free speech clause—even more so than invocation of the free exercise clause—has became the primary tactic used by religious groups seeking to gain access to public space and other public resources for religious expressive activities. Examples include cases like *Widmar v. Vincent*, 454 U.S. 263 (1981), which involved access to university facilities for meetings by a religious club, and *Rosenberger v. University of Virginia*, 515 U.S. 819 (1995), which involved access to university-mandated student fees to subsidize a religious student group's publications. In such cases, conservative religious groups have relied on the free speech clause's requirement of viewpoint-neutrality to invalidate discriminatory restrictions on their expressive activities—and have achieved considerable success in doing so.

Private associations seeking to defend exclusionary membership requirements have also used freedom of association—a constitutional mandate derived from free speech guarantees—as a shield to insulate their discriminatory decisions from the reach of civil rights laws.

For instance, in *Hurley v. Irish American Gay, Lesbian and Bisexual Group of Boston*, 515 U.S. 557 (1995), the Court held that the free speech clause allowed organizers of the St. Patrick's Day parade in Boston to exclude a gay contingent from marching in the event. Similarly, in *Boy Scouts of America v. Dale*, 530 U.S. 640 (2000), the Court concluded that freedom of association gave the Boy Scouts immunity to discriminate against a gay scoutmaster—despite a New Jersey statute purporting to outlaw such discrimination.

Finally, commercial speech—often involving advertising communicated to consumers by large corporate interests—is now close to receiving the same level of protection provided to traditional expression. That means that businesses now enjoy both freedom from regulation of their own expressive activities and immunity from being compelled to make contributions to someone else's speech.

In cases involving the tobacco industry and agribusiness, corporate interests have successfully invoked free speech principles in ways that would have seemed exotic a generation ago. And as a recent beef advertising case, *Veneman v. Livestock Marketing Ass'n*, 541 U.S. 1062 (2004), illustrates, corporate America continues to invoke the free speech clause now that corporate interests have been awakened to understanding just how much protection the First Amendment may provide.

These lines of authority and others (I do not suggest that this list is necessarily exhaustive) provide a lot of utility for conservative purposes. Indeed, they have proven so beneficial that conservatives now have a new and serious relationship with freedom of speech. At the same time, freedom of speech has retained most of its liberal adherents. For the most part, they haven't forgotten America's earlier history—or its lesson. They remember that free speech is the "fella that brung them" to the political dance in the first place. It is that combination of conservative and liberal support, I submit, that makes freedom of speech an enduring constitutional principle for the foreseeable future.

But the contours of that principle continue to evolve, and some folks are unhappy that speech protections have been extended in a way that might obscure the core concern over speech critical of government and speech relating to self-governing. And some also wonder whether the extension of free speech protection has sacrificed other constitutional values such as racial equality and personal autonomy and dignity.

This book provides an introduction to America's free speech journey. I have offered materials that relate to history, theory, and doctrine to give readers a sense of the actual terms on which free speech debates are waged.

I begin in part I with some historical discussions. Freedom of thought and expression is taken so much for granted in America and other Western democracies that we tend to forget how recently it has come to be accepted. The three centuries that elapsed between the appearance of the first book printed in England in 1476 and America's Declaration of Independence in 1776 provide the immediate background of the American constitutional system, and the struggles of this period may prove particularly relevant. The evolution of the law of treason and the evolution of jury powers in the area of sedition libel (libel that undermines government) in England and France in the 1700s are discussed in Blackstone's canonical "Commentaries," first published in 1765. In addition to Blackstone, I have provided excerpts from other commenters, Professors Chaffee, Heyman, Mayton, and Anderson, who present their sense of the historical backdrop.

These materials hopefully will provide some context to help readers to decide whether, as a matter of so-called original intent—even if in England the phrase "freedom of the press" may well have meant only freedom from prior restraint—the First Amendment should be read more broadly. My own view is that it should, even as a matter of history. In England, Parliament was sovereign. Under such a regime, it made perfect sense that rights were designed only against executive and judicial officials, such as Crown-appointed licensers. But in America's system based on popular sovereignty, the protection of speech sensibly seems broader. James Madison, on the very day he introduced the Bill of Rights, explained the key difference between the British system of governmental sovereignty and the American system of popular sovereignty. In 1794, he was emphatic: "If we advert to the nature of Republican Government, we shall find that the censorial power is in the people over the Government, and not in the Government over the people." Under this new historical conception in America, the First Amendment has to mean more than mere freedom from prior restraint.

Part II moves from history to theory: Even if the First Amendment is not limited to prior restraints frowned upon in England, what, exactly, does "freedom of speech" protect? All constitutional rulings must harmonize text and context into some overarching system of principles and ideas. Several are offered and analyzed in the various excerpts provided from works of Professors Schauer, Sunstein, Baker, Meiklejohn, and Karst; the theoretical paradigms they offer include the so-called marketplace of ideas, metaphor, the need for government to overcome market imperfections, a robust modern vision of popular sovereignty and empowerment, and the equality norm that infuses much of the rest of the Constitution. Also discussed in these materials is the question of how much First Amendment protections ought to give way to other government interests—how much (and what kind of) "balancing" ought to be allowed.

The last part of the book, part III, involves the translation of notions of history and theory into judicial doctrine. Free speech is waged in a huge variety of contexts, and courts necessarily have crafted rules and tests to administer all the various settings in which free speech questions arise. Why the government is regulating, what kind of speech is being uttered, where it is taking place, to whom it is being uttered, what nonspeech dimensions are wrapped up with the speech, how coerced the speech is, what the effects of the speech upon vulnerable persons might be, and so on, are all doctrinal factors—variables, if you will—that courts have plugged into the various formulas that are applied. These and related questions are taken up in the excerpts of works from Professors Stone, Brownstein, Kalven, Akhil Amar, Matsuda, Post, Sullivan, and me. There is, of course, far too much doctrine to canvass in any single volume, let alone a book this size. I have not tried to provide a discussion of all the important modern battlegrounds. Instead, I have chosen a small but significant number of doctrinal areas—regulation of the content as distinguished from the time, place, or manner of speech; regulation of speech on public property; regulation of hate speech; regulation of speech that takes the form of conduct; regulation of compelled subsidized speech; regulation of political monetary donations and expenditures; and the possibly distinctive role of the institutionalized media—to give a sense of the ways in which doctrines are forged and interrelate.

*   *   *

Notes on style. I have indicated the removal of material by the use of ellipses and asterisks and have used brackets for any textual material I have added. I have removed all footnotes from the excerpts I provide without indicating that fact and I have added notes of my own that cite important cases mentioned in the excerpts. The footnotes I have added thus do not correspond to any original numbering in the essays when they were first published.

Vikram Amar
Davis, California
June 2008

NOTE

1. Akhil Reed Amar, foreword, "The Document and the Doctrine," *Harvard Law Review* 114, no. 26 (2000): 58.

Part I

HISTORICAL FOUNDATIONS

COMMENTARIES ON THE LAWS OF ENGLAND
Sir William Blackstone

In this, and the other instances which we have lately considered, where blasphemous, immoral, treasonable, schismatical, seditious, or scandalous libels are punished by the English law, some with a greater, others with a less degree of severity; the *liberty of the press*, properly understood, is by no means infringed or violated. The liberty of the press is indeed essential to the nature of a free state: but this consists in laying no *previous* restraints upon publications, and not in freedom from censure for criminal matter when published. Every freeman has an undoubted right to lay what sentiments he pleases before the public: to forbid this, is to destroy the freedom of the press: but if he publishes what is improper, mischievous, or illegal, he must take the consequence of his own temerity. To subject the press to the restrictive power of a licenser, as was formerly done, both before and since the revolution* is to

---

Sir William Blackstone, "Commentaries on the Laws of England," vol. 4, pp. 151–53.
    *The art of printing, soon after its introduction, was looked upon (as well in England as in other countries) as merely a matter of state, and subject to the coercion of the crown. It was therefore regulated with us by the king's proclamations, prohibitions, charters of privilege and of licence, and finally by the decrees of the court of Starchamber; which limited the number of printers, and of presses which each should employ, and prohibited new publications unless previously approved by proper licensers. On the demolition of this odious jurisdiction in 1641, the long parliament

subject all freedom of sentiment to the prejudices of one man, and make him the arbitrary and infallible judge of all controverted points in learning, religion, and government. But to punish (as the law does at present) any dangerous or offensive writings, which, when published, shall on a fair and impartial trial be adjudged of a pernicious tendency, is necessary for the preservation of peace and good order, of government and religion, the only solid foundations of civil liberty. Thus the will of individuals is still left free; the abuse only of that free will is the object of legal punishment. Neither is any restraint hereby laid upon freedom of thought or enquiry: liberty of private sentiment is still left; the disseminating, or making public, of bad sentiments, destructive of the ends of society, is the crime which society corrects. A man (says a fine writer on this subject) may be allowed to keep poisons in his closet, but not publicly to vend them as cordials. And to this we may add, that the only plausible argument heretofore used for restraining the just freedom of the press, that it was necessary "to prevent the daily abuse of it," will entirely lose its [*sic*] force, when it is shewn (by a seasonable exertion of the laws) that the press cannot be abused to any bad purpose, without incurring a suitable punishment: whereas it never can be used to any good one, when under the control of an inspector. So true will it be found, that to censure the licentiousness, is to maintain the liberty, of the press.

---

of Charles I, after their rupture with that prince, assumed the same powers as the Starchamber exercised with respect to the licensing of books; and in 1643, 1647, 1649, and 1652 (Scobell, i. 44, 134. ii. 88, 230.) issued their ordinances for that purpose, founded principally on the Starchamber decree of 1637. In 1662 was passed the Statute 13 & 14 Car. II. c. 33. which (with some few alterations) was copied from the parliamentary ordinances. This act expired in 1679, but was revived by Statute I Jac. II. c. 17. and continued till 1692. It was then continued for two years longer by Statute 4 W. & M. c. 24. but, though frequent attempts were made by the government to revive it, in the subsequent part of that reign (Comm. Journ. 11 Feb. 1694. 26 Nov, 1695. 22 Oct. 1696. 9 Feb. 1697. 31 Jan. 1698.), yet the parliament resisted it so strongly, that it finally expired, and the press became properly free, in 1694; and has ever since so continued.

FREE SPEECH IN WAR TIME
Zechariah Chafee Jr.

Never in the history of our country, since the Alien and Sedition Laws of 1798, has the meaning of free speech been the subject of such sharp controversy as to-day.... The United States Supreme Court has recently handed down several decisions upon the Espionage Act, which put us in a much better position than formerly to discuss the war-time aspects of the general problem of liberty of speech, and this article will approach the general problem from that side....

*   *   *

At the outset, we can reject two extreme views in the controversy. First, there is the view that the Bill of Rights is a peace-time document and consequently freedom of speech may be ignored in war. This view has been officially repudiated. At the opposite pole is the belief of many agitators that the First Amendment tenders unconstitutional any Act of Congress without exception "abridging the freedom of speech, or of the press," that all speech is free, and only action can be restrained and punished. This view is equally untenable. The provisions of the Bill of Rights cannot be applied with absolute literal-

From *Harvard Law Review* 32 (1919).

ness but are subject to exceptions. For instance, the prohibition of involuntary servitude in the Thirteenth Amendment does not prevent military conscription, or the enforcement of a "work or fight" statute. The difficulty, of course, is to define the principle on which the implied exceptions are based, and an effort to that end will be made subsequently.

Since it is plain that the true solution lies between these two extreme views, and that even in war time freedom of speech exists subject to a problematical limit, it is necessary to determine where the line runs between utterance which is protected by the Constitution from governmental control and that which is not. Many attempts at a legal definition of that line have been made, but two mutually inconsistent theories have been especially successful in winning judicial acceptance, and frequently appear in the Espionage Act cases.

One theory construes the First Amendment as enacting Blackstone's statement that "the liberty of the press...consists in laying no *previous* restraints upon publications and not in freedom from censure for criminal matter when published." The line where legitimate suppression begins is fixed chronologically at the time of publication. The government cannot interfere by a censorship or injunction *before* the words are spoken or printed, but can punish them as much as it pleases *after* publication, no matter how harmless or essential to the public welfare the discussion may be. This Blackstonian definition found favor with Lord Mansfield, and is sometimes urged as a reason why libels should not be enjoined. It was adopted by American judges in several early prosecutions for libel, one of which was in Massachusetts, whence Justice Holmes carried it into the United States Supreme Court.[1] Fortunately he has now repudiated this interpretation of freedom of speech,[2] but not until his dictum had had considerable influence, particularly in Espionage Act cases.[3] Of course if the First Amendment does not prevent prosecution and punishment of utterances, the Espionage Act is unquestionably constitutional.

This Blackstonian theory dies hard, but has no excuse for longer life. In the first place, Blackstone was not interpreting a constitution but trying to state the English law of his time, which had no censorship and did have extensive libel prosecutions. Whether or not he stated that law correctly, an entirely different view of the liberty of the press was soon afterwards enacted in Fox's Libel Act, so that Blackstone's view does not even correspond to the English law of the last hundred and twenty-five years. Furthermore, Blackstone is notoriously unfitted to be an authority on the liberties of American colonists, since he upheld the right of Parliament to tax them, and was pronounced by one of his own colleagues to have been "we all know, an anti-republican lawyer."[4]

Not only is the Blackstonian interpretation of our free speech clauses inconsistent with eighteenth-century history, soon to be considered, but it is contrary to modern decisions, thoroughly artificial, and wholly out of accord with a common-sense view of the relations of state and citizen. In some respects this theory goes altogether too far in restricting state action. The prohibition of previous restraint would not allow the government to prevent a newspaper from publishing the sailing dates of transports or the number of troops in a sector. It would render illegal removal of an indecent poster from a billboard or the censorship of moving pictures before exhibition, which has been held valid under a free speech clause. And whatever else may be thought of the decision under the Espionage Act with the unfortunate title, *United States v. The Spirit of '76*, it was clearly previous restraint for a federal court to direct the seizure of a film which depicted the Wyoming Massacre and Paul Revere's Ride, because it was "calculated reasonably so to excite or inflame the passions of our people or some of them as that they will be deterred from giving that full measure of co-operation, sympathy, assistance, and sacrifice which is due to Great Britain, as an ally of ours," and "to make us a little bit slack in our loyalty to Great Britain in this great catastrophe."

*   *   *

A second interpretation of the freedom of speech clauses limits them to the protection of the use of utterance and not to its "abuse." It draws the line between "liberty" and "license." Chief Justice White rejects

> the contention that the freedom of the press is the freedom to do wrong with impunity and implies the right to frustrate and defeat the discharge of those governmental duties upon the performance of which the freedom of all, including that of the press, depends.... However complete is the right of the press to state public things and discuss them, that right, as every other right enjoyed in human society, is subject to the restraints which separate right from wrong-doing.[5]

*   *   *

To a judge obliged to decide whether honest and able opposition to the continuation of a war is punishable, these generalizations furnish as much help as a woman forced, like Isabella in "Measure for Measure," to choose between her brother's death and loss of honor, might obtain from the pious maxim, "Do right." What is abuse? What is license? What standards does the law afford? To argue that the federal Constitution does not prevent punishment for criminal utterances begs the whole question, for utterances within its protection are not crimes. If it only safeguarded lawful speech, Congress could escape its operation at any time by making any class of speech unlawful. Suppose, for example, that Congress declared any criticism of the particular administration in office to be a felony, punishable by ten years' imprisonment. Clearly, the Constitution must limit the power of Congress to create crimes. But how far does that limitation go? Cooley suggests that the legislative power extends only to speech which was criminal or tortious at common law in 1791. No doubt, conditions then must be considered, but must the legislature leave them unchanged for all time? Moreover, the few reported American cases before 1791 prove that our common law of sedition was exactly like that of England, and it would be extraordinary if the First Amendment enacted the English sedition law of that time, which was repudiated by every American and every liberal Englishman, and altered by Parliament itself in the very next year, 1792. Clearly, we must look further and find a rational test of what is use and what is abuse. Saying that the line lies between them gets us nowhere. And "license" is too often "liberty" to the speaker, and what happens to be anathema to the judge.

*   *   *

How about the man who gets up in a theater between the acts and informs the audience honestly but perhaps mistakenly that the fire exits are too few or locked? He is a much closer parallel to Schenck or Debs. How about James Russell Lowell when he counseled, not murder, but the cessation of murder, his name for war? The question whether such perplexing cases are within the First Amendment or not cannot be solved by the multiplication of obvious examples, but only by the development of a rational principle to mark the limits of constitutional protection.

*   *   *

It is obvious that under this law liberty of the press was nothing more than absence of the censorship, as Blackstone said. All through the eighteenth century, however, there existed beside this definite legal meaning of liberty of the press, a definite popular meaning: the right of unrestricted discussion of public affairs. There can be no doubt that this was in a general way what freedom of speech meant to the framers of the Constitution. As Schofield says, "One of the objects of the Revolution was to get rid of the English common law on liberty of speech and of the press.... Liberty of the press as declared in the First Amendment, and the English common-law crime of sedition, cannot co-exist." I must therefore strongly dissent, as would Professor Schofield, from the conclusion of Dean Vance in a recent article on the Espionage Act, that the founders of our government merely intended by the First Amendment "to limit the new government's statutory powers to penalize utterances as seditious, to those which were seditious under the then accepted common-law rule." The founders had seen seventy English prosecutions for libel since 1760, and fifty convictions under that common-law rule, which made conviction easy. That rule had been detested in this country ever since it was repudiated by jury and populace in the famous trial of Peter Zenger, the New York printer, the account of which went through fourteen editions before 1791. Nor was this the only colonial sedition prosecution under the common law, and many more were threatened. The First Amendment was written by men to whom Wilkes and Junius were household words, who intended to wipe out the common law of sedition, and make further prosecutions for criticism of the government, without any incitement to law breaking, forever impossible in the United States of America.

It must not be forgotten that the controversy over liberty of the press was a conflict between two views of government, that the law of sedition was a product of the view that the government was master, and that the American Revolution transformed into a working reality the second view that the government was servant, and therefore subjected to blame from its master, the people. Consequently, the words of Sir James Fitzjames Stephen about this second view have a vital application to American law.

"To those who hold this view fully and carry it out to all its consequences there can be no such offence as sedition. There may indeed be breaches of the peace which may destroy or endanger life, limb, or property, and there may be incitements to such offences, but no imaginable censure of the government, *short of a censure which has an immediate tendency to produce such a breach of the peace*, ought to be regarded as criminal."

*   *   *

It is now clear that the First Amendment fixes limits upon the power of Congress to restrict speech either by a censorship or by a criminal statute, and if the Espionage Act exceeds those limits it is unconstitutional. It is sometimes argued that the Constitution gives Congress the power to declare war, raise armies, and support a navy, that one provision of the Constitution cannot be used to break down another provision, and consequently freedom of speech cannot be invoked to break down the war power.[6] I would reply that the First Amendment is just as much a part of the Constitution as the war clauses, and that it is equally accurate to say that the war clauses cannot be invoked to break down freedom of speech. The truth is that all provisions of the Constitution must be construed together so as to limit each other. In war as in peace, this process of mutual adjustment must include the Bill of Rights. There are those who believe that the Bill of Rights can be set aside in war time at the uncontrolled will of the government. The first ten amendments were drafted by men who had just been through a war. Two of these amendments expressly apply in war. A majority of the Supreme Court declared the war power of Congress to be restricted by the Bill of Rights in *Ex parte Milligan*,[7] which cannot be lightly brushed aside, whether or not the majority went too far in thinking that the Fifth Amendment would have prevented Congress from exercising the war power under the particular circumstances of that case. If the First Amendment is to mean anything, it must restrict powers which are expressly granted by the Constitution to Congress, since Congress has no other powers. It must apply to those activities of government which are most liable to interfere with free discussion, namely, the postal service and the conduct of war.

*   *   *

... [T]o put the matter another way, it is useless to define free speech by talk about rights. The agitator asserts his constitutional right to speak, the government asserts its constitutional right to wage war. The result is a deadlock. Each side takes the position of the man who was arrested for swinging his arms and hitting another in the nose, and asked the judge if he did not have a right to swing his arms in a free country. "Your right to swing your arms ends just where the other man's nose begins." To find the boundary line of any right, we must get behind rules of law to human facts. In our problem, we must regard the desires and needs of the individual human being who wants to speak and those of the great group of human beings among whom he speaks. That is, in technical language, there are individual interests and social interests, which must be balanced against each other, if they conflict, in order to determine which interest shall be sacrificed under the circumstances and which shall be protected and become the foundation of a legal right. It must never be forgotten that the balancing cannot be properly done unless all the interests involved are adequately ascertained, and the great evil of all this talk about rights is that each side is so busy denying the other's claim to rights that it entirely overlooks the human desires and needs behind that claim.

NOTES

1. *Patterson v. Colorado,* 205 U.S. 454 (1907).

2. *Schenck v. United States,* 249 U.S. 47 (1919).

3. *Masses Pub. Co. v. Patten,* 246 Fed. 24 (C. C. A. 2d, 1917); *United States v. Coldwell,* Bull. Dept. Just., No. 158 (D.C. R. I.) 4.

4. J. Willes, in Dean of St. Asaph's Case, 4 Doug. 172 (1784).

5. *Toledo Newspaper Co. v. United States,* 247 U.S. 402 (1900).

6. *United States v. Marie Equi,* Bull. Dept. Just., No. 172, 21 (Ore., 1918), J. Bean.

7. 4 Wall. (U.S.) 2 (1866).

RIGHTING THE BALANCE
AN INQUIRY INTO THE FOUNDATIONS
AND LIMITS OF FREEDOM OF EXPRESSION

Steven J. Heyman

INTRODUCTION

* * *

Despite its unusual facts, the Baker incident in many ways is representative of contemporary disputes over the First Amendment. Whether they focus on hate speech, pornography, flag burning, abortion-clinic demonstrations, publishing the names of rape victims, tobacco advertising, violent entertainment, the National Endowment for the Arts, Internet regulation, or other issues, such controversies tend to have a common structure. Those who advocate regulation of a particular form of expression contend that it causes substantial harm to individuals, groups, or the community at large. Opponents are often skeptical about the seriousness of this harm. In any event, they argue, the First Amendment denies government the power to prevent such harm through the suppression of speech.

Of course, few people would deny that there are situations in which speech may be regulated without violating the First Amendment. Yet we have

From *Boston University Law Review* 78, no. 5 (1998). Courtesy of *Boston University Law Review*.

no well-developed and generally accepted view of when regulation is legitimate. In the absence of any common ground or standard to appeal to, contemporary free speech disputes often appear to be irresolvable.

It is difficult to see how this impasse can be broken without a more general account of the scope of free expression—a view that integrates both the justifications and the limits of that freedom into a coherent whole. This Article makes a start toward the development of such a theory. Its central thesis is that free speech is a right that is limited by the fundamental rights of other individuals and the community as a whole.

... [T]his idea was regarded as axiomatic when the First Amendment was adopted. Eighteenth-century Americans understood freedom of speech within the framework of natural rights theory. Free speech was a right inherent in human nature and republican citizenship. Like all such rights, however, it was bounded by the rights of others. Because government was instituted to protect rights, it had an obligation not only to respect liberty of speech, but also to ensure that this liberty was not used to violate other fundamental rights.

In this way the natural rights tradition provided a standard by which to assess the legitimacy of laws regulating free speech. The possibility of such a standard was undermined, however, by the rise of legal positivism and utilitarianism, which repudiated the concept of natural rights. In modern jurisprudence, First Amendment issues are conceived of not as conflicts of rights, but as clashes between free speech and "social interests"—a term within which the rights of others have been absorbed. There is, however, no clear way to resolve such conflicts. This is a key reason why contemporary First Amendment problems so often appear to involve clashes of irreconcilable values.

*   *   *

... Rights represent what it means to be a free person in various spheres of life—not only in relation to the external world, but also in one's inner life and its expression to others, in social relationships and community life, and in the intellectual and spiritual realm. These four elements of liberty correspond to the major justifications that have been advanced for freedom of speech: that it is an aspect of external freedom; that it is essential for individual self-realization; that it is central to democratic self-government; and that it safeguards the search for truth....

* * *

I. Natural Rights, Social Welfare, and the First Amendment

* * *

Any effort to determine the scope of First Amendment rights must begin with the constitutional text: "Congress shall make no law ... abridging the freedom of speech, or of the press...." At first glance, this language appears absolute, leaving no room for regulation. Yet on closer examination several questions arise. First, what is meant by "the freedom of speech"? On one hand, the term might be understood in a purely descriptive way, to refer to the absence of external restrictions on speech. On this reading, the Amendment's protection would apply to all acts of speech, regardless of whether they might be considered rightful or wrongful. Alternatively, "freedom of speech" may be taken in a normative sense, to refer to the rightful exercise of the capacity for expression. "Abridging" raises a similar issue: do all regulations of speech abridge its freedom, or only those that are unjustified or illegitimate? Again, what should we make of the fact that the Amendment refers only to Congress? Even if we assume that the Amendment imposes an absolute ban on federal regulation, is the same true when the principle of free speech is applied to the states through the Fourteenth Amendment? Issues of this sort are critical to an understanding of the First Amendment, yet they cannot be resolved by reference to the text alone. Instead, the Amendment's meaning must be understood in relation to our developing conception of freedom of expression and its place within the American legal, political, and social order.

* * *

A. THE NATURAL RIGHTS ORIGINS OF THE FIRST AMENDMENT

1. The English Background

To articulate the basis and scope of liberty of speech and press, eighteenth-century Americans drew on a variety of sources, including the common law and the civic-republican tradition. But the most comprehensive framework they looked to was provided by the theory of natural rights and the social contract.

As developed in the works of John Locke, this theory sought to determine the purpose and limits of government by tracing its rise from a state of nature. In that condition, individuals have a right to natural liberty, defined as the power to control one's own person, actions, and possessions without interference by others. This liberty is not unbounded, however, but is subject to the constraints of the law of nature, which enjoins individuals to respect the freedom, equality, and rights of others. In the state of nature, natural law has little power to restrain the violation of rights, for it lacks effective means of enforcement. For this reason, individuals agree to form a society for mutual protection. In so doing, they alienate a portion of their natural liberty to the community, which is empowered to regulate individual conduct to the extent necessary to protect rights and promote the common good.

Locke insists, however, that some elements of liberty are inalienable. Although such rights are not subject to legislative regulation for the public good, they are nevertheless limited by the rights of others. In addition to liberty of conscience, the category of inalienable rights includes freedom of thought in general. This right is not only inherent in individuals, but lies at the foundation of liberty. According to Locke, human freedom is ultimately grounded in reason—in our capacity as rational beings to determine our own thoughts and actions. Locke therefore condemns rulers who seek to "enslave" their subjects "in that which should be the freest part of Man, their Understandings."

As this discussion suggests, Locke's account of freedom of thought has not only an individual but also a political dimension. When individuals enter into the social contract, they give up their natural liberty to judge of and defend their own rights, and transfer this power to the community, to be used for the protection of its members. Thus all political authority is originally vested in the community. In turn, the community generally entrusts this power to a particular government. According to Locke, however, the people always retain the right to judge whether the government, as their "Trustee or Deputy," has acted contrary to its trust. In this way, Locke not only justifies a right to revolution, but implicitly lays the foundation for the eighteenth-century libertarian doctrine of political freedom of speech.

These implications of Lockean thought were developed more fully by later writers, especially the radical Whigs John Trenchard and Thomas

Gordon. In *Cato's Letters*, first published in the 1720s, Trenchard and Gordon defended and popularized Locke's theory of natural rights, the social contract, and the right of revolution. At the same time, they fused that theory with a strong civic-republican emphasis on the active role of the people in politics. …Drawing not only on English history but also on classical republican writers such as Livy, Plutarch, and Tacitus, Cato asserted that freedom of speech was "the great bulwark of liberty," protecting the people against tyranny by preventing and exposing abuses of power.

For Cato, the right to "think what you would, and speak what you thought" was not merely a barrier against government oppression; it was also an essential element of natural liberty.… The natural right to free speech was limited only by the obligation to respect the rights of others, by "injur[ing] neither the society, nor any of its members." For example, private defamation was wrongful because it violated the individual right to reputation. But Cato expressed strong reservations about the traditional law of seditious libel, which punished even true statements defamatory of the government or its officials. Although he acknowledged that political libels might occasionally foment causeless discontents among the people, he argued that this harm was outweighed by the benefits of having "some check upon [official] behaviour, …as well as by warning other people to be upon their guard against oppression." The law of libel had to be carefully confined if it was not to become an instrument of tyranny. In particular, Cato asserted that truthful accusations of public wrongdoing "can never be a libel in the nature of things."

*   *   *

The most powerful conservative response to this view came from Sir William Blackstone, whose *Commentaries on the Law of England* appeared in the late 1760s. Although he conceded that "[t]he liberty of the press is…essential to the nature of a free state," Blackstone insisted that "this consists in laying no *previous* restraints upon publications, and not in freedom from censure for criminal matter when published." Thus the traditional common law, which punished not only private libels but also seditious, blasphemous, and offensive publications, was fully consistent with a free press.

To a modern reader, Blackstone's position appears not merely narrow but almost incomprehensible. How can liberty of the press allow one to publish whatever one chooses, yet afford no protection against subsequent punishment? To understand Blackstone's view, we must briefly explore his political theory.

Following Locke, Blackstone held that "the principal aim of society is to protect individuals in the enjoyment of those absolute rights, which were vested in them by the immutable laws of nature." He identified those rights as life (and, more broadly, personal security), personal liberty, and private property. A major objective of the *Commentaries* was to rationalize the English constitution and common law by showing the ways in which they protected these rights.

Yet despite his common ground with Locke and Cato, Blackstone portrayed natural liberty in a less positive light. Although he held that such freedom is "a right inherent in us by birth, and one of the gifts of God to man at his creation," Blackstone also subscribed to the traditional Christian doctrine that human nature has become fallen and corrupt. Natural liberty was a "wild and savage" condition which was "infinitely [less] desirable" than the "legal obedience and conformity" that characterizes organized society. For Blackstone, the function of society was not merely to protect natural rights but also to civilize human beings. He therefore emphasized the extent to which natural liberty was alienable, and subject to regulation by laws made by the community for the public good—a good that encompassed not only the rights of individuals, but also social values such as order, morality, and religion.

Blackstone also gave a different account of political authority. Distancing himself from the Lockean doctrine that all power is initially vested in the people, Blackstone stated that, when individuals enter into society, they agreed to submit to the authority of those they regarded as best capable of governing for the public good. The evidence of this general consent was longstanding tradition. In England, the legislative authority, which was the supreme power in any state, was vested in a Parliament consisting of the king, the aristocracy, and representatives of the people themselves, while the executive power belonged to the king alone.

In contrast to Locke and Cato, Blackstone stressed the hierarchical relationship between rulers and their subjects. Indeed, the very idea of law was that of a "rule of action, which is prescribed by some superior, and which the inferior is bound to obey." A "due subordination of rank" was essential in a well-governed society, so that "the people may know...such as are set over them, in order to yield them their due respect and obedience."

Consistent with the Whig tradition, Blackstone recognized that the king's powers as supreme executive were limited by laws declaring the rights of the people, such as the Magna Carta and Bill of Rights. Moreover, he defended the English Revolution of 1688, in which the Lords and Commons determined that King James II's attempts to subvert the constitution amounted to an abdication of the throne. At the same time, however, Blackstone criticized the Lockean theory of revolution, endorsed by "some zealous republicans," which "would have reduced the society almost to a state of nature," leveled all distinctions of property, rank, and authority, overturned all positive laws, and left the people free to establish a new social and political regime. In short, while *Cato's Letters* synthesized natural rights theory with civic republicanism, Blackstone fused that theory with the ideology of the traditional legal, political, and social order.

We are now in a better position to understand Blackstone's views on liberty of the press. For Blackstone, freedom of thought and expression were elements of natural liberty. It would be inconsistent with that liberty to compel the press to submit to prior censorship, for that would make the executive "an arbitrary and infallible judge of all controverted points in learning, religion, and government." The press "became properly free" in 1694 when Parliament refused to renew the law authorizing such censorship. The result, however, was merely to place publication on a par with other forms of liberty. For Blackstone, expression was an alienable right which was subject to regulation for the common good. Publications that violated laws against seditious, blasphemous, or immoral writings constituted not liberty but licentiousness. Accordingly, Blackstone argued that to subject such writings to subsequent punishment under the law was "necessary for the preservation of peace and good order, of government and religion, the only solid foundations of civil liberty." This was especially true of libels against public officials; whether true or false, such accusations undermined the respect for authority upon which government depends.

2. Natural Rights and the Founding of the American Republics

Although the revolutionary ideology of Locke and the radical Whigs was marginal in eighteenth-century England, it had a profound influence on American political thought. In addition to providing the justification for the American Revolution, this ideology clearly emerges from the bills of rights affixed to most of the first state constitutions. Thus, the Pennsylvania Declaration of Rights opens with the assertion that "all men are born equally free and independent, and have certain natural, inherent and inalienable rights, amongst which are, the enjoying and defending life and liberty, acquiring, possessing and protecting property, and pursuing and obtaining happiness and safety." "[A]ll power," the Declaration continues, is "originally inherent in, and consequently derived from, the people; therefore all officers of the government, whether legislative or executive, are their trustees and servants, and at all times accountable to them." In addition to many other personal rights, the Declaration asserts that "the people have a right to freedom of speech, and of writing, and publishing their sentiments: therefore the freedom of the press ought not to be restrained."

In this way Pennsylvania placed liberty of speech and press squarely within the framework of natural rights and popular sovereignty. Similarly, the Virginia Declaration of Rights echoed *Cato's Letters* in asserting that "the freedom of the Press is one of the greatest bulwarks of liberty, and can never be restrained but by despotick Governments." At the same time, Americans agreed with Cato that, as a natural right, free expression was limited by the rights of others, including the right to reputation. For example, while the Massachusetts Declaration provided that the liberty of the press "ought not ...to be restrained in the Commonwealth," it also declared that "[e]ach individual in the society has a right to be protected by it," and therefore "ought to find a certain remedy, by having recourse to the laws, for all injuries or wrongs which he may receive in his person, property, or *character*."

When a new Federal Constitution was proposed in 1787, the most powerful objection leveled against it was that it lacked a bill of rights. Among the most important of these rights, Antifederalists contended, were freedom of speech and press, which they characterized as inalienable rights of human nature and invaluable bulwarks against tyranny. In response, Federalists argued that a bill of rights was unnecessary....

Yet arguments of this sort were unable to overcome the desire for a bill of rights. Several state conventions accompanied their ratifications with recommended amendments, or declined to ratify in the absence of such amendments. The proposed amendments were derived largely from the state declarations of rights and reflected their radical Whig principles. The first state proposal relating to freedom of expression, which came from the Virginia convention, read: "That the people have a right to freedom of speech, and of writing and publishing their sentiments; that the freedom of the press is one of the greatest bulwarks of liberty, and ought not to be violated." This recommendation, which was to form the basis for James Madison's draft of the First Amendment, combined the Pennsylvania Declaration's focus on free speech as a natural right of individuals with the Virginia Declaration's Catonic description of liberty of the press as a safeguard against abuse of power.

In June 1789, Madison introduced his proposal for a bill of rights in the First Congress. In an important speech, he explained that the purpose of such a document was "to limit and qualify the powers of Government, by excepting out of the grant of power those cases in which the Government ought not to act, or to act only in a particular mode." Such limitations, he implied, were subject to judicial enforcement. Madison identified two categories of rights that were protected in bills of rights: (1) natural rights, or "those... which are retained when particular powers are given up to be exercised by the legislature"; and (2) "positive rights" such as trial by jury, which were equally "essential to secure the liberty of the people." Madison's notes cite freedom of speech as a paradigmatic instance of a natural right. Following the proposal of the Virginia Convention, Madison's draft of the First Amendment provided: "The people shall not be deprived or abridged of their right to speak, to write, or to publish their sentiments; and the freedom of the press, as one of the great bulwarks of liberty, shall be inviolable." Although sparse, the legislative history of the Amendment also contains other indications that it was understood in the context of natural rights.

In his groundbreaking study of the origins of the First Amendment, Leonard Levy argued that the Amendment reflected Blackstone's narrow conception of liberty of the press as a mere ban on prior restraints rather than subsequent punishment. A basic flaw in this argument was the assumption that anyone who believed that expression could be subjected to subsequent punishment must have shared Blackstone's position. As we have seen, however, virtually everyone in the eighteenth century, from Blackstonian conservatives to libertarians like Cato and Jefferson, held that free expression, like other forms of liberty, was bounded by law. But whereas conservatives regarded expression as an ordinary liberty that was subject to plenary regulation for the public good, libertarians inclined to view it as an inalienable right that was limited only by the rights of others.

It is certainly true that, at the time the Constitution and Bill of Rights were adopted, some Americans described freedom of the press in Blackstonian terms. In part, as Levy observes, this reflected the persistence of "the taught traditions of [the] law," of which Blackstone was the foremost expositor. There were also political reasons for invoking Blackstone. As Gordon Wood has shown, the movement for a stronger federal constitution drew much of its support from conservatives who believed that, under the post-Revolutionary state governments, America suffered from an excess of popular liberty and democracy. For such conservatives, Blackstone's insistence that the liberty of the press did not prevent regulation of its "licentiousness" was quite appealing. More generally, this concern about excessive liberty may help to explain the Federalists' resistance to a bill of rights.

Yet if the Constitution was partly motivated by conservative concerns, the demand for a bill of rights represented a reassertion of the radical Whig ideology that animated the Revolution. For this reason it is a mistake to regard Blackstone as the key to the original meaning of the First Amendment. As we have seen, Blackstone's approach rested on the view that freedom of expression was an aspect of natural liberty that was alienable and subject to legislative regulation for the common good. By contrast, the object of the Bill of Rights was to specify those freedoms that Americans regarded as essential or *inalienable*, and to reserve them from government control. Freedom of speech and press fell in this category, not only as inherent rights of individuals but also as indispensable means by which the people could hold public officials to account—a view that was contrary to Blackstone's position that the government, not the people, was sovereign. In these respects, Blackstone's view was fundamentally inconsistent with the logic and purpose of the First Amendment.

*   *   *

Although Republicans denied all federal power over the press, they did not regard the freedoms of speech and press themselves as absolute. Some accepted the law of seditious libel, as modified by the defense of truth, while others repudiated that law. Virtually all Republicans, however, believed that freedom of expression was limited by the rights of other individuals, especially the right to reputation. But Republicans insisted that the protection of those rights belonged to the states rather than the federal government. In Madison's words, individuals were required to seek "a remedy for their injured reputations, under the same laws, and in the same tribunals, which protect their lives, their liberties, and their properties."

In this section, I have suggested that the First Amendment reflected the libertarian tradition of the radical Whigs more than the conservatism of

Blackstone.... [B]oth views found considerable support in late eighteenth-century America, and the debate between them continued for some time to come. As with other constitutional provisions, this makes it difficult to attribute any precise original meaning to the First Amendment. Nevertheless, this review of the history may enable us to identify not only sharp disagreements, but also a substantial area of consensus. In the late eighteenth century, Americans generally believed that freedom of thought, belief, and expression were among the natural rights of individuals. These freedoms were also regarded as inherent in republican citizenship, allowing the people to express their views on public affairs and to guard their liberties against governmental encroachment—a right which extended at least to making true allegations against public officials, as even the Sedition Act recognized. At the same time, there was broad agreement that, as natural rights, freedom of speech and press were limited by the rights of others.

*   *   *

C. THE TRANSFORMATION OF FREE SPEECH THEORY

... [This] natural rights background ... suggests a rather straightforward principle: that free speech is limited by the fundamental rights of others, and that the law may protect these rights against speech that violates them. Although this principle was widely held when those Amendments were adopted, it no longer holds a central place in American constitutional theory or doctrine. Instead, we generally view First Amendment issues in terms of an opposition between freedom of speech and state interests.

To understand this shift, we must explore the transformation of American jurisprudence after the Civil War. During the late nineteenth and early twentieth centuries, the theory of natural rights gave way to a more positivist and utilitarian conception of law. On this view the function of law was not to protect the inherent rights of individuals, but to promote the social good as defined by the community or the state.

One of the leading figures in this development was Oliver Wendell Holmes, Jr. Although Holmes "enlisted in the Civil War 'as a convinced abolitionist,'" his experience of its bloodshed and upheaval led him to regard natural rights doctrines as a threat to social order—an attitude that "he shared with much of late-nineteenth-century American culture." In his jurisprudential writings, Holmes rejected Lockean and Kantian notions of the inherent freedom and dignity of individuals. In particular, he insisted that legal and constitutional interpretation should be divorced from ideas of "the rights of man in a moral sense." Rights had no independent existence, but derived their force from positive law, which aimed to promote social ends. At bottom, legal disputes involved clashes of social interests, which could be resolved only by "weighing considerations of social advantage."

*   *   *

In criticizing individual-rights theories and emphasizing the social purposes of law, Holmes... articulated themes that were to become central to early twentieth-century Progressive thought. In this way, [his] views played an important role in the legal and constitutional revolution that culminated in the New Deal.

Although the Progressive critique of rights was directed primarily against the extreme defense of property symbolized by *Lochner v. New York*,[1] that critique also had implications for the status of civil liberties. In particular, Holmesian positivism and sociological jurisprudence had the effect of undermining the traditional American rationale for freedom of expression. Rather than a right of nature or republican citizenship, free speech on this view represented merely one interest to be weighed against others. There was nothing distinctive about expression that entitled it to special protection, or that placed it beyond the authority of the state to regulate like any other form of activity.

This perspective is evident in *Schenck v. United States*,[2] the Supreme Court's first important effort to address the meaning of the First Amendment. Writing for a unanimous Court, Justice Holmes upheld the convictions of Socialist Party members for conspiring to obstruct recruitment by sending anti-draft leaflets to men who had been called for military service in the First World War. Although he conceded that individuals ordinarily had a right to express their views, Holmes held that this right did not protect speech that endangered other social interests. "The question in every case," he wrote, "is whether the words used are used in such circumstances and are of such a nature as to create a clear and present danger that they will bring about the substantive evils that Congress has a right to prevent." As *Schenck* and other cases made clear, this standard was satisfied whenever, in the legislature's judgment, speech had a tendency to cause social harm.[3]

In this way the rejection of natural rights threatened to undermine the constitutional basis for protecting free speech.... A leading effort in this direction came from Zechariah Chafee, Jr.... In a 1919 article and a book published the following year, Chafee criticized *Schenck* and other Espionage Act decisions for treating free speech "as merely an individual interest, which must readily give way like other personal desires the moment it interferes with the social interest in national security." Instead, Chafee argued that the most important purpose served by free speech was the social interest in "the discovery and spread of truth on subjects of general concern."

This approach was soon adopted by Justice Holmes himself. Dissenting in *Abrams v. United States*,[4] Holmes began by observing that, when the expression of opinions threatens important social objectives, suppression appears to be a "perfectly logical" response—essentially the basis of his decision in *Schenck*. Nevertheless, he continued, "when men have realized that time has upset many fighting faiths, they may come to believe even more than they believe the foundations of their own conduct that the ultimate good desired is best reached by free trade in ideas—that the best test of truth is the power of the thought to get itself accepted in the competition of the market, and that truth is the only ground on which their wishes safely can be carried out." ... In this way, he laid the foundations of modern free speech jurisprudence on the ruins of the natural rights theory which originally supported the First Amendment.

*   *   *

Although Progressives were critical of the notion of fundamental rights, they nevertheless recognized that free speech was important for individuals as well as for society.... The role of the First Amendment in protecting individual liberty was a central theme of Justice Jackson's majority opinion in *West Virginia State Board of Education v. Barnette*,[5] which held that a compulsory flag salute "invade[d] the sphere of intellect and spirit which it was the purpose of the First Amendment...to reserve from all official control." Earlier, Justice Brandeis had characterized this liberty in more positive terms, asserting that the First Amendment had been adopted in the belief "the final end of the state was to make men free to develop their faculties."[6] This individual-liberty view has gained increased momentum since the 1960s.

D. CLASSICAL VERSUS MODERN FREE SPEECH THEORY

...It may therefore seem that we have come full circle, and that the result of modern First Amendment theory has been to reproduce the essential features of classical libertarian theory. But this impression would be mistaken. To begin with, the classical theory regarded the values of free speech as a relatively unified whole, while the modern justifications are sometimes represented as distinct from, or even opposed to, one another. Over time, however, these different rationales have often come to be seen as elements of a more general theory of freedom of expression.

A more fundamental difference relates to the nature of the justifications offered by the classical and modern views. Whereas the former sought to justify free speech primarily on intrinsic grounds, as a right of human nature and republican citizenship, the modern approach is more instrumental, focusing on the individual and social interests that speech serves. On this view, our constitutional commitment to free expression ultimately rests on an empirical judgment as to the best means of promoting the social good. In Justice Holmes' words, it is "an experiment...based upon imperfect knowledge," which is subject to revision or rejection in light of experience.[7]

Most importantly for the purposes of this Article, the classical and modern views conceptualize First Amendment issues in fundamentally different ways. For the classical view, many free speech problems involved rights on both sides. As we have seen, Progressive jurisprudence recharacterized rights as interests, and held that individual interests had value only insofar as they promoted those of society. In this way, individual rights came to be absorbed into the concept of social interests. Initially, First Amendment problems were reconceived as conflicts between two sets of social interests: those that were promoted by free speech and those that might be injured by it. Over time, free expression has once more come to be regarded as a right, whether for intrinsic or instrumental reasons or both. But this revival of rights in First Amendment jurisprudence has not extended to the values that may be harmed by speech, which continue to be characterized as social interests. In this way, we have come to a hybrid position which conceives of First Amendment issues as conflicts between free speech rights and social interests.

*   *   *

The classical and modern views differ not only on the substantive nature of First Amendment problems, but also on their formal structure. For the classical view, such problems involved a trilateral relationship between (1) those who desired to speak or listen to others speak; (2) those whose rights might be affected by that speech; and (3) the state, which was bound to respect and protect the rights of both sides. On the modern view, the rights of others are reconceived as social interests, and the state is regarded as the representative of such interests. Indeed, despite Pound's efforts to distinguish them, the terms "social interests" and "state interests" are generally used interchangeably. In this way, First Amendment problems come to be viewed in terms of a bipolar opposition between the state and those who wish to engage in expression—a view that is applied not only to cases involving political speech or criticism of government, but also to cases involving speech that impacts on private parties.

E. THE DILEMMA OF MODERN FIRST AMENDMENT THEORY

In short, modern First Amendment theory perceives an inherent conflict between freedom of speech and the state's efforts to promote other social values. There are three basic approaches that one may take to First Amendment problems when they are understood in this way: (1) a statist position, which would generally defer to the government's power to regulate for the common good; (2) a civil libertarian view, which would generally protect freedom of speech; and (3) an approach that would seek to balance free speech and state interests. Each of these approaches suffers from serious difficulties, however—a result that should lead us to reexamine the conceptual framework of modern First Amendment theory.

The statist view would allow government broad power to regulate speech in the same way that it regulates conduct. Although this approach affords protection to the social interests that may be injured by expression, it provides little or no protection to freedom of speech. For this reason, it is clearly inadequate as an interpretation of the First Amendment.

By contrast, the civil libertarian view seeks maximal protection for free expression (and other individual rights) against state power. Yet just as statism fails to define the bounds of that power, civil libertarianism is unable to identify appropriate limits to free speech. Since it no longer appears possible, within a modern framework, to distinguish between legitimate and illegitimate restrictions, the modern defense of free speech tends toward absolutism.

*   *   *

[Individual liberty views are] subject to a more general objection.... While such arguments may establish the priority of free speech over social interests in general, they fail to demonstrate its priority over other fundamental rights, because the same sorts of arguments can be made on behalf of those rights. For example, while it is true that democratic self-government depends on political free speech, the latter seems to depend on individual liberty of speech and thought. Unless they enjoy such liberty, individuals will be incapable of participating in self-government. It may seem, therefore, that individual free speech is a more fundamental right than its political counterpart. In another sense, however, the reverse may be true: as Meiklejohn contends, individual liberties may depend on the existence of political freedom. In this way, it becomes clear that these two aspects of free speech are interdependent, and that neither is more basic than the other. Freedom of speech must be viewed as a unified system, which includes both individual and collective elements.

The argument may now be revised to assert that it is *freedom of speech as a whole* that has precedence over other social interests. Once more, however, the same kinds of arguments can be made for the priority of other rights. For instance, individuals cannot speak freely if they are not secure against violence. In this way, free speech depends on the right to personal security. Again, it does not necessarily follow that the latter is more fundamental than the former. Instead, just as individual and political free speech turned out to be interdependent, the same is true of free speech and other fundamental rights. It is only when these rights are taken as a whole, as a system of constitutional liberty, that they have priority over other interests.

*   *   *

In summary, while civil libertarianism provides strong protection for free speech, it is unable to identify the limits of that freedom....

The third approach, balancing, seeks to avoid the pitfalls of both statism and civil libertarianism. In recognizing that both free speech and competing interests have important value, and that neither should be unreasonably sacrificed to the other, balancing is appealing from a common sense standpoint. From a theoretical perspective, however, balancing is perhaps the least coherent of the three approaches, for it is difficult to see how free speech and state interests are to be balanced against each other. As originally conceived by Pound and others, a major purpose of interest jurisprudence was to reduce competing values to common terms—those of social welfare—so that they could be weighed on the same scale. On this view, applied by Chafee to the First Amendment, free speech and other interests should be measured in order to determine what result would most promote the common good. Yet the common good provided only an indeterminate standard for deciding between social interests. Moreover, balancing social interests is often thought to be an essentially legislative function.[8] Thus, this approach—what may be called quantitative balancing—failed to ensure strong protection for free speech.

For this reason, the thrust of most modern First Amendment theory has been to reverse the efforts of...Chafee, and to show that freedom of speech is *qualitatively different* from other social interests. When we view free speech in this way, however, it is difficult to see what it would mean to balance free speech against other social interests. This is even more true when free speech is reconceived as an individual right. In short, while a quantitative approach to balancing fails to adequately protect expression, a qualitative approach appears to be impossible.

*   *   *

CONCLUSION

At the heart of contemporary disputes over the First Amendment is an apparent conflict between freedom of expression and other fundamental values such as dignity, equality, and community. This conflict results from the tendency of modern First Amendment theory to conceive of issues in terms of an opposition between free speech and other social interests. Because of the difficulty of finding common ground between these disparate values, First Amendment problems often appear to be intractable.

*   *   *

The rights-based theory thus acknowledges what is most powerful in an absolutist approach to the First Amendment—its refusal to compromise the principles underlying free speech—while at the same time recognizing that these principles also justify protection of other rights. The value of free speech is ultimately strengthened rather than weakened by this recognition of its normative limits....

NOTES

1. 198 U.S. 45 (1905).
2. 249 U.S. 47 (1919).
3. See, e.g., *Debs v. United States*, 249 U.S. 211 (1919).
4. 250 U.S. 616 (1919).
5. 319 U.S. 624 (1943).
6. *Whitney v. California*, 274 U.S. 357 (1927) (J. Brandeis, concurring).
7. *Abrams v. United States*, 250 U.S. 616 (1919) (J. Holmes, dissenting).
8. See *Dennis v. United States*, 341 U.S. 494 (1951) (J. Frankfurter, concurring in judgment).

SEDITIOUS LIBEL AND THE LOST GUARANTEE OF A FREEDOM OF EXPRESSION

William T. Mayton

*   *   *

The framers...thought...external limitations, consisting of identified personal rights, were about the best that could be done in the case of a nation, such as England, where the government already held general lawmaking powers. But given the opportunity, as was then uniquely available in America, a stronger first line of protection could be achieved by internally adjusting the structure of government. So, through limitations and dispersals of government power in the original, unamended Constitution, they extended a strong guarantee of liberty of expression.

The first amendment was meant to affirm, and not to disturb, this structural guarantee. Still, as it was added to the Constitution, we were warned that its beguiling promise of a "freedom of speech" might diminish this guarantee by inviting a wholly rights-based and external mode of protecting speech. Levy has in much this way succumbed, and in his work he has excluded or treated as insignificant a wealth of evidence about the internal and structural protections of the liberty of expression under the original Constitution.

From *Columbia Law Review* 91 (1984). Courtesy of *Columbia Law Review*.

Taken together these protections eliminate the power to suppress seditious libel that Levy believes was absorbed and ratified by the first amendment. This Article advances a new understanding of the original guarantee of the liberty of expression and the limits and dispersals of power that it encompasses. This original guarantee was made possible by federalism, by an allocation to the states rather than to the federal government of an authority to suppress speech harmful to person and property. The Constitution's treason clause is an explicit manifestation of this original guarantee. The treason clause, as it acknowledges and defines government's traditional power to punish conduct injurious to it, specifically limits this power to conduct involving "overt acts." In this way, the federal government was to be precluded from using this power to suppress dissident speech, as had happened in England....

*   *   *

I. HISTORICAL FACT, CONSTITUTIONAL METHOD, AND THE RATIFICATION PROCESS

The argument that the American Constitution was meant to permit the punishment of seditious libel rests on a historical fact—the eighteenth-century English practice of punishing seditious libel—and on the view that the first amendment incorporates this practice through its open-ended "freedom of speech" phraseology. Because the first amendment was added to the Constitution without much debate as to precisely what "freedom of speech" was supposed to mean, it seems altogether plausible to give content to this provision by incorporating past practice. But to understand the full constitutional protection of speech, we must look past the first amendment and consider the entire Constitution. When we do so, the plausibility of the first amendment's incorporating past practice is considerably dissipated. The original process of drafting and ratifying the Constitution provided both the opportunity and the incentive to break with history and to discontinue the practice of seditious libel. Moreover, the original Constitution, unlike the first amendment, carries with it a source of strong extrinsic evidence—the state ratification debates—concerning the extent and nature of the constitutional protection of speech. This evidence is missed by focusing solely on the first amendment.

The process of drafting the Constitution provided the framers with the opportunity to break the historical link between seditious libel and government. The practice of seditious libel most often has been a product of factional politics, the irrepressible tendency of the "government for the time" to suppress speech detrimental to it. But at the constitutional convention the framers were in something of a disinterested position concerning speech and might for the moment have been insulated from the political forces that normally incline lawmakers toward suppression. Factions that would maintain their incumbency by using the national government to stifle dissident speech were not yet entrenched.

That the framers were in a position to break with past practice does not necessarily mean that they did.... The adoption of the Constitution was ultimately a federal rather than a national act: the Constitution had to be ratified by "conventions of the people" assembled in each state. For several reasons a national power to punish seditious libel would have been greatly disfavored at these conventions and very prejudicial to the prospects of the ratification of the Constitution. Studies have shown that in the years surrounding the framing and adoption of the Constitution a robust freedom of speech flourished in America, and that the press was a trenchant and persistent critic of government and government officials. Additionally, a certain independence and insular sense of community and locale was characteristic of Americans. ... Thus, to secure ratification the framers could not present the ratifying conventions with such a document. Instead, they had to proffer a document that eliminated the means by which the central government might indulge the inclination to suppress dissident speech.

In the state ratification debates, the power of the national government to suppress speech was drawn into issue. The debates on this power thus provide an important source of information about the structure of the Constitution as it relates to speech. More importantly, in these debates the understanding was reached that the Constitution as drafted at Philadelphia disarmed the national government of such power. For this reason, James Madison, the primary author of the first amendment, explained that it was altogether improper to define the first amendment's protection of speech by means of an external referent such as Blackstone's depiction of a freedom of speech in England. Instead, the first amendment's "freedom of speech" provision should first of all be given content by reference to the whole of the Constitution. Moreover, as Madison pointed out, the means by which the Constitution protected a liberty of expression could and should be identified by "the reasoning which then justified the original, unamended Constitution, and *invited its ratification*."

II. THE ENGLISH EXPERIENCE: OF A SUPPRESSION OF SPEECH BY THE GOVERNMENT FOR THE TIME

The "reasoning which then justified the Constitution" had its uniquely American components, federalism and a central government of limited powers. This reasoning, however, was developed against a background of suppression in England and cannot be fully understood except by reference to that background. This suppression was accomplished in three ways: constructive treason, seditious libel, and prior restraints. . . .

*   *   *

In order to understand fully the modern abuse of our constitutional protection of speech, it is necessary to disentangle constructive treason and seditious libel. These two modes of suppression, parallel and overlapping, served the same end: suppression of dissident speech by means of the criminal law. The newer doctrine of seditious libel, however, appears to have been created to avoid the legal safeguards that had attached to the older doctrine of constructive treason. Uncovering this motive for creating seditious libel is important, because history has here been repeated. In the United States we have devised criminal statutes in the nature of constructive treason, but have instead characterized them as sedition or espionage laws, and thereby have avoided one of our own constitutional safeguards—the treason clause—against such laws.

A. CONSTRUCTIVE TREASON

Treason is an offense against the state; under English law it was an act "against the person or government of the King."[1] . . . Edward III approved a statute that limited the crime largely to three situations: "levying war against our lord the king," "adhering to the king's enemies in his realm, giving to them aid and comfort," and "compassing or imagining the death of our lord the king."[2]

The "compassing" the king's death category was in turn limited by the condition that it could be established only by an "open deed," that is, an *overt act.* So limited, this category reached attempts and conspiracies, with the overt act requirement explained as "conspire[ing] the death of the king and the maner, and thereupon provid[ing] weapons, powder, harness, poison, or send[ing] letters of the execution thereof." Speech, in and of itself, was not, however, generally thought to constitute treason or "an overt act of compassing [the King's] death."[3] The Statute of Treasons, therefore, excluded merely dissident speech from its definition of crimes against the Crown. Accordingly, the statute was extolled for its "protection to what we ... now call political agitation and discussion."[4]

* * *

The way in which new treasons, without the overt act requirement and aimed at dissident speech, were created by new statutes is also shown by the reign of Henry VIII. Two of these statutes illustrate the typically broad and indeterminate nature of these treasons. One statute made it treason "[s]landerously or maliciously to publish ... by express writing or words, that the King our sovereign Lord is an heretic, schismatic, tyrant, infidel, or usurper."[5] This statute also defined as treason words or writing that deprived the King of his "dignity."[6] Another punished words or writing that "maliciously" led to a "disturbance of the king's enjoyment of his crown."[7] Adhering to the now familiar pattern, the statutes of Henry VIII were repealed after his death and the Statute of Edward III was again reinstated. And so, the waves of suppression rose, subsided, and continued.

These statutes enacted without the overt act limitation were not, however, the only source of constructive treasons. Starting at roughly the beginning of the seventeenth century, these treasons were also created by an enlargement of the "compassing or imagining the king's death" provision of the Statute of Treasons. As a consequence of this enlargement, speech, at least in written form, was considered an overt act of compassing the King's death, a suppression of written speech that roughly coincided with the rise of printing in England....

* * *

In America the framers moved to block such suppression of political comment. They did so specifically and in the text of the Constitution—by means of the treason clause.

B. SEDITIOUS LIBEL

In 1606, the public offense of seditious libel was created, ad hoc, by the Star Chamber decision in *de Libellis Famosis*. Thereafter, much of the repression previously accomplished by means of constructive treason in common law courts was transferred to the Star Chamber. Later, Blackstone was to present seditious libel as a common law doctrine, but its history is inconsistent with his view of the common law....

*   *   *

... [I]t appears that the offense of seditious libel was created to gain Star Chamber jurisdiction, to avoid the constraints of common law procedure, and to avoid the overt act limitation of constructive treason. Moreover, the misdemeanor classification of the doctrine—necessary for Star Chamber jurisdiction—should not disguise the fact that punishment, which included life imprisonment and mutilation, was vicious.

The third line of suppression in England, laws that required the licensing of all printed matter, was also a Star Chamber production. These laws, requiring virtually all printed matter to be approved by agents of the Crown prior to publication, established a bureaucratic network of suppression. Although the Star Chamber was abolished in 1641, the licensing laws that it had created did not die with it, at least not immediately. Instead, they were continued by acts of Parliament for fifty years or so until they lapsed, permanently, in 1694 when Parliament refused to renew them.

As the licensing laws were expiring, however, seditious libel, that other Star Chamber creation[,] was moved to a new home. In 1679 the Whig Parliament had deliberately let the licensing laws expire temporarily. This loosening of censorship failed, however, because of "the triumph of the king through the law courts."[8] In a proclamation grounded in an advisory opinion by the judges of the King's Bench, then led by Chief Justice Scroggs, Charles II assumed an executive authority to resume the licensing laws. In a similar manner the Crown assured the continuing vitality of the offense of seditious libel. Assisted by the same judges and in response to petitions against his proroguing of Parliament, Charles first proclaimed that "tumultuous petitioning" was unlawful. This round of "censorship by proclamation" was completed as Scroggs and the "twelve high judges of England," in conference at Charles II's direction with his privy council, proclaimed that seditious libel was an offense under the common law, and therefore within the jurisdiction of the King's Bench.

*   *   *

III. A LEGACY OF IDEALISM

*   *   *

A strong statement of the fundamental illegitimacy of government suppression of speech, one that distinguished between speech and acts, is that of Benedict de Spinoza in *A Theological-Political Treatise*. Spinoza reasoned that because of the discernible bad externalities of some acts—for example, the injury to the victim of theft—the individual under government "justly cedes the right of free action" in order to "preserve the peace." But the liberty of speech, he thought, was something else again: Government "should merely have to do with actions and every man should think what he likes and say what he thinks."[9]

This limitation of government power over speech was, at one level, based on an "indefeasible natural right" of the individual. By "natural right" Spinoza meant those rights "wherewith we conceive every individual to be conditioned by nature, so as to live and act in a given way." And every individual is conditioned by nature "to think what he likes and say what he thinks." Government control of such a natural right is unjust, Spinoza reasoned, in that it requires a standard of conduct which can hardly be met. "[I]t is impossible," Spinoza said, "to deprive men of the liberty of saying what they think." But while the government could not eliminate speech by its laws, it could burden it, and Spinoza saw this burden as being especially unfortunate in that it fell disproportionately upon worthier individuals. Accordingly, Spinoza wrote of "useless laws, which can only be broken by those who love virtue and the liberal arts, thus paring down the state till it is too small to harbour men of talent."

*   *   *

The inevitability of... [a] discretion[ary definition of permitted speech] and its abuse, and the use of the overt acts requirement as a means of containment, were publicly acknowledged in colonial America. For example, in the preamble for the Virginia Bill for Establishing Religious Freedom, Thomas Jefferson wrote:

> [T]o suffer the civil magistrate to intrude his powers into the field of opinion and to restrain the profession or propagation of principles on supposition of their ill tendency is a dangerous falacy, which at once destroys all religious liberty, because he being of course judge of that tendency will make his opinions the rule of judgment, and approve or condemn the sentiments of others only as they shall square with or differ from his own; that it is time enough for the rightful purposes of civil government for its officers to interfere when principles break out into overt acts against peace and good order....

The power of government to punish speech that might be injurious to it was roundly condemned in eighteenth-century political philosophy. A distinction was drawn, however, between the government's acting to protect itself and the government's acting to protect private interests. Speech might impair a reputation, and opening the courts to private actions for damages from such injury was considered socially useful. Also, an acknowledged duty of government was to protect its citizens from speech that might cause injury to their "life[,] limb or property"—to protect against injury such as might result from "falsely shouting fire in a crowded theatre."[10] This duty to protect private citizens against injury to person and property, however, need not lead to a leveling of the liberty to speak freely about public matters, especially when an allocation of powers among various parts of a government is possible. The writings of Benjamin Franklin lend perspective as to how this leveling might be avoided.

In support of a state defamation law, and with some irony, Franklin advocated the "liberty of the cudgel," that is, a bit of self-help on the part of a person defamed. "[I]f an impudent writer attacks your reputation," Franklin wrote, then "break his head."[11] Franklin was not, of course, intent on promoting physical assaults. His point was that "[i]f . . . it should be thought that this proposal of mine may disturb the public peace," then the legislature of the state of Pennsylvania should provide an alternative, a legal remedy for injuries to private reputation. Franklin made it abundantly clear, however, that he was only advocating a remedy for private injury; in no sense was he approving anything approximating seditious libel laws. If liberty of the press, he wrote, was "understood to be merely the liberty of discussing the propriety of public measures and political opinions, let us have as much of it as you please." Franklin, moreover, expected that state governments, and not a national government, would provide a remedy for such private injury.

Franklin's discourse therefore presaged the constitutional scheme that was to emerge: a national government deliberately disabled of the power to suppress speech, but with the states retaining the power to redress or deter private injuries caused by speech. Furthermore, in line with the eighteenth-century insight that laws against speech, because of their peculiar indeterminacy, could not be limited to socially useful applications, the constitutional scheme that was to emerge protected speech by eliminating any power to make such laws.

IV. THE FRAMING AND RATIFICATION

*   *   *

The evidence shows that the framers of the original Constitution rejected the practice of seditious libel and instead created protections of speech more consistent with eighteenth-century ideals. These protections, however, are not spelled out in the text of the original Constitution. While the treason clause is a specific limit on the power of the national government to make dissident speech a crime, this particular limit is understandable only by reference to constructive treason and the eighteenth-century overt act requirement. In addition to the treason clause, the more general and more important protections of speech are lodged in the structure of government created by the Constitution. Fortunately, as the Constitution was explained in the crucial state ratification debates, the existence and essence of these protections emerged with some clarity.

A. THE TREASON CLAUSE

*   *   *

In the ratification convention in North Carolina, the fear was voiced that "any man who will complain of their oppressions, or write against their usurpation, may be deemed a traitor." In response, Richard Dobbs Spaight, a member of the Philadelphia convention, pointed to the treason clause:

Why did not the gentleman look at the Constitution, and see their powers? Treason is there defined. It says, expressly, that treason against the United States shall consist only in levying war against them, or in adhering to their enemies, giving them aid and comfort. Complaining, therefore, or writing, cannot be treason.

Similar assurances were recorded in Virginia. The treason clause was also praised in the ratification debates in Massachusetts and Pennsylvania.

*   *   *

Still, I wish to be careful not to overstate the relative importance of the treason clause. I agree with Taylor's assessment of it as a free speech provision; and as I discuss in more detail, its overt act requirement is an important containment of the use of the criminal law as an instrument of political oppression. Nonetheless, to the framers the more important protection of speech lay in a Constitution structured to deny the national government power over speech.

B. A LIMITATION OF POWER

To the framers, the limitation of federal powers was more than an accommodation to state government; it was as well a means of preserving individual liberty.... Once a legislature, and especially the national Congress, gains the power to punish speech to serve its estimate of the collective good, any assertion of that power carries with it certain pressures, such as public sentiment and the weight of a judgment of a coordinate branch of government, that make judicial protection of conflicting individual rights rather difficult....

How this method of preserving liberty by limiting power applied to speech was explained in the state ratification debates and at the convention in Philadelphia. James Wilson, in the ratification debate in Pennsylvania, explained that the press was protected from suppression by the national government in that "it will be found that there is given to the general government no power whatsoever concerning it; and no law, in pursuance of the Constitution, can possibly be enacted to destroy that liberty." Similarly, James Iredell in North Carolina explained that "the future Congress will have no other authority over [the press] than [copyright laws].... If the Congress should exercise any other power over the press than this, they will do it without any warrant from this Constitution, and must answer for it as for any other act of tyranny." This consensus included those opposed to the Constitution. Richard Henry Lee, one of the more learned and influential of the Constitution's opponents was, as he said, bound to "confess I do not see in what cases the congress can, with any pretense of right, make a law to suppress the freedom of the press."

At the constitutional convention in Philadelphia there was but a single recorded reference to speech. But in light of the assurances about speech made at the state ratification debates it was a significant one. A motion was made to include in the Constitution the declaration that "the liberty of the press should be inviolably observed." But after the explanation that "[i]t is unnecessary—[t]he power of Congress does not extend to the Press," the motion was defeated.[12]

The evidence, then, is that an understanding was reached at the convention and during the ratification process that the national government had no power over speech. Indeed, the ratifying convention in Virginia expressly conditioned its ratification on this understanding. At this convention, Patrick Henry's motion to make ratification contingent upon the addition of a bill of rights to the Constitution was defeated. Instead, the Constitution as submitted to the convention was approved by a resolution predicated on the understanding that:

> Whereas the powers granted under the proposed Constitution are the gift of the people, and every power not granted thereby remains with them, ... and, among other essential rights, liberty of conscience and of the press cannot be cancelled, abridged, restrained, or modified, by any authority of the United States.

Given this understanding about the limitation on federal power over speech, the first amendment, if interpreted along the lines of Blackstone, upsets the scheme of the original Constitution. It presumes to acknowledge a power of suppression that the original Constitution was understood to deny.

*   *   *

V. THE ALIEN AND SEDITION ACTS AND THE ORIGIN OF THE BLACKSTONIAN MEASURE OF A FREEDOM OF EXPRESSION UNDER THE U.S. CONSTITUTION

The... Constitution's protection of a liberty of expression is not contained in one sentence. [The] central "freedom of speech" phrase must first be defined by reference to the rest of the Constitution. The first amendment may then add to the protections of speech provided by the whole Constitution, but it cannot diminish them, certainly not by reference to an external measure such as Blackstone. Unfortunately, this straightforward construction of the first amendment has been distorted. The initial and main occasion for this distortion was the enactment of the Alien and Sedition Acts, where the first amendment was read both to imply and to ratify a national power to make dissident speech a crime.

* * *

... [I]n 1794, the power of the national government to burden dissident speech was successfully contained. Over the next few years, however, as the Adams Administration was stung by a critical press and as a reconstituted Federalist Party saw its hegemony threatened by the Jeffersonians, the irrepressible specter of factional politics emerged. It grew until, in 1798, just nine years after the Constitution had been ratified, a Federalist majority of Congress succeeded in passing a sedition act, as part of the Alien and Sedition Acts. This act imposed fines and imprisonment on "any person who shall write, print, utter or publish... any false, scandalous and malicious writing or writings against the government of the United States, or either House of Congress ... or the President... [or] to bring them... into contempt or disrepute."[13]

* * *

As a consequence of the Federalist's self-serving reliance on Blackstone, the history of freedom of expression in the United States has been stood on its head. The prevailing view, as developed by Levy in *Legacy of Suppression*, is that the Alien and Sedition Acts inspired a new and original exposition of freedom of expression under the Constitution. This exposition, as Levy sees it, was necessary in order to counter an entrenched Blackstonian measure of this liberty, *a measure that was part of the original understanding about speech.* This depiction of the original understanding, however, is upside down: Blackstone's view, as we have seen, was not and could not have been a part of the original understanding about speech and the Constitution. Nowhere in the constitutional convention or the state ratification debates is there anything close to an understanding that the Constitution was meant to impart or to countenance a federal power to punish seditious libel. Instead, the consensus of these debates was that the federal government had not been given any power that would allow it to indulge this practice. Moreover, there is nothing in the debate accompanying the first amendment that upsets this consensus. A Blackstonian measure of "the freedom of speech" was, therefore, simply a piece of post hoc grafting, done by a successful faction in Congress to provide a modicum of legitimacy for the first federal sedition act.

*   *   *

VII. MODERN IMPLICATIONS OF THE ORIGINAL GUARANTEE

*   *   *

...Today there remains a flabbiness in our rights-oriented free speech jurisprudence that permits the continuation of such costs. We presume the existance of government power, and then depend upon the courts to protect individual rights from this power. But not every government-imposed cost to speech presents an issue in a form susceptible of resolution by the courts,[14] and not every individual is hardy enough to risk a court contest and to absorb the costs of it. The idea of the framers, of course, was that where possible—and they knew it was possible with respect to the national government—such costs were to be wholly eliminated by removing the source: a government power over speech.

*   *   *

CONCLUSION

*   *   *

Under the original understanding the power to protect person and property from injuries caused by speech was assigned to the states. With this original allocation in mind, a significant part of modern case law about speech can be put in a perspective more in keeping with the relevant constitutional framework. In its seminal *Chaplinsky* dictum, the Supreme Court identified a range of speech—"the lewd and obscene, the profane, the libelous, and the insulting or 'fighting' words"—as outside the first amendment.[15] The Court did so by weighing the "slight social value" of such speech against the "social interest" in order and morality. But instead of indulging in balancing, the Court could have reached the same result by simply acknowledging that regulation of such speech was originally assigned to the states and was for this reason outside the first amendment. Such speech, however, should still enjoy a constitutional protection, as part of the conditioned liberty of expression protected by the due process clauses of the fifth and fourteenth amendments.

Unlike this conditioned due process protection, the first amendment was meant to preserve an unconditioned liberty to speak freely about public matters. The first amendment succeeded to this central function inasmuch as it was meant to affirm the guarantee of the original Constitution. This central function should not be diminished by means of due process-like balancing. Nor should it be diminished by an entirely rights-oriented jurisprudence. The objective underlying the Bill of Rights was to identify those personal liberties that were to be protected against otherwise legitimate assertions of government power. This objective though, is one that invites conflict and compromise in a contest between individual rights and the collective interests that government seeks to advance. Consequently, the courts, in their task of protecting individual rights, have claimed the discretion to compromise these rights as well as the opposing governmental interest. In the area of public speech, the result of this "balancing" has often been tragic. Merely human judges, while extolling the right to speak, have sacrificed it to fear, to the passion of majorities, and to base, self-serving politics. More mundanely, they have compromised speech because of their own bad guesses about the public interest.

*   *   *

NOTES

1. M. Hale, *The History of the Pleas of the Crown*, vol. 1, 59.

2. Ibid., at 89.

3. See, e.g., Pine's Case, 79 Eng. Rep. 703 (K. B. 1629).

4. J. Stephen, *History of the Criminal Law of England*, vol. 2, 247 (1883).

5. Hen. 8, chap. 13, vol. 26 (1534).

6. J. Stephen, vol. 2, *supra* note, at 256.

7. Hen. 8, chap. 7, vol. 28 (1533), quoted in translation from the original French in M. Hale, *The History of the Pleas of the Crown*, vol. 1, 276.

8. Havighurst, "The Judiciary and Politics in the Reign of Charles II," pt. 2, *Law Q. Review* 66 (1950): 229, 241.

9. R. Elwes, *The Chief Works of Benedict de Spinoza*, vol. 1, 265 (1951).

10. W. Holdsworth, *A History of English Law*, vol. 8, 338 (1926).

11. *The Works of Benjamin Franklin*, vol. 12, 134 (J. Bigelow ed. 1907).

12. M. Farrand, *The Records of the Federal Convention of 1787*, vol. 2, 617–18 (1966) (remarks of Roger Sherman, delegate from Connecticut).

13. Act of July 14, 1798, chap. 74, § 2, 1 Stat. 596, 596.

14. See *Laird v. Tatum*, 408 U.S. 1 (1972).

15. *Chaplinsky v. New Hampshire*, 315 U.S. 568, 571–72 (1942).

THE ORIGINS OF
THE PRESS CLAUSE

David A. Anderson

I. INTRODUCTION

* * *

I make no claim that the Framers' understanding of the press clause should be controlling today; I share Professor Nimmer's view that what they said may turn out to be more important than what they meant.[1] But text and meaning ultimately are inseparable; to understand what the Framers said, we inevitably seek to discover what they meant. In this instance, history provides some clues. The press clause had a substantial legislative history in the First Congress and, more important, a number of antecedents in state constitutions and other declarations of the revolutionary period. This article explores those sources and then reexamines, in the light of this history, Leonard Levy's conclusion that freedom of the press meant no more than freedom from prior restraint.

Reprinted from *UCLA Law Review* 30 (1983). Courtesy of the Regents of the University of California and the author.

II. THE LEGISLATIVE HISTORY OF THE PRESS CLAUSE

*   *   *

A. Pre-Revolutionary Declarations

The history of the press clause begins a generation before the actual drafting of the first amendment. In 1768, the *Boston Gazette*, the leading organ of radicalism in Massachusetts, accused the royal governor of misrepresenting the position of the Massachusetts House to the British secretary of state. The Royal Council condemned the article as a seditious libel, and Governor Bernard asked the House to turn the matter over to a grand jury for prosecution. The House, dominated by the radical leader Sam Adams, refused to do so and instead adopted a resolution stating: "The Liberty of the Press is a great Bulwark of the Liberty of the People: It is, therefore, the incumbent Duty of those who are constituted the Guardians of the People's Rights to defend and maintain it." As we shall see later, this language appears to have been adapted from one of "Cato's Letters" that had been republished in the *Gazette* only a few months earlier.

A more elaborate declaration came in 1774, on the eve of the War for Independence. The Continental Congress, hoping to make allies of the settlers in Quebec, approved a declaration explaining to the northern neighbors the goals of the American endeavor:

> The last right we shall mention, regards the freedom of the press. The importance of this consists, besides the advancement of truth, science, morality, and arts in general, in its diffusion of liberal sentiments on the administration of Government, in its ready communication of thoughts between subjects, and its consequential promotion of union among them, whereby oppressive officers are shamed or intimidated, into more honourable and just modes of conducting affairs.[2]

Three things should be noted about the Quebec Address. First, its view of the purposes of freedom of the press was not limited to scrutiny of government, but also included broader intellectual and cultural objectives. Second, the declaration said nothing about freedom of speech. Although it reflects values we associate today with freedom of speech, or freedom of expression generally, it viewed the press as the means by which these values were to be vindicated. Third, the declaration must be read as an expression of American aspirations rather than accomplishments. The press freedom that the Continental Congress so ardently commended to the inhabitants of Quebec was poorly protected by law in America. The colonial press had no legal protection in 1774 other than the common law prohibition against prior restraints— hardly a sufficient safeguard for the ambitious role outlined for the press in the Quebec Address.

B. THE STATE CONSTITUTIONS

The Massachusetts resolution and Quebec Address were not law, of course. The first legally effective press clauses appeared in the eleven state constitutions adopted during the War for Independence. Of those, nine included provisions on freedom of the press, all phrased in general terms.

There were essentially four versions of these early press clauses. The first was the provision drafted by George Mason in 1776 for the Virginia Declaration of Rights. It read: "That the freedom of the Press is one of the greatest bulwarks of liberty, and can never be restrained but by despotick Governments." This was copied almost verbatim in the North Carolina Declaration of Rights, later in 1776.

The second model was that of Maryland, which said simply: "That the liberty of the press ought to be inviolably preserved." This was adopted verbatim in the Delaware Declaration of Rights, and with minor deviations in the constitutions of Georgia and South Carolina.

The Massachusetts Constitutional Convention of 1780 produced its own version of the press clause. It read: "The liberty of the press is essential to the security of freedom in a state: it ought not, therefore, to be restrained in this Commonwealth." New Hampshire copied this model in its Bill of Rights of 1783.

The only state whose press clause did not follow one of these models was Pennsylvania; it had the only original state constitution that protected freedom of speech as well as press. The Pennsylvania provision read: "That the people have a right to freedom of speech, and of writing, and publishing their sentiments; therefore the freedom of the press ought not to be restrained."

This is the provision invariably referred to as "the press clause" of the Pennsylvania Constitution, and as we shall see, this language eventually played an important role in the evolution of the first amendment. But the Pennsylvania Constitution of 1776 contained a second provision relating to the press. This second press clause has been little noticed because it was contained not in the Declaration of Rights, where the other press clause was located, but in the main body of the constitution, called the "Plan or Frame of Government for Commonwealth or State of Pennsylvania." This second press clause reads as follows: "The printing presses shall be free to every person who undertakes to examine the proceedings of the legislature, or any part of government."

It is impossible to know exactly what this provision meant. It may have been an exhortation to printers to open their columns to opposing viewpoints on government. We usually think of the colonial newspapers as being intensely partisan, and most of them were. But many of them also served as forums for public debate. The *South Carolina Gazette*, which Benjamin Franklin helped found, was a forum for religious and political controversy throughout the pre-revolutionary period. As late as 1775, James Rivington, a leading Tory publisher, affirmed that his *New York Gazetteer* was open to all parties and that he considered his press "in the light of a public office, to which every man has a right to have recourse."[3] Merrill Jensen, an indefatigable reader of the newspapers of the period, wrote that "most newspaper publishers believed that it was a part of their public duty to print materials on all sides of a question, even when they were counter to a particular publisher's own views."[4]

Moreover, impartiality and accessibility seem to have been universally acknowledged as ideals, however often they may have been ignored in practice. Even the most partisan papers invariably claimed impartiality, and when printers were attacked for publishing unpopular viewpoints, they often defended [themselves] by appealing to the public's appreciation of the value of free and open discussion. Thus, even though the press did not come to view itself as primarily a neutral conduit of information until much later, the ideal of impartiality already was powerful enough to have inspired the second Pennsylvania press clause.

* * *

D. The State Ratifying Conventions

* * *

Virginia's ratifying convention was the first to adopt a proposed press clause, in June of 1788. Its press clause read: "That the people have a right to freedom of speech, and of writing and publishing their sentiments; that the freedom of the press is one of the greatest bulwarks of liberty and ought not to be violated."

This proposal is remarkable for three reasons. First, it is almost identical to the language that Madison used when he introduced the Bill of Rights in Congress. Second, it is not Madison's language, or even George Mason's. It is essentially Pennsylvania's language from the 1776 Pennsylvania Constitution. It includes the Virginia Constitution's "bulwark of liberty" rhetoric, but the substance is purely Pennsylvania's. This choice was crucial, because of all the original states, only Pennsylvania protected freedom of speech. Had the Virginia Ratifying Convention used its own state constitution as the model, rather than that of Pennsylvania, Madison's proposed bill of rights might not have included freedom of speech. Third, the Virginians ignored a Pennsylvania modification designed to adapt the state press clause to the federal context. The press clause unsuccessfully proposed that the Pennsylvania ratifying convention used the phrase "shall not be restrained by any law of the United States." The Virginia convention chose a more universal prohibition similar to that of the Pennsylvania Constitution: "ought not to be violated." Why Virginia chose the Pennsylvania press clause is a mystery, particularly since most of the rest of its proposals came from the Virginia Declaration of Rights.

*   *   *

The most notable fact about the ratifying conventions is that they generated few new ideas. Despite the clamor for bills of rights in general and freedom of the press in particular, the recommendations of the ratifying conventions merely repeated language from the state constitutions. Significantly, most of them saw no need to revise the language for application to the federal government; there was no mention of Congress or the federal government except in the recommendations of the Pennsylvania minority, and that recommendation was not picked up by any of the other ratifying conventions. If the ratifying conventions viewed freedom of the press in the federal context differently from the way it was viewed in the states, their language did not reflect it.

E. The First Congress: Writing the First Amendment

*   *   *

1. Madison's Proposals in the House

*   *   *

Madison's bill of rights included two amendments relating to freedom of the press. The second, which was aimed at the states, came to naught. The first evolved into the present speech-and-press clause. It read: "The people shall not be deprived or abridged of their right to speak, to write, or to publish their sentiments; and the freedom of the press, as one of the great bulwarks of liberty, shall be inviolable." The language was essentially that suggested by the Virginia Ratifying Convention of the previous year.

On July 21, this amendment—along with all the others—was sent to the select committee. Although the committee did not greatly change the substance of Madison's proposals, it played an important role in the legislative history of the first amendment. It rewrote Madison's speech-and-press provision and combined it with his separate clause protecting the rights of assembly and petition. The committee's language was much closer to the present first amendment than to Madison's draft. It read as follows: "The freedom of speech and of the press, and the right of the people peaceably to assemble and consult for their common good, and to apply to the Government for the redress of grievances, shall not be infringed."

*   *   *

After this [an] intense debate on instructing representatives, the vote on the amendment itself was anticlimactic. The records merely state that the question was taken on the speech-press-assembly-petition clause as reported by the select committee and that it was "agreed to"; there is no record of the vote or of comments opposing the clause. The House spent six more days debating other bill of rights provisions and, on August 24, adopted a resolution formally proposing the amendments that had been agreed upon.

2. The First Amendment in the Senate

Records of the First Senate are far sketchier than those of the House. Senate proceedings were closed to the public, and no detailed record of debates was kept. The Senate Journal and the History of the Proceedings and Debates report only the actions taken, without further elucidation. The Journal shows that the House version of what is now the first amendment came before the Senate on September 3. An attempt to insert a right to instruct representatives was rejected by a vote of two to fourteen.

* * *

... [On] September 4, a new version of the language appeared, for the first time limiting the prohibition to Congress. It read: "That Congress shall make no law, abridging the freedom of speech, or of the press, or the right of the people peaceably to assemble and consult for their common good, and to petition the government for a redress of grievances" ...

In any event, the change made the construction parallel to that of the religion clause as adopted by the House, which also began with the words "Congress shall make no law." At the end of the Senate debate, on September 9, the Senate combined the two amendments into one, covering the same subjects as the present first amendment. It also deleted the phrase "and consult for their common good."

* * *

Contrary to occasional flights of Newspaper Week oratory, the position of the first amendment did not indicate that the Framers attached primacy to the freedoms of speech and press. The provision we know as the first amendment was third on the list submitted to the states. It became first only because Amendments One and Two were not ratified. If the order of amendments represented their importance to the Founders, then we know that nothing was as important to them as the election (Amendment One) and compensation (Amendment Two) of congressmen. In fact, freedom of press or speech was never first on anyone's list. It was the last right mentioned in the Address to the Inhabitants of Quebec. It was article twelve of the Pennsylvania Declaration of Rights, the sixteenth of twenty amendments proposed by the Virginia

Ratifying Convention, and the second clause of the fourth proposition in Madison's proposed bill of rights.

*   *   *

4. Some Observations on Congress's Work

From the first amendment's journey through Congress, three conclusions may be drawn. First, freedom of the press only gradually came to be seen as part of a larger parcel of related rights. In most of the state constitutions, freedom of the press was treated as a separate, distinct right. In the ratifying conventions, its relationship to freedom of speech was recognized, and in Madison's initial version of the first amendment, speech and press were coupled. The House select committee joined those with the rights of assembly, consultation, and petition, combining in one amendment all of the major rights relating to freedom of expression. The Senate apparently also saw a relationship to free exercise of religion and freedom from governmentally established religion. The amalgamation of the religion clauses with those previously joined by the House made the first amendment what it is today—a cluster of distinct but related rights, complementary means by which thought, belief, and expression are protected from governmental interference.

Second, Congress unequivocally refused to protect freedom of the press from encroachment by the states. The House's unspecific prohibition— "freedom of the press...shall not be infringed"—was made specific by the Senate: "*Congress* shall make no law...." Madison and his colleagues in the House obviously assumed that, even without the word "Congress," a specific prohibition against state infringement would be required. But the Senate specifically rejected the state free-press amendment, and the House acquiesced in that decision. The legislative intent to limit only the federal government could hardly be more clear.

Finally, so far as we can tell, Congress never debated the merits or meaning of freedom of the press. The arguments concerned either peripheral matters or questions about the advisability of a bill of rights generally. No one asserted that freedom of the press was not an appropriate or necessary element of a bill of rights. No one expressed any fear that the guarantee might make the press irresponsible or too powerful. No one suggested that "freedom of the press" was too expansive, or that the prohibition was too absolute to be taken literally.

*   *   *

III. INTERPRETING THE LEGISLATIVE HISTORY

The legislative history of the press clause is, of course, inconclusive, not only in the sense that history is always inconclusive, but also because the Framers simply did not articulate what they meant by "freedom of the press." Until some further evidence of their views turns up (which seems unlikely, in view of the vast amount of attention historians already have devoted to the Framers and their writings), attempts to divine the "original understanding" of the press clause must begin with this sketchy history of its framing. Nevertheless, some conclusions may be drawn.

First, freedom of the press, whatever it meant, was a matter of widespread concern. Nine of the eleven original states that adopted revolutionary constitutions protected freedom of press. It was included in the bill of rights proposed at the constitutional convention; after that proposal was rejected, it was the only right proposed independently. Of the seven bills of rights that were proposed in the ratifying conventions, five contained press clauses. By the time the First Congress began preparing a bill of rights, there was little doubt that one of the rights would be freedom of the press. Every version of the Bill of Rights considered by the First Congress contained a press clause; there was never any suggestion that it should be deleted. Freedom of the press occupied a secure place in the framers' catalogue of essential rights.

Second, the press clause had its own origins, separate and distinct from the other first amendment rights. Freedom of the press was neither equated with nor viewed as a derivative of freedom of speech. Most of the state constitutions protected freedom of the press, but only one protected speech. As Levy showed, freedom of speech, unlike freedom of the press, had little history as an independent concept when the first amendment was framed. "It developed as an offshoot of freedom of the press, on the one hand, and on the other, freedom of religion—the freedom to speak openly on religious matters." The hypothesis that the press clause was merely "complementary to and a natural extension of Speech Clause liberty,"[5] advanced by Chief Justice Burger, is not supported by the historical evidence. Epistemologically, at least, the press clause was primary and the speech clause secondary.

"Freedom of expression," the notion of an interrelated complex of protections for thought, belief, and expression, is a modern concept. To impose it retrospectively on the framers is anachronistic. Although they gradually recognized a relationship between the freedoms of press, speech, petition, assembly, and religion, the process was inductive, rather than deductive. The Framers began not with a general theory of intellectual freedom, but with specific solutions to concrete grievances. The first amendment must be viewed (historically, at least) as the sum of its parts, not as a divisible integer.

Third, there is no evidence that the framers intended to protect freedom of the press qualifiedly. Whatever the concept meant to them, they sought to protect it fully. Not one of the state press clauses included the Blackstonian limitation, "being responsible for the abuse thereof," which appeared in a number of later state constitutions. None of the proposals of the ratifying conventions contained any such limitation, nor did any of the versions in the First Congress. The only attempt to impose any limitation—the proposal in the Senate to protect the press only "in as ample a manner as hath at any time been secured by the common law"—was defeated. In the debates of the Constitutional Convention and the First Congress, no one expressed any fear of the power of the press or any apprehension of abuse of its power. No one suggested that it was necessary to balance the freedom of the press against other interests. The Framers either did not appreciate, or appreciated but did not fear, the consequences of a free press.

Fourth (and most important), freedom of the press was viewed not merely as a desirable civil liberty, but as a matter integral to the structure of the new government. The press clause was the product of revolutionary ferment. There were no guarantees of press freedom in colonial charters and little agitation to add them. The demand for legal protection of the press was contemporaneous with the demand for independence and self-government. The rhetoric often came from the pens of Englishmen, such as John Wilkes, "Cato," and "Father of Candor," but the realities that made the rhetoric relevant were the confrontations of American printers like John Peter Zenger and Eleazer Oswald with royal governors and other local representatives of the crown.

*   *   *

Nothing makes the structural role of press freedom clearer than the "bulwark of liberty" metaphor with which the ideal was expressed. The phrase, as well as many of the ideas that it represented, came from *Cato's Letters*. Cato was a pseudonym for the English journalists John Trenchard and William Gordon. Their essays have been described as "the most popular, quotable, esteemed source of political ideas in the colonial period."[6] Essay No. 15, entitled "Of Freedom of Speech: That the same is inseparable from Publick Liberty," first employed the bulwark metaphor: "Freedom of Speech is the great Bulwark of Liberty. . . ." Liberty, in eighteenth-century America, meant political liberty; it was not a guarantee of personal autonomy or self-fulfillment. Cato touted freedom of speech, not for its own sake, but for its value in combating governmental oppression and tyranny.

> This sacred Privilege is so essential to free Government that the Security of Property; and the Freedom of Speech, always go together; and in those wretched Countries where a Man cannot call his Tongue his own, he can scarce call any Thing else his own. Whoever would overthrow the Liberty of the Nation, must begin by subduing the Freedom of Speech; a Thing terrible to publick Traytors.[7]

*   *   *

The revolutionary context from which the press clause sprang, the concerns of those who demanded it, and the language in which its role was expressed, all suggest that Justice Stewart was right: the Framers viewed the press clause as a structural provision of the Constitution. "The primary purpose of the constitutional guarantee of a free press was . . . to create a fourth institution outside the Government as an additional check on the three official branches."

*   *   *

The Stewart . . . view of the press clause seems so thoroughly supported by the legislative history that one may wonder why it has not been universally accepted. The answer lies, I think, in the puzzle of seditious libel and in the hegemony of Leonard Levy's interpretation of first amendment history. If the Framers expected the press to operate as an effective check on government, how could they have tolerated the law of seditious libel, which made criticism of government a crime? And if they really understood the value of a free press, how could they have behaved so repressively toward it when they held power?

*   *   *

V. THE MEANING OF FREEDOM OF THE PRESS IN 1789

*   *   *

A. SEDITIOUS LIBEL IN AMERICA, PRE-1798

*   *   *

[W]e must remember that the Framers were inveterate seditious libelers themselves. Many of them were outspoken critics of the existing government under the Articles of Confederation. Under the Blackstonian view of freedom of the press, that criticism made them guilty of seditious libel. Levy implies that they were oblivious to this anomaly, but Madison, at least, was not. If sedition acts had been enforced against the press during the revolutionary period, he asked rhetorically, "might not the United States have been languishing at this day, under the infirmities of a sickly confederation?"

It is difficult to believe that the Framers' attitudes toward criticism of government were unaffected by the revolutionary experience. Even if they were not prepared to articulate a new theory that would repudiate seditious libel explicitly, they may well have believed that the hopeful generality "freedom of the press"—an idea that took root (whatever its meaning) during the revolutionary period—would somehow accommodate criticism of government.

B. The Sedition Act of 1798

There remains the rather large fact of the Sedition Act of 1798. If the Framers intended by the press clause to protect criticism of government, how could they have enacted, only nine years later, a federal statute whose avowed purpose was to prevent such criticism? There can be no doubt that the Sedition Act was inconsistent with the checking-function theory of the press clause. The Act made it a crime to "write, print, utter or publish...any false, scandalous and malicious writing or writings against the government of the United States, or either house of the Congress of the United States, or the President of the United States, with intent to defame."[8]

*   *   *

1. The Sedition Act and "The Framers"

... [Because the Sedition Act was passed so soon after the First Amendment,] we sometimes assume the actors must have been more or less the same, or at least must have shared the same basic ideas. Neither assumption is true.

Both America and the Congress changed dramatically in the 1790s. The triumphant self-confidence that produced "the great experiment" was being eroded by xenophobia, sectionalism, and partisanship. The visions of anarchy generated by the French Revolution and the reality of war between the European powers must have seemed genuinely threatening to many in the politically immature and militarily weak new republic. The period has been described as "the most awkward decade in American history, bearing little relation to what went on immediately before or after."[9]

The Fifth Congress reflected the changes that were occurring in the country during that decade. Of the ninety-five senators and representatives who served in the First Congress, only eighteen remained when the Sedition Act was enacted in July 1798, and of those only ten voted "aye." It was thus not, in any literal sense, "the Framers" who passed the Sedition Act. Nor was it that subset of the Framers called "the Federalists." The Sedition Act was, of course, the project of the Federalist Party. The party's leader, President Adams, did much to incite anti-Republican sentiment in Congress, approved the Act's passage, and specifically authorized its enforcement against his critics. The premier Federalist, Alexander Hamilton, urged Adams to enforce the Act even more vigorously and sought passage of even more drastic limitations on criticism of government officials.

*   *   *

The Sedition Act has a stench of political expediency about it that robs much of its force as evidence of its proponents' fundamental beliefs. The avowed purpose of the Act was to silence the Federalists' domestic critics, thereby presenting to the world a united front and refuting French claims that the American people did not support their government. But the Federalists used the Act in an attempt to weaken the Republicans before the elections of 1800.

* * *

The argument that the Sedition Act must have been consistent with the Framers' understanding of the first amendment because they (or men who shared their ideas) passed it is untenable. Neither of the alternative premises is sound. The Federalists who sought to prevent criticism of government by passing the Sedition Act were not the Framers, nor did they share the Framers' views. Because they were members of the same generation as the Framers, their views on the meaning of the press clause are entitled to somewhat greater weight than we should give to those of a contemporary Congress, but their views cannot be controlling. That the Fifth Congress might have passed an act inconsistent with the original understanding of the Constitution is hardly impossible.

2. Irreconciliation

Let us assume for a moment that the Federalists of 1798 must have known what the press clause originally meant and that their Sedition Act was consistent with that meaning. What could that meaning have been? The obvious answer is "no prior restraint." If the press clause merely constitutionalized that Blackstonian prohibition, the Sedition Act would not be inconsistent; it did not, after all, authorize injunctive relief. The subsequent punishments authorized by the Act would be perfectly consistent with that view of the press clause.

But this interpretation is still inconsistent with everything we know about the Framers' intentions because the Sedition Act was a *federal* law. The one point upon which the Framers did make their intention clear was that Congress had no legitimate power to pass *any* law respecting the press.

* * *

The Framers were unanimous: the Constitution gave Congress no power to regulate the press. The Sedition Act therefore was utterly inconsistent with the original understanding of the Constitution, no matter what the press clause meant. It is doubly inconsistent with the Levy thesis. He argues not only that the original Constitution gave Congress no power over the press, but that by adding the first amendment, the Framers meant to give added assurance that Congress was to be "totally without power to enact legislation respecting the press." Levy acknowledges, as he must, that the Sedition Act is inconsistent with his interpretation of the press clause.

Under any view of the matter, the Sedition Act was a breach of the Framers' understanding. It is therefore futile to look for the meaning of the press clause in that Act.

* * *

VI. CONCLUSION

* * *

In the minds of members of the First Congress, the press clause was part of the new plan of government, no less than if it had been in the original Constitution. To the Anti-Federalists, it was an essential modification of the original Constitution; to the Federalists, it expressed what was already implicit in the Constitution. Their quarrel was only over the necessity of specifically guaranteeing freedom of the press. Neither side doubted its utility. Its value lay, as Professor Blasi says, in "checking the inherent tendency of government officials to abuse the power entrusted to them."[10] Because it plays this role, it is, in Justice Stewart's words, "a *structural* provision of the Constitution."

* * *

I do not challenge [the] conclusion that colonial America was a repressive society in which there was little meaningful freedom of speech or press. But I think the relevant experience, so far as the press clause is concerned, was the revolution, not the colonial period. And the press during the revolutionary period was free, in fact if not in law, to criticize the government seditiously and even licentiously. That the American patriots did not extend this freedom to the Tory press is beside the point. They may not have been sophisticated enough to realize that true freedom of expression must include freedom for even the most dangerous ideas, but they had seen the connection between press criticism and political change. Moreover, I accept [the] conclusion that as legislators, judges, and executives, the Framers often behaved inconsistently with any expansive notion of freedom of expression; the Framers sometimes seemed as eager to silence dissent as George III had been. But in this I share George Anastaplo's view: they meant for us to do as they said, not as they did.[11] The behavior of our leaders was no more a reliable indicator of the meaning of the Constitution then than it is today. Our executive still seeks to impose prior restraints on publication;[12] our Supreme Court denies full protection of the first amendment to our most popular medium of mass communication;[13] Congress attempts to control mailing of political propaganda.[14] If we do not accept these actions as definitive today, we should not assume that the actions of the Framers define the original understanding of the press clause.

*   *   *

The sense one gets from that history is that most of the Framers perceived, however dimly, naively, or incompletely, that freedom of the press was inextricably related to the new republican form of government and would have to be protected if their vision of government by the people was to succeed.

NOTES

1. Melville Nimmer, "Introduction—Is Freedom of the Press a Redundancy: What Does It Add to Freedom of Speech?" *Hastings Law Journal* 26 (1975): 639.

2. Address to the Inhabitants of Quebec (1774) in Bernard Schwartz, *The Bill of Rights: A Documentary History*, vol. 1 (New York: Chelsea House Publishers, 1971), p. 223.

3. E. Emery and M. Emery, *The Press and America: An Interpretative History of the Mass Media*, 4th ed. (Englewood Cliffs, NJ: Prentice-Hall, 1978), p. 55.

4. Merrill Jensen, *The New Nation: A History of the United States during the Confederation, 1781–1789* (1958), p. 430.

5. *First National Bank v. Bellotti*, 435 U.S. 765, 800 (1978) (C. J. Burger, concurring).

6. Clinton Rossiter, *Seedtime of the Republic: The Origin of the American Tradition of Political Liberty* (New York: Harcourt, Brace, 1953), p. 141.

7. *Cato's Letters: Essays on Liberty, Civil and Religious, and Other Important Subjects*, vol. 1, p. 96.

8. James Morton Smith, *Freedom's Fetters: The Alien and Sedition Laws and American Civil Liberties* (Ithaca, NY: Cornell University Press, 1956), p. 442.

9. B. Bailyn, D. Davis, D. Donald, J. Thomas, K. Wiebe, and G. Wood, *The Great Republic* (1977), p. 341.

10. Blasi, "The Checking Value in First Amendment Theory," *Am. B. Found. Research Journal* (1977): 521, 538.

11. Anastaplo, "Book Review," *NYU Law Review* 39 (1964): 735, 739.

12. See, e.g., *New York Times Co. v. United States*, 403 U.S. 713, 718–19 (1971); *United States v. Progressive, Inc.*, 467 F. Supp. 990, 1000 (W.D. Wis. 1979), appeal dismissed, 610 F.2d 819 (7th Cir. 1979).

13. See, e.g., *FCC v. Pacifica Found.*, 438 U.S. 726 (1978); *Red Lion Broadcasting Co. v. FCC*, 395 U.S. 367 (1969).

14. See *Lamont v. Postmaster Gen.*, 381 U.S. 301 (1965).

Part II

THEORETICAL PARADIGMS

MUST SPEECH BE SPECIAL?

Frederick Schauer

*   *   *

From 1919 until about twenty years ago, discussion about freedom of speech in the context of the first amendment took place largely in the "How much?" mode. The courts and first amendment theorists commonly acknowledged, as Holmes put it, that the first amendment was not "intended to give immunity for every possible use of language."[1] Thus, the various exceptions to the coverage of the first amendment—commercial advertising, defamation, obscenity, and fighting words—were rarely called into serious question. Moreover, even with respect to political and other speech that the first amendment plainly covered, the battle lines were narrowly drawn. No one doubted that free speech was a good thing, at least in the abstract, and consequently there was little concern for *why* free speech was valued. Instead the problems centered around the weight to be given freedom of speech when it conflicted with other universally acknowledged values, most commonly national security and public order. Although in retrospect it seems that this debate could have been illuminated by closer attention to the philosophical foundations of the principles of free speech, that was not the course taken.

From *Northwestern University Law Review* 78 (1983). Reprinted with permission.

Rather, the tired metaphors of the marketplace of ideas and the search for truth served as stage props for a debate over how much the values of free speech would have to yield in the face of exigent public concerns.

This is not to say that the issues present in this phase were easy. On the contrary, the judicial and academic divisions during this period of growth of free speech doctrine—roughly from 1919 to the mid-1960s—were as sharp as they have ever been. But the combatants seemed relatively unconcerned with the deeper meaning of free speech. First amendment partisans took it as a given that maximum protection of free speech was a good thing, and devoted their efforts to arguing that the perceived dangers of speech were not nearly as great as was often assumed. And those who were wary of excess protection of speech were similarly unconcerned with the deep theory of the first amendment. They saw no reason to doubt the value of free speech in the abstract, but were unwilling in real cases to sacrifice many of their fears about dangers to security, order, and the stability of the state.

The 1960s and 1970s brought a new phase to free speech theory, a phase that substituted for the question "How much?" the seemingly simpler question of "How?" This was, of course, a period of intense solicitude for individual rights, and free speech was no exception. There was no call to examine the reasons for accepting the principle of free speech, for everyone agreed without question that maximum freedom of speech (and most other things as well) was desirable. As a result, most disputes focused on the strategies for achieving maximum protection. This search for how to attain optimal free speech protection pervaded not only the academic commentary, but the work of the courts as well. For it was during this phase that those studying the first amendment witnessed the judicial creation of the various devices that have now become acknowledged weapons in the first amendment arsenal— vagueness, overbreadth, the chilling effect, special procedural protection, and many others. With free speech once again taken as a given in this search for methods of protecting it, there was, as in the previous phase, little occasion for concentrated attention on the "Why?" rather than the "How?" or the "How much?" of the first amendment.

From the foregoing two phases, a first amendment emerged that was, at its core, quite strong. Although perhaps it was not strong enough to satisfy those who exalt free speech above all other values, there is little doubt that *Brandenburg v. Ohio*,[2] *New York Times Co. v. Sullivan*,[3] and *Cohen v. California*[4] represent a profound commitment to virtually unlimited discussion of political, moral, and social questions of all types. Moreover, this strong core was well guarded by a host of procedural and subsidiary doctrines that seem to make it relatively safe from erosion.

From this secure core, arguments in the current phase of free speech theory have centered around the broadening of the first amendment. The most prominent example of the *broadening* of the first amendment is of course commercial advertising, but the same phenomenon exists with respect to campaign contributions, speech by public employees during working hours, nude dancing, and the choice by government of the books or entertainment that it will offer in *its* facilities. In each of these areas, recent developments have made first amendment considerations applicable to issues that in the recent past were considered well without the boundaries of the first amendment. Moreover, for every instance of judicial broadening of the first amendment, there seem to be at least ten attempts in the academic literature to have the first amendment swallow up one more segment of society or of governmental action.

With this process of broadening, or at least arguing about broadening, has come the reemergence of theory. For although the accepted assumptions, traditional metaphors, and standard platitudes about the value of free speech might have been largely sufficient to deal with the issues of the past, they are clearly inadequate to confront the questions we must ask when trying to determine the extent to which, if at all, the courts should broaden the coverage of the first amendment to encompass a wide range of activities seemingly so far from the comprehension of the classical free speech theorists that the relevance of classical theory has become attenuated. In the place of the classical theories have come new attempts to ask about the "Why?" of the first amendment, in the hope of developing a theory that will explain the values that the concept of free speech is designed to serve. With such a theory in place, of course, it becomes much easier to confront the questions raised by the broadening of the first amendment. For if we know *why* we have the principles of free speech, then we can determine in the new case whether that class of activities is the type that the first amendment is designed to promote.

Would that it be so easy! The problem, of course, is that there are numerous candidates for the appropriate underlying theory of the free speech and free press clauses of the first amendment. Indeed, the concentration in this Symposium on deep theory, either explicitly or implicitly, is strong evidence of the way that debate about freedom of speech has shifted. In order to shed some light on the debate about the philosophical/sociological/political/historical foundations of free speech, it seems appropriate to set some ground rules, or at least some standards that an adequate theory must satisfy. Surprisingly, hardly any attention has been devoted to this task. On second thought, it probably is not so surprising. Almost everyone would prefer being the star quarterback to being the referee or a member of the rules committee. Yet if there were no rules, and no referees, there would be no star quarterbacks, so someone has to do the job, and that is part of what I want to accomplish here. But it is also too large a task to complete in this forum, so I want to concentrate on only part of it. I want to deal with the question of whether, and if so to what extent, an adequate theory of free speech must explain the way in which the activities encompassed by the first amendment are importantly distinct from activities that do not receive such uniquely cherished protection. In other words, must speech be special?

I

*   *   *

The question of whether speech is special has a descriptive side and a normative side. On the descriptive side, the question is whether one can identify relevant differences between speech and activities not covered by the first amendment. But on the normative side, the question is whether such a difference is necessary for a satisfactory underlying theory of the first amendment. For it is by no means inconceivable, and indeed may very well be the case, that what is analytically necessary for a satisfactory theory of the first amendment is unattainable given the existing state of the world. Yet that is getting ahead of things. For the moment, it is sufficient to note that the question "Must speech be special?" is analytically distinct from the question "Is speech special?"

In dealing with these issues, I want to discuss one particular strand of free speech theory that presents the problems most starkly. This strand I will call the "self-development" theory, and I use that designation precisely because it is different from the titles of the various theories that I believe comprise it. I mean to include within the category those theories relying variously on self-realization, self-fulfillment, self-expression, and variants on the individual liberty core of all of these theories. Conversely, I mean to exclude from the category the leading consequentialist justifications for a principle of freedom of speech, including most prominently the search for truth/marketplace of ideas theories, the popular sovereignty/democratic process theories, and the distrust of government theories.

… [T]the focus is on what free speech can do for the individual, either as speaker, or as listener, or both.[] But the most striking feature of all of these self-development theories is that they identify as the value underlying the principle of freedom of speech a value that is not peculiar to speech. In every variant at issue the value that self-development theorists urge is a value that can undoubtedly be promoted by speech. Nevertheless, that same value can also be promoted by other activities that do not involve communication, and self-development theorists offer no particular reason why communicative activities can serve the goal more completely or more frequently than other activities that are not in any significant sense communicative.

* * *

… [T]he theories under discussion provide the ideal vehicle for discussing whether it is necessary for a satisfactory theory of the first amendment that speech be in some way special. For under these theories and their variants, speech is not claimed to be special, or significantly distinguishable from the other activities that may also contribute to the value that provides the basis of the theory. If it is necessary to a satisfactory theory of the first amendment that some such distinguishing feature be provided, then all of these theories must be considered to be failures.

II

The *locus classicus* of objections to self-development theories is a paragraph in an article by Robert Bork in which Bork scrutinizes the claimed benefits from speech of "development of individual faculties and the achievement of pleasure."[5] He finds both of these justifications wanting for precisely the reason that I am discussing here:

> [T]he important point is that these benefits do not distinguish speech from any other human activity. An individual may develop his faculties or derive

pleasure from trading on the stock market, following his profession as a river port pilot, working as a barmaid, engaging in sexual activity, playing tennis, rigging prices or in any of thousands of other endeavors. Speech with only the first two benefits can be preferred to other activities only by ranking forms of personal gratification. These functions or benefits of speech are, therefore, to the principled judge, indistinguishable from the functions or benefits of all other human activity. He cannot, on neutral grounds, choose to protect speech that has only these functions more than he protects any other claimed freedom.[6]

This argument draws its significance from the fact that the first amendment protects speech more than it protects non-speech conduct. Without this contrast the first amendment serves no function. To the extent that the argument from self-development in all of its forms collapses into an argument for general liberty, then no argument has been presented for a principle of free speech that is stronger than a general principle of personal liberty. Because in American constitutional doctrine we protect personal liberty only by application of the minimal scrutiny of the rational basis standard, a justification that fails to distinguish the activities protected by the stringent standard of the first amendment from the activities protected by the minimal scrutiny of the rational basis test has failed in its task of explaining the protection of freedom of speech under the first amendment.

III

*   *   *

As a question of social and political philosophy, the argument against the adoption of the self-development principle is premised on a point about the nature of moral and practical reason. If a specific principle is generated by a broader principle, and if we accept the broader principle, then we must, at the risk of self-contradiction, accept every other specific principle also generated by the broader principle, unless we can give particular and articulated reasons for drawing a distinction. If we accept X, and if X generates a, b, and c, then we must be willing, if we are to act rationally, to accept a, b, and c, and not just the one or two of those that happen to strike our fancy at the moment.

In the context of the principle of freedom of speech, then, if we say that we value free speech because it is a form of self-development, and if we accept self-development as a given, then, if we have not justified any qualification, we must be willing to protect every form of self-development as much as we protect speech. Yet many forms of self-development, as I am using that term, can cause harm to other individuals or to society in general. It would be implausible to suppose that the state is or could be significantly disabled to prevent harms merely because the cause of those harms was, in the process, engaged in self-expression, self-fulfillment, or self-realization. Thus we acknowledge that, in general, the prevention of harm is a proper function of the state, regardless of how nice the causing of harm may make someone feel.

But if speech is merely one category within the larger universe of self-developing actions, then it would seem, again to be consistent, that we would have to accept the principle that speech may be restricted when it causes harm to others. Yet then what is the point of a principle of free speech? Many communicative acts, including many that our pre-theoretical understanding of the nature of free speech would lead us to want to protect, have the capacity for causing significant harm to others or to society in general. Indeed, if I may return to American constitutional law for a moment, it is hard to think of any first amendment case in which the communicative acts at issue did not cause some degree of harm, or at least offense. The anguish caused by the Nazis in Skokie,[7] the offense and annoyance of Cohen's jacket[8] and Cantwell's phonograph,[9] the damage to Damron's reputation and career,[10] the economic losses of even the innocent merchants of Claiborne County,[11] the distortion of the election process by money or misleading promises,[12] and the humiliation caused by publicity about the victim of a sex offense[13] are but a small sample of instances in which the principle of freedom of speech is understood to prevent the government from intervening to deal with the kinds of harm that are normally taken to be sufficient to justify use of the state's coercive powers.

Thus, we want to protect speech not because it causes no harm, but *despite* the harm it may cause. Our search for a justification, therefore, is a search for a reason to distinguish speech from the entire range of intentional actions. This is exactly the distinction that the various arguments from self-development fail to provide. As a result, these arguments tell us why we should protect liberty in general, but in the process they also become arguments for giving speech no greater protection than that given to the full range of other intentional actions. As a question of social and political theory, therefore, the arguments from self-development fail to provide a reason for recognizing a principle that grants greater protection for speech against state intervention than it grants to anything else the individual might wish to do.

IV

Let us now turn from abstract political theory, and attempt to look at this question as one arising in the attempt to formulate a theory of *this* Constitution's first amendment. In order to do this, we must rely on the notion of principled adjudication. Unfortunately, however, the idea of principled adjudication, or of neutral principles, has been the subject of so much redefinition and misinterpretation that I would like to use an alternative term, confessing in the process that this term merely reflects an idea already well-established in the literature, if only one is willing to wade through all the drivel.

Thus, I want to refer to the notion of *articulate consistency*. This term is designed to emphasize that we are dealing with a question of consistency and not of the rightness or wrongness of principles, and that the particular notion at issue is largely controlled by the way that a court chooses to articulate its reasons for a decision. The constraint of articulate consistency suggests that when we justify a decision by reference to a principle (or a reason, rule, standard, justification, or theory) we must be willing to apply the principle, as articulated in the first decision, to all cases coming within the verbal description of that principle. When a court provides, without qualification, a reason for its decision, it must be willing to apply that reason in future cases, absent particularly strong reasons to the contrary. The key feature of articulate consistency is the way in which it is normatively neutral, or procedural. The requirements of articulate consistency can apply to good reasons, bad reasons, or reasons totally unjustified by the judicial role. If a court sticks to what it says, if it is willing to take seriously its own statements, then it has satisfied the requirements of articulate consistency. And this is no less true if the original reasons or justifications are wrong, outrageous, or whatever.

We can see, therefore, that the court in the first case has a great deal of control over how much of a constraint the notion of articulate consistency is going to be. If the court in the first case justifies its decision by a very narrow principle, festooned with caveats, qualifications, and exceptions, then it is unlikely that the constraint of articulate consistency will be a significant barrier to what the court decides to do in the next case. On the other hand, if the court in the first case justifies its decision by a broad and generally unqualified principle, then the necessity of remaining faithful to this principle will exercise a substantial constraint on future decisions. Thus, the extent to which a principle applies in future cases is controlled by the justification that the court has provided in the first case.

We can now return to the principle of free speech, for it is the notion of articulate consistency that provides the link between the points made in the previous section and the same issue in the context of constitutional law. If a court says that it is protecting act x under the first amendment because x is an instance of self-expression, self-fulfillment, or self-realization, and the first amendment protects self-expression, self-fulfillment, or self-realization, then the court must be willing to apply that same principle in future cases. But since any intentional action can and usually is an instance of self-expression, self-fulfillment, or self-realization, then the constraints of articulate consistency would require the court to protect all intentional actions under the first amendment. The court, to be consistent, must be willing to apply the reason given in the first case to subsequent cases fitting within the description of the principle. If the principle is described merely as self-expression, then the first amendment must protect all self-expressive actions. Yet of course it is not true that all self-expressive actions are protected by the first amendment, or even by any other part of the Constitution. Thus, the problem with the entire range of self-development justifications for the first amendment is that they fail the test of articulate consistency. Without more, they offer a rationale that is far broader than we are willing to accept, which if consistently applied would protect almost all activities to the same extent that we protect certain communicative activities. Because we are unwilling to do this, these justifications might just as well not have been mentioned at all. A reason we are not willing to follow is no reason at all.

V

... [T]here [i]s a point in having written and authoritative constitutions, or at least that an authoritative constitution must be taken as such. In order to be faithful to this conviction, I must deal with the textual response to the arguments I have just presented. Thus, it is freedom of speech and press, and not freedom of liberty in general, that is specifically set forth in the text for special protection. Even if the justification would, to be fully consistent, have to be applied to a far wider range of cases, only part of this range is picked out by the constitutional text for special attention. The reason we do not apply the self-development arguments to their full reach is that we lack the constitutional mandate for so doing. Because we have that mandate in the case of speech, we can proceed to apply that justification in speech cases. The relevant distinction under this argument—what makes speech special—is the very fact that the constitutional text says it is.

One might call this the argument from coincidence. Even if there is no good reason for treating speech specially, the text says we must, and that is sufficient to justify the special protection for speech. And to the extent that the text is clear, we cannot legitimately avoid it. Thus, there may be no completely justifiable reason for limiting the presidency to those thirty-five years old or older, or for giving equal representation in the Senate to Delaware and California, but these are the mandates from the text, so we follow them. And so too, picking out speech for special treatment is the mandate from the text, and that's that. Speech is special by stipulation, even though now the stipulation may seem a bit odd.

But this loses sight of why we are looking at justifications at all. The very reason we are concerned about the underlying theoretical justification for the principle of freedom of speech, in a way that we are not with respect to the age of the presidency and equal representation in the Senate, is that the text is not clear, and we are therefore required to work out a theory of free speech so that we can intelligently apply the vague words of the document. The argument from coincidence is therefore circular. It calls upon us to note the presence of speech and not action in general in the text, but it is the very unclarity of the text that is the impetus for the entire enterprise. If we assume we cannot have a literal interpretation of the first amendment, then we must interpret it in light of some underlying purpose or theory. But if that underlying theory says nothing in particular about speech, if it does not set speech apart from a vast range of other conduct, then there is no principled stopping point after we leave the domain of what is very specifically and unequivocally mentioned in the text. To put it bluntly, the argument from coincidence might support applying the first amendment to all self-expressive or self-fulfilling instances of *speech* (taken literally) or press (taken literally), but the argument is of no assistance if we are trying to figure out why or how to apply the first amendment to oil paintings and handwritten manuscripts but not to nude bathing or riding a motorcycle without a safety helmet.

VI

... [T]here might be reasons why *speech* relating to or causing self-expression, self-fulfillment, or self-realization might be more important than other forms of conduct relating to or causing self-expression, self-fulfillment, or self-realization. Alternatively, there might be greater danger in regulating the communicative aspects of, say, self-expression than in regulating the non-communicative aspects of self-expression.

I have no desire whatsoever to refute any of these arguments, because these arguments, unlike the argument from coincidence, acknowledge the very point at issue. Indeed, they do more than acknowledge it, they concede it; for the qualifications about speech being a more important form of self-expression, or about the regulation of speech-related self-expression being particularly dangerous, are concessions of the very point under dispute. If there is some reason to treat self-expressive speech differently from other forms of self-expressive activities (and the same would apply to activities that foster self-fulfillment or self-realization), then that reason becomes part of the underlying theoretical justification for the first amendment. In other words, a reason has just been given for treating speech specially.

*   *   *

VII

Although the foregoing discussion has taken place in the context of self-development values that are argued to provide the foundations for the principle of free speech, the self-development justification is offered merely as an example of the larger question of the extent to which speech is or must be special. When I claim that a principle of free speech is "independent," therefore, I am not claiming that the principle is or can be entirely self-standing. Nor do I claim that free speech is an end in itself, or an ultimate, irreducible value, although I do believe that ultimate irreducible values exist. Thus, free speech, perhaps because it is so counter-intuitive in protecting a wide panoply of harmful and obnoxious activities, must especially be justified by reference to some other, presumably more fundamental, principle or principles.

When we engage in the process of searching for these more fundamental principles, we must, as I have argued, be willing to accept all of the conclusions that follow from acceptance of the more fundamental principle, or provide some distinction between speech and the other activities generated by the principle. If we justify free speech by reference to a principle of democracy, or some broader principle or scheme of political liberty, for example, then we must be willing to accept not only a principle of free speech, but also those other more specific principles that follow from a general principle of democracy or political liberty. In fact we do precisely that, because we protect voting and other activities related to the process of government as strongly as we protect freedom of speech, albeit in different ways and with different doctrines. An argument based on democracy, therefore, even without any further qualifications, satisfies the constraint of articulate consistency in a way that an argument from self-expression *simpliciter* does not.

Thus, we cannot distinguish free speech, or speech itself, from all other activities. That is undoubtedly impossible. It nevertheless remains crucial that we treat freedom of speech as being independent from general liberty, because of two interrelated problems. First, we want to protect speech *more* than we protect many other activities that are part of some conception of general liberty. For example, we want to protect speech more than we protect economic activity, although under some theories economic activity is an important and perhaps even central part of liberty in general. We also want to protect free speech more than we want to protect a wide range of non-communicative lifestyle choices, although once again these choices are to some an important component of liberty in general. The second point, inseparable from the first, is that we are unwilling to disable ourselves from dealing with harmful, offensive, obnoxious, dangerous behavior in general in the way that we are with reference to speech.

*   *   *

VIII

In searching for an underlying theoretical justification for the principle of freedom of speech, it is possible that we will find a number of different justifications. Although some theories are indeed unitary, and although there need not be anything inherently wrong with a unitary theory, so, too, there need not be anything wrong with a multi-valued theory.

When I refer to a multi-valued theory of the first amendment, I am actually including two different types of multi-valued theories. One type views the language of the free speech and free press clauses of the first amendment as the umbrella under which are located a number of more or less distinct separate principles, each with its own justification, and each directed toward a separate group of problems. Under such a view, for which I acknowledge considerable sympathy, we might in fact have several first amendments. We might have one first amendment directed primarily to the problem of government suppression of its critics. The justifications for this first amendment might be largely of the democratic theory and abuse of governmental power varieties, and this first amendment might be the one that is most applicable to cases such as *New York Times Co. v. Sullivan,* . . . just to take one famous . . . example[]. Another first amendment might be directed primarily toward the problem of open inquiry in the sciences and at academic institutions, being based primarily on the heritage of Galileo and the search for truth marketplace of ideas justifications for the principle of free speech. Perhaps this is the first amendment, albeit with some overlap with the one mentioned previously, that lurks around cases such as *Sweezy v. New Hampshire*[14] and *Board of Education, Island Trees Free Union School District v. Pico.*[15] A third first amendment might be a reaction to an excess of historical censorship of the arts, leading to cases such as *Southeastern Promotions, Ltd. v. Conrad*[16] and *Jenkins v. Georgia,*[17] and perhaps even based in part on notions of self-realization. This list of possible first amendments is of course representative rather than exhaustive, but I think I have made the point.

Alternatively, the other variety of multi-valued theory might say that speech represents a unique mix of various different characteristics, not duplicated in other human endeavors. This unique mix of self-expression, self-realization, capacity for influencing political change, and so on, is then said to justify special protection for speech. This is by no means an implausible view, but it seems somewhat sticky in application, at least at the margin. That is, what do we do when we are unsure of first amendment coverage in a close case? I suspect that here it would be futile to inquire into whether this instance presents the same kind of unique mix of characteristics that justifies the special protection of speech. Rather, we would look at the particular components of that mix that were present in the case at hand, and when that happens this second type of multi-valued theory collapses into the first.

IX

[T]he development of constitutional principles need not be based solely on the dictionary definition of the words in the text, nor on the specific understandings of those who drafted the provisions at issue. Thus, the task of the courts, in attempting to interpret the open-ended and morally loaded constitutional provisions—freedom of speech, equal protection, cruel and unusual punishment, and so on—is to develop a theory of these clauses, a theory that will be significantly philosophical but will include a large dose of precedent.

When we are engaged in theory construction in this sense, we can proceed in alternative ways. One approach is to attempt to work out an ideal political theory independent of the particular constitutional provision at issue, such as freedom of speech, and then proceed to apply that clause to the extent that it supports that theory. I have little sympathy for this approach, in large part because its chief analytical tool seems to be the shoehorn. To the extent that the text does not fit the preconceived theory, then a little pushing and pulling, huffing and puffing, bending and slicing, and—*voila*—one's preconstructed political theory just happens to be embodied in the Constitution, with nothing left out.

An alternative approach, and one much more consistent with my vision of constitutionalism, is one that starts with the particular clause as the mandate for building a narrow theory *of that clause.* We start with freedom of speech, for example, because freedom of speech is written down in the authoritative document, and then proceed to work out a theory of freedom of speech. Under this approach we accept the presupposition that speech is special, because the text imposes that presupposition on us. Then we try as hard as we can to derive an underlying theory that is consistent with the textual presupposition. It is this process that I have implicitly described throughout this article. We are required to accept the view that the Constitution gives speech and press special protection, that in close cases we must develop an underlying theory of the first amendment, and that this underlying theory must be consistent with, and preferably supportive of, the special protection for speech given by the document. It is in this sense that I maintain that speech must be special.

X

There is an intellectual ache in all of this, and it may be shared by many people now engaged in the process of trying to explore the theoretical foundations of the principle of freedom of speech. As we reject many of the classical platitudes about freedom of speech and engage in somewhat more rigorous analysis, trying to discover why speech—potentially harmful and dangerous, often offensive, and the instrument of evil as often as of good— should be treated as it is, our intuitions about the value of free speech, solid as they may be, are difficult to reconcile with this analysis. The ache, it seems to me, is caused by the fact that although the answer to "Must speech be special?" is probably "Yes," the answer to "*Is* speech special?" is probably "No." Reconciling this inconsistency is the agenda we cannot avoid.

NOTES

1. *Frohwerk v. United States*, 249 U.S. 204, 206 (1919).
2. 395 U.S. 444 (1969).
3. 376 U.S. 254 (1964).
4. 403 U.S. 15 (1971).
5. Robert Bork, "Neutral Principles and Some First Amendment Problems," *Indiana Law Journal* 47 (1971): 25.
6. Ibid.
7. *Collin v. Smith*, 578 F.2d 1197 (7th Cir.), *stay denied*, 436 U.S. 953, *cert. denied*, 439 U.S. 916 (1978).
8. *Cohen v. California*, 403 U.S. 15 (1971).
9. *Cantwell v. Connecticut*, 310 U.S. 296 (1940).
10. *Ocala Star-Banner Co. v. Damron*, 401 U.S. 295 (1971).
11. *NAACP v. Claiborne Hardware Co.*, 458 U.S. 886 (1982).
12. *Brown v. Hartlage*, 456 U.S. 45 (1982); *Citizens against Rent Control v. Berkeley*, 454 U.S. 290 (1981).
13. *Globe Newspaper Co. v. Superior Court*, 457 U.S. 596 (1982).
14. 354 U.S. 234 (1957).
15. 457 U.S. 853 (1982).
16. 420 U.S. 546 (1975).
17. 418 U.S. 153 (1974).

FREE SPEECH NOW

Cass R. Sunstein

*   *   *

For those who believe either that the judiciary should play a limited role in American government or that the Constitution's meaning is fixed by the original understanding of its ratifiers, the First Amendment is a particular embarrassment. The current state of free speech in America owes a great deal to extremely aggressive interpretations by the Supreme Court, which has invalidated legislative outcomes on numerous occasions. These decisions cannot be justified by reference to the original understanding of the First Amendment. Such decisions also involve a highly intrusive judicial role in majoritarian politics.

There is some continuity, however, between current practice and the original understanding, and between current practice and principles of democratic government. The continuity lies in the distinctive American contribution to the theory of sovereignty. In England, sovereignty lay with the King. "In the United States," as James Madison explained, "the case is altogether different. The People, not the Government, possess the absolute sovereignty." The placement of sovereignty in the people rather than in the government has important implications for freedom of speech. As Madison understood it, the

From *University of Chicago Law Review* 59 (1992). Reprinted with permission.

new conception of sovereignty entailed a judgment that any "Sedition Act" would be unconstitutional. The power represented by such an Act ought, "more than any other, to produce universal alarm; because it is levelled against that right of freely examining public characters and measures, and of free communication among the people thereon, which has ever been justly deemed the only effectual guardian of every other right."

With Madison's pronouncements in mind, we might think of the American tradition of free expression as a series of struggles to understand the relationship between this conception of sovereignty and a system of free speech. The extraordinary protection now accorded to political speech can well be understood as an elaboration of the distinctive American understanding of sovereignty.

My goal in this article is to defend this basic proposition and to evaluate the current system of free expression in light of it. As we will see, an effort to root freedom of speech in a conception of popular sovereignty shows that our current understandings are off the mark. Those understandings misdirect the basic inquiry, protect speech that should not be protected, and worst of all, invalidate democratic efforts to promote the principle of popular sovereignty under current conditions.

I. THE NEW FIRST AMENDMENT

American children watch a good deal of television—about twenty-seven hours per week—and American television contains a good deal of advertising. For adults, every hour of television contains nearly eight minutes of commercials. For most of its history, the Federal Communications Commission (FCC) imposed limits on the amount of advertising that broadcasters could air on shows aimed at children. In 1984, the FCC eliminated the limits.

In the wake of deregulation, some stations air between eleven and twelve minutes per hour of commercials during children's programming on weekends, and up to fourteen minutes on weekdays. Some shows are actually full-length commercials, because the lead characters are products.

In 1990 Congress imposed, for children's programming, a limit of ten and one half minutes of television commercials per hour on weekends, and twelve minutes on weekdays. President Bush withheld his approval, invoking the First Amendment. According to the President, the First Amendment "does not contemplate that government will dictate the quality or quantity of what Americans should hear—rather, it leaves this to be decided by free media responding to the free choices of individual consumers." The President did "not believe that quantitative restrictions on advertising should be considered permissible...."

Nonetheless, the Children's Television Act of 1990 has become law....

This episode reveals that something important and strange has happened to the First Amendment. Whereas the principal First Amendment suits were brought, in the 1940s, 1950s, and 1960s, by political protestors and dissidents, many of the current debates involve complaints by commercial advertisers, companies objecting to the securities laws, pornographers, businesses selling prerecorded statements of celebrities via "900" numbers, people seeking to spend large amounts of money on elections, industries attempting to export technology to unfriendly nations, newspapers disclosing names of rape victims, and large broadcasters resisting government efforts to promote diversity in the media. How has this happened?

To attempt an answer, we must step back a bit. From about 1940 to 1970, American constitutional debate over freedom of expression was divided along clear lines. On one side were those accepting what came to be the dominant position, a form of First Amendment "absolutism." On the other side were the advocates of "reasonable regulation." One could identify the two sides by their commitment to, or rejection of, four central ideas.

The first idea is that the government is the enemy of freedom of speech. Any effort to regulate speech, by the nation or the states, is threatening to the principle of free expression. More subtly, an effort to regulate speech is defined as a governmental attempt to interfere with communicative processes, taking the existing distribution of entitlements—property rights, wealth, and so on—as a given. I will discuss this point in more detail below.

The second idea is that we should understand the First Amendment as embodying a commitment to a certain form of neutrality. Government may not draw lines between speech it likes and speech it hates. All speech stands on the same footing. Thus the protection accorded to speech extends equally to Communists and Nazis, the Ku Klux Klan and the Black Panthers, Martin Luther King Jr. and George Wallace. Government should ensure that broadcasters, newspapers, and others can say what they wish, constrained only by the impersonal pressures of the marketplace. This conception of neutrality among different points of view is the government's first commitment.

The third idea is that we should not limit the principle of free expression to political speech, or to expression with a self-conscious political component. It is extremely difficult to distinguish between political and nonpolitical speech. Any such distinction is likely to reflect illegitimate partisan politics. Thus the free speech principle extends to more than self-conscious efforts to contribute to democratic deliberation. It extends equally to sexually explicit speech, music, art, and commercial speech. Under this view, the First Amendment sets out a principle not limited to its particular historical wellsprings. "Speech," in the First Amendment, means all speech.

The final idea is that any restrictions on speech, once permitted, have a sinister and inevitable tendency to expand. Principled limits on government are hard to articulate; to allow one kind of restriction is in practice to allow many other kinds as well. "Slippery slope" arguments therefore deserve a prominent place in the theory of free expression. As far as possible, "balancing" ought to play no role in free speech law. Judges should not uphold restrictions on speech simply because the government seems to have good reasons for the restriction in the particular case. They must protect against the likely effect of the decision on future government action.

In the past quarter-century these four principles have commanded enormous respect. The press insisted on them with special enthusiasm. It was joined by many teachers in law schools and political science departments, and by numerous litigators, most notably the American Civil Liberties Union.

One can easily identify the components of the opposing position. On this view, balancing is an inevitable part of a sensible system of free expression, and "reasonable regulation" should be upheld. The meaning of the First Amendment should be determined by reference to its history, in particular by reference to the relatively limited aims of the Framers and the complexities of the Supreme Court's own precedents. Certain categories of speech—advocacy of crime, especially dangerous speech, commercial speech, hate speech, sexually explicit speech, and libel—fall outside the First Amendment altogether. The government, according to this view, plays a role in maintaining a civilized society. This means that it may guard, for example, against the degradation produced by obscenity or the risks posed by speech advocating over-throw of the government. Large-scale neutrality makes no sense.

From the perspective of the 1990s, it may be hard to remember the vigor and tenacity with which the opposing camps struggled over their respective positions. The basic commitments of the absolutist view are now clichés, even dogma. Despite that view's novelty and the lack of direct historical support on its behalf, it has won a dramatic number of victories in the Supreme Court. This is so especially with restrictions of speech on the basis of its content, where special scrutiny is now routine, except in quite narrow categories of excluded speech. Thus constitutional protection has been accorded to most commercial speech; to most sexually explicit speech; to many kinds of libel; to publication of the names of rape victims; to the advocacy of crime, even of violent overthrow of the government; to large expenditures on electoral campaigns; to corporate speech; in all likelihood to hate speech; and of course to flag burning.

It is not an overstatement to say that, taken all together, these developments have revolutionized the law of free expression. For many, the new law is an occasion for a sense of triumph and, perhaps, a belief that the principal difficulties with First Amendment law have been solved. The remaining problems are thought to be ones of applying hard-won doctrinal wisdom to ever-present threats of censorship.

In the last decade, however, the commitments that emerged from the last generation of free speech law have come under extremely severe strain. Emerging controversies have appeared over such issues as campaign finance regulation, hate speech, "dial-a-porn," the securities laws, scientific speech, nude dancing, commercial advertising, selective funding of expression, pornography, and regulation designed to produce quality and diversity in broadcasting. With these developments, previous alliances have come apart. Sometimes the new disputes seem to resurrect the belief in "reasonable regulation." Often they draw one or more of the four basic commitments of the absolutists into sharp question.

The ironies in all this are abundant. The new coalitions have spurred plausible arguments of hypocrisy, with free speech advocates claiming that the new challengers abandoned the liberal commitment to free speech as soon as the commitment became inconvenient, or required protection for unpopular causes. Indeed, it has been charged that, for many, the commitment to free speech stands revealed as contingent and convenient, and not principled at all.

On the other hand, the enthusiasm for broad application of free speech principles to the new settings is ironic as well. The constitutional protection accorded to commercial speech, for example, is relatively new. Justices Douglas and Black, probably the most vigorous advocates of free expression in the history of the Court, rejected protection for commercial speech, as did many others. The notion that the First Amendment protects libel of ethnic groups, or hate speech, is a quite modern development, if it is a development at all. Until recently, no one thought that the First Amendment cast any doubt on the securities laws. Until the last few decades, the states had very broad authority to regulate sexually explicit material. And the interaction of the free speech principle with campaign spending and broadcasting surely raises complex and novel issues.

Under these circumstances, it seems peculiar to insist that any regulatory efforts in these areas will endanger "the First Amendment" or inevitably pave the way toward more general incursions on speech. Insistence on the protection of all words seems especially odd when it is urged by those who otherwise proclaim the need for judicial restraint, for the freeing up of democratic processes from constitutional compulsion, and for close attention to history. These ideas would seem to argue most powerfully against reflexive invocation of the First Amendment.

Current law, then, faces a new set of constitutional problems, raising issues that have shattered old alliances and that promise to generate new understandings of the problem of freedom of expression. In this article, I propose and evaluate two responses to the current state of affairs. The two responses have the same source. That source is the distinctive American contribution to the theory of sovereignty.

The first proposal calls for a New Deal with respect to speech. It applies much of the reasoning of the New Deal attack on the common law to current questions of First Amendment law. Such an approach would produce significant changes in existing understandings of the nature of the free speech guarantee. It would call for a large-scale revision in our view of when a law "abridges" the freedom of speech. At a minimum, it would insist that many imaginable democratic interferences with the autonomy of broadcasters or newspapers are not "abridgements" at all. The New Deal for speech would also argue that such autonomy, because it is guaranteed by law, is itself sometimes an abridgement. I believe that there is much to be said in favor of this approach, and in certain, well-defined settings, it should be accepted.

*   *   *

Ultimately, I argue that an insistence that the First Amendment is fundamentally aimed at protecting democratic self-government, combined with modest steps in favor of a New Deal for speech, would resolve most of the current problems in free speech law without seriously compromising the First Amendment or any other important social values. But in order to reach this conclusion, it will be necessary to abandon, or at least qualify, the basic principles that have dominated judicial and academic thinking about speech in the last generation.

II. A NEW DEAL FOR SPEECH?

A. BACKGROUND

Perhaps we need a New Deal for speech, one that would parallel what the New Deal provided to property rights during the 1930s, and that would be rooted in substantially similar concerns. A brief review follows.

Before the New Deal, the Constitution was often understood as a constraint on government "regulation." In practice, this meant that the Constitution was often invoked to prohibit governmental interference with existing distributions of rights and entitlements. Hence minimum wage and maximum hour laws were seen as unjustifiable exactions—takings—from employers for the benefit of employees and the public at large. The Due Process Clause insulated private arrangements from public control, especially if the government's goals were paternalistic or redistributive. In operating under the police power, government must be neutral in general, and between employers and employees in particular. A violation of the neutrality requirement, thus understood, would count as a violation of the Constitution.

On the pre-New Deal view, existing distributions marked the boundary not only between neutrality and partisanship, but between inaction and action as well. Government inaction consisted of respect for existing distributions. Government action was understood as interference with them. The rallying cry "laissez-faire" embodied such ideas. The fear of, and more important, the very conception of "government intervention" captured this basic approach.

The New Deal reformers argued that this entire framework was built on fictions. Their response is captured in President Roosevelt's references to "this man-made world of ours" and his insistence that "we must lay hold of the fact that economic laws are not made by nature. They are made by human beings." The pre-New Deal framework treated the existing distribution of resources and opportunities as prepolitical, when in fact it was not. It saw minimum wage and maximum hour laws as introducing government into a private or voluntary sphere. But the New Dealers pointed out that this sphere was actually a creation of law. Rules of property, contract, and tort produced the set of entitlements that ultimately yielded market hours and wages.

To New Deal reformers, the very categories of "regulation" and "government intervention" seemed misleading. The government did not "act" only when it disturbed existing distributions. It was responsible for those distributions in the first instance. What people owned in markets was a function of the entitlements that the law conferred on them. The notion of "laissez-faire" thus stood revealed as a conspicuous fiction.

To the extent that property rights played a role in market arrangements—as they inevitably did—those arrangements were a creature of positive law, including, most notably, property law, which gave some people a right to exclude others from "their" land and resources. On this view, market wages were a result of legal rules conferring rights of ownership on certain groups. Rather than superimposing regulation on a realm of purely voluntary interactions, minimum wage laws substituted one form of regulation for another.

The fact that an existing distribution is not natural or prepolitical provides no argument against it. When one regulatory system is superimposed on another, it is not true that all bets are off, or that we cannot evaluate them in constitutional terms, or for their ability to diminish or to increase human liberty, or other things we value. Here the New Deal reformers were often too cavalier. A system of private property is a construct of the state, but it is also an important individual and collective good. In general, a market system—for property or for speech—promotes both liberty and prosperity, and its inevitable origins in law do not undermine that fact.

To their basic point, then, the New Dealers added a claim that existing distributions were sometimes inefficient or unjust. Different forms of governmental ordering had to be evaluated pragmatically and in terms of their consequences for social efficiency and social justice. The fact that markets are a creature of law meant not that they were impermissible, but that they would be assessed in terms of what they did on behalf of the human beings subject to them. Markets would not be identified with liberty in an a priori way; they would have to be evaluated through an examination of whether they served liberty or not.

The New Dealers were not socialists; they generally appreciated the contributions of markets to prosperity and freedom. At the very least, however, a democratic judgment that markets constrained liberty—embodied in a law calling for maximum hours or minimum wages—was plausible and entitled to judicial respect.

*   *   *

We could generate, from the suggested First Amendment "New Deal," a large set of proposals for constitutional reform. I describe those proposals in summary fashion here. A more detailed discussion would be necessary in order fully to come to terms with any one of them.

*   *   *

2. Campaign finance

Many people have justified restrictions on campaign expenditures as an effort to promote political deliberation and political equality by reducing the distorting effects of disparities in wealth. On this view, such laws promote the system of free expression by ensuring that less wealthy speakers do not have much weaker voices than wealthy ones. But some have forcefully challenged campaign finance laws as inconsistent with "the marketplace of ideas." Indeed, some say these laws effect a kind of First Amendment taking from rich speakers for the benefit of poor ones. On this rationale, the Supreme Court invalidated certain forms of campaign finance regulation in *Buckley v Valeo*.[1] In the crucial passage, the Court said that "the concept that government may restrict the speech of some elements of our society in order to enhance the relative voice of others is wholly foreign to the First Amendment...."

Buckley reflects pre-New Deal understandings. We should view it as the modern-day analogue of *Lochner v New York*:[2] a decision to take the market status quo as just and prepolitical, and to use that decision to invalidate democratic efforts at reform. Reliance on markets is governmental neutrality. Use of existing distributions for political expenditures marks out government inaction.

From what I have said thus far, it should be clear that elections based on those distributions are actually subject to a regulatory system made possible and constituted through law. That law consists, first, in legal rules protecting the present distribution of wealth, and more fundamentally, in legal rules allowing candidates to buy speech rights through markets.

Because it involves speech, *Buckley* is even more striking than *Lochner.* Efforts to redress economic inequalities, or to ensure that they do not translate into political inequalities, should not be seen as impermissible redistribution, or as the introduction of government regulation where it did not exist before. Instead we should evaluate campaign finance laws pragmatically in terms of their consequences for the system of free expression. There are some hard questions here. The case for controls on campaign expenditures is plausible but hardly clear-cut. An inquiry into these considerations would raise issues quite different from those invoked by the *Buckley* Court.

*   *   *

6. The public forum doctrine

We would also have to rethink the public forum doctrine. Current law appears to take roughly the following form. The state may not close off streets, parks, and other areas held open to the public "from time immemorial"; here the public has earned a kind of First Amendment easement. Courts will uphold reasonable regulations, but government cannot eliminate the basic right of access. The same rules apply to other areas if they have been "dedicated" to the public, that is, if the state has generally opened them for expressive activities. But still other areas—and this is a very large category—need not be open at all. Courts will uphold any restrictions so long as they are minimally rational.

This system turns on common law rules. It gives access if the area has been "dedicated," by tradition or practice, for public access, and this determination is based on whether, at common law, the area in question was held open. In a period in which streets and parks were principal places for communicative activity, this historical test was sensible functionally. It well served the goal of the public forum doctrine, which was the creation of access rights to places where such rights were most effective and crucial.

The streets and parks no longer carry out their common law roles. Other areas—mailboxes, airports, train stations, broadcasting stations—are the modern equivalents of streets and parks. It is here that current doctrine is ill-suited to current needs. To keep the streets and parks open is surely important, but it is not enough to allow broadly diverse views to reach the public.

For this reason the Court should abandon the common law test and look instead to whether the government has sufficiently strong and neutral reasons for foreclosing access to the property. Certainly airports and train stations should be open to communicative efforts.

7. Content-based versus content-neutral restrictions

We would also need to reassess the distinction between content-based and content-neutral restrictions on speech—the most central distinction in contemporary free speech law.

Under current law, the Court views with considerable skepticism any law that makes the content of speech relevant to restriction. If, for example, Congress tries to prevent speech dealing with a war from appearing on billboards, it is probably acting unconstitutionally. By contrast, if Congress bars all speech on billboards, courts will subject the measure to a balancing test, because this type of restriction on speech is content-neutral. It does not skew the thinking process of the community, and it is unlikely to reflect an impermissible governmental motivation.

There is a great deal to be said in favor of this conception of neutrality. In certain respects, however, it reproduces the framework of the *Lochner* era. It takes the market status quo as natural and just insofar as it bears on speech. It sees partisanship in government decisions to alter that status quo, and neutrality in decisions that basically respect it. But there may be no neutrality in use of the market status quo when the available opportunities are heavily dependent on wealth, on the common law framework of entitlements, and on the sorts of outlets for speech that are made available, and to whom. In other words, the very notions "content-neutral" and "content-based" seem to depend on taking the status quo as if it were preregulatory and unobjectionable.

At least two things follow. The first is that many content-neutral laws have content-differential effects. They do so because they operate against a backdrop that is not prepolitical or just. In light of an unjust status quo, rules that are content-neutral can have severe adverse effects on some forms of speech. Greater scrutiny of content-neutral restrictions is therefore appropriate. Above all, courts should attend to the possibility that seemingly neutral restrictions will have content-based effects. The government's refusal to allow Lafayette Park (across the street from the White House) to be used as a place for dramatizing the plight of the homeless is a prominent example.

Second, we should draw into question a familiar justification for skepticism about content-based regulation of speech. That justification is that such regulation "skews" the marketplace of ideas. This idea has two infirmities. First, we do not know what a well-functioning marketplace of ideas would look like. The preconditions of an economic marketplace can be specified by neoclassical economics; the same is not true for the preconditions of a system of free expression. Second, the idea depends on taking the "marketplace" as unobjectionable in its current form. If it is already skewed, content-based regulation may be a corrective. It would be exceptionally surprising if there were no such skewing. The point bears especially on the debate over pornography, where critics often say that the "preregulatory" status quo is in fact a regulatory system—one that is skewed in favor of sexual inequality.

In general, the existence of an unjust status quo is not a good reason to allow content regulation. For one thing, any inquiry into the speech status quo is probably beyond governmental capacity. There is a serious risk that judicial or legislative decisions about the relative power of various groups, and about to whom redistribution is owed, will be biased or unreliable. Judgments about who is powerful and who is not must refer to some highly controversial baseline. The resulting judgments are not easily subject to governmental administration. Indeed, government will inevitably be operating with its own biases, and those biases will affect any regulatory strategy. This risk seems unacceptable when speech is at stake.

What is distinctive about regulation of speech is that such regulation forecloses the channels of change; it prevents other views from being presented at all. Instead of allowing restrictions, we should encourage efforts to promote a better status quo. I have discussed some of these in connection with the broadcasting market.

*   *   *

8. "Unconstitutional conditions"?

Finally, it would be necessary to reemphasize that there are limits on government's power to affect deliberative processes through the use of government funds. On this point, it is exceptionally hard to unpack the Court's cases. Some of these decisions suggest that when allocating funds, government cannot discriminate on the basis of point of view. It would follow that government could not allocate funds only to people who will speak in favor of a certain cause. Other cases draw a distinction between a "subsidy" and a "penalty," permitting government to refuse to subsidize speech, but prohibiting government from penalizing it.

The Court's most recent decision suggests that so long as the government is using its own money and is not affecting "private" expression, it can channel its funds however it wishes. The problem in *Rust v Sullivan*[3] arose when the Department of Health and Human Services issued regulations banning federally funded family planning services from engaging in (a) counseling concerning, (b) referrals for, and (c) activities advocating abortion as a method of family planning. The plaintiffs claimed that these regulations violated the First Amendment, arguing that the regulations discriminated on the basis of point of view.

The Court disagreed. In the key passage, it said,

> The Government can, without violating the Constitution, selectively fund a program to encourage certain activities it believes to be in the public interest, without at the same time funding an alternate program which seeks to deal with the problem in another way. In so doing, the Government has not discriminated on the basis of viewpoint; it has merely chosen to fund one activity to the exclusion of the other.

In response to the claim that the regulations conditioned the receipt of a benefit on the relinquishment of a right, the Court said that "here the government is not denying a benefit to anyone, but is instead simply insisting that public funds be spent for the purposes for which they were authorized."

Rust seems to establish the important principle that government can allocate funds to private people to establish "a program" that accords with the government's preferred point of view. In fact the Court seems to make a sharp distinction between government coercion—entry into the private realm of markets and private interactions—and funding decisions. So made, this distinction replicates pre-New Deal understandings. But there is no fundamental distinction among the law that underlies markets, the law that represents disruption of markets, and the law that calls for funding decisions. Courts must assess all of them in terms of their purposes and effects for free speech.

Notwithstanding the apparent implications of *Rust*, it would be intolerable to say that government can target funds, or jobs, or licenses, or anything else that it owns only for speech with which it agrees. Suppose, for example, that the government decides to fund only those projects that speak favorably of Democrats. However government is acting, the First Amendment constrains the purposes for which government may act, and the effects of its actions. The notion that the First Amendment is directed only at criminal punishment or civil fines depends on an outmoded notion of what government does, and on a pre-New Deal understanding of "interference" with constitutional rights. A government decision to sponsor speech favorable to one or another party platform would run afoul of a central commitment of the First Amendment.

For this reason funding decisions that discriminate on the basis of viewpoint are at least ordinarily impermissible. The proposition that government may allocate funds however it chooses is rooted in anachronistic ideas about the relationship between the citizen and the state. It poses a genuine threat to free speech under modern conditions.

D. Conclusion: A New Deal for Speech

A reformulation of First Amendment doctrine of this general sort has much to be said in its favor. Above all, such a reformulation would reinvigorate processes of democratic deliberation, by ensuring greater attention to public issues and greater diversity of treatment of those issues.

Some qualifications are necessary here. A system of markets in speech—surrounded by the law of property, contract, and tort—has major advantages over other forms of regulation. Such systems are content-neutral, at least on their face. This is an important point, above all because in markets, no government official is authorized to decide, in particular cases, who will be allowed to speak. There is no need to emphasize the risk of bias when government decides that issue.

In addition, markets are highly decentralized. With respect to both the print and electronic media, there are numerous outlets. Someone unable to find space in the New York Times or on CBS may well be able to find space elsewhere. A great advantage of a market system is that other outlets generally remain available. At least some other forms of regulation do not have this salutary characteristic. In any case it is important to ensure that any regulation does not foreclose certain points of view.

But our current system of free expression does not serve the Madisonian ideal. Free markets in expression are sometimes ill-adapted to the American revision of the principle of sovereignty. If we are to realize that principle, a New Deal for speech, of the sort outlined above, would be highly desirable.

NOTES

1. 424 U.S. 1 (1976).
2. 198 U.S. 45 (1905).
3. 500 U.S. 173 (1991).

SCOPE OF THE FIRST AMENDMENT
FREEDOM OF SPEECH

C. Edwin Baker

This paper develops three theories of the scope of speech protected by the first amendment: two different marketplace of ideas theories, which I will call the *classic model* and the *market failure model*, and a third, the *liberty model*.

* * *

I. THE CLASSIC MARKETPLACE OF IDEAS THEORY

A. THE THEORY

According to classic theory, truth is discovered through its competition with falsehood for acceptance. This result depends on certain crucial assumptions. First, truth must be "objective" or "discoverable." Truth is able to outshine falsity in debate or discussion only if truth is there to be seen. If, instead, truth were subjective, chosen or created, an adequate theory must explain why the competition among various viewpoints leads to the "best choice" or why protecting this competition provides a proper or legitimate process of choice or

---

From *UCLA Law Review* 25 (1978). Courtesy of C. Edwin Baker.

creation. Second, people must possess the capacity correctly to perceive truth or reality. One can distinguish two aspects of this rationality assumption. First, people's social location must not control the manner in which they perceive or understand the world. If perceptions are social creations and if people's social experiences are radically different, then mere discussion would be inadequate for discovering what truth or which perspectives are correct or best; one could not hope that employing reason in discussion would provide an unbiased insight into reality. Instead, perceptions of truth would vary, and dominance of one perception over another would depend on arbitrary circumstances and power relations among social groups.

Second, people's rational faculties must enable them to sort through the form and frequency of message presentation in order to evaluate the core notions. Otherwise, the marketplace of ideas would only promote acceptance of those perspectives which were adequately packaged and promoted.

The premise that this marketplace of ideas uniformly promotes human interests implies that cultural pluralism will be progressively diminished and that no intractable conflict of values exists in society. Intractable value conflicts and permanent or progressive diversity would imply either a lack of uniform, stable content of truth or the insufficiency of truth as a basis for human action; the usefulness of the robust debate could not then be assumed but would depend on whether it operated to advance or obstruct the interests of the group whose values one adopts. Nevertheless, given the theory's assumptions about the objective nature of truth, the rational capabilities of humans, and the unity of the real aims of people, limiting the marketplace of ideas necessarily undermines the discovery and recognition of truth and impedes wise, well-founded decision making. Given the theory's assumptions, the presentation of conflicting arguments and insights aids people in discovering the truth in each position.

B. JUDICIAL ADOPTION

The Supreme Court steadfastly relies upon a marketplace of ideas theory in determining what speech is protected. Marketplace imagery (competition of ideas, the value of robust debate) pervades Court opinions and provides justification for their first amendment "tests."

*   *   *

C. FAILURE OF ASSUMPTIONS

The assumptions on which the classic marketplace of ideas theory rests are almost universally rejected today. Because of this failure of assumptions, the hope that the marketplace leads to truth, or even to the best or most desirable decision, becomes implausible. First, truth is not objective. Even in the sciences, the presumed sanctuary of objectively verifiable truth, often only those values to which the scientists personally give allegiance provide criteria for judging between competing theories. Criteria for choice of paradigms include the theory's ability to provide answers to currently pressing questions, its usefulness in suggesting further applications or new investigatable problems, and its simplicity or aesthetic appeal. The moderns appear unwilling to believe in Platonic forms or intelligible essences. Instead, knowledge depends on how people's interests, needs, and experiences lead them to slice and categorize an expanding mass of sense data. In fact, the greater diversity and conflict in people's social interests, needs, and experiences may explain why social life has a greater number of, and more constant conflict among, competing paradigms than is usually the case within a "science." And even if "rational" debate can play some role in advancing understanding within a given paradigm, discussion appears insufficient by itself to evaluate different paradigms. This failure of discussion results, in part, precisely because the value oriented criteria— interests, desires, or aesthetics—which guide the development of perceptions, appear ungrounded, incapable of objective demonstration. However, one premise of my latter constructive argument will be that one must assume the value of the free development of people's humanity; and that this value provides an initial basis from which something can be said about differing paradigms and even more can be said about the desirable features of a structure of paradigm conflict and about the process of developing or creating knowledge. One could also, but I will not here, argue that this value of free development of people's humanity has been progressively unfolding in human history.

*   *   *

This observation about the consequences of rejecting the assumption of "objective truth" leads directly to an evaluation of the other assumptions of the model. The first aspect of rationality required by the marketplace model, that people can use reason to comprehend a set reality, is undermined once one rejects the assumption of objective truth, for no set reality exists for people to understand. The sociology of knowledge provides a more precise basis for a critique of this rationality assumption. People's perspectives and understanding are greatly influenced, if not determined, by their experiences and their interests, both of which reflect their location in a specific, historical socio-economic structure. Two implications of the sociology of knowledge should be relatively uncontroversial. First, dialogue cannot completely eliminate conflicts and divergences between people's perspectives as long as the social structure is such that people have very different experiences and conflicting interests. More specifically, social change—changes in the family, social, economic, or political order—not the marketplace of ideas, will have the greater impact on these divergent notions of "truth." Second, and in consequence of the first comment, not only will robust discussion be insufficient for advancing understanding (since it is at best one determinant of understanding), but also, if one continues to hope for a process of progressive development of understanding (the classic model's search for truth), the process of development will depend on the existence of a realm in which new experiences and interests can become actualities; thus, progress requires protection of some realm of conduct and of everyday activity beyond mere discussion.

The classic model also requires that people be able to use their rational capacities to eliminate distortion caused by the form and frequency of message presentation and to find the core of relevant information or argument. This assumption cannot be accepted. Emotional or "irrational" appeals have great impact; "subconscious" repressions, phobias, or desires influence people's assimilation of messages; and, most obviously, stimulus-response mechanisms and selective attention and retention processes influence understanding or perspectives. In fact, these psychological processes partially explain at the level of the individual what the sociology of knowledge observes at the level of the group. One is rewarded for adopting perspectives that further one's interests.

Since interests vary with social position, the perspectives that are reinforced will also vary. These differential rewards explain *why* the sociology of knowledge finds that people maintain perspectives which promote one's interest even when presented with contrary information or alternative perspectives. The psychological technique of selective attention and retention, as well as the insights of cognitive dissonance and balance theories, suggest *how* people preserve these perspectives.

*　*　*

II. THE MARKET FAILURE MODEL

Society has found that the invisible hand does not always produce the results desired in the marketplace of goods; various forms of market failures require state intervention to achieve efficient allocations or desired distributions. Critics of the classic marketplace of ideas theory, relying either on the failure of the assumptions described in Part I or specifically on failures of the economic market (such as monopolization of communication channels or difficulties of organizing interest groups), have advocated various forms of governmental intervention to improve market functioning. The specific solutions proposed relate to the particular problem or market failure identified—identifications which have varied considerably among the critics.

A. The Reform Proposals

To clarify the content of the market failure model(s) I will outline the major reform positions, analyze the assumptions justifying each, and give a few examples of specific reform proposals.

Reformers generally take one of four positions: (1) that economic market failures be corrected to the extent possible without restricting anyone's speech freedom; (2) that all viewpoints be guaranteed adequate, but not necessarily equal, access to the market; (3) that all viewpoints have equal access to the marketplace of ideas (e.g., equal time for each candidate); or (4) that all individuals have equal access. (I should note that implementing many proposals suggested by the first two positions would be compatible with, but not necessarily required by, the liberty theory of the first amendment advanced in Part III.)

The first view—that economic market failures require government intervention—is based on the observation that inefficient resource allocations to speech activities may be caused by monopolization or by the difficulty which racial, sexual, or ethnic groups, consumers, the poor, or environmentalists, and other large, unorganized groups have, due to organization costs and free-loading, in achieving efficient levels of advocacy. Often, critics of this form of market failure propose invigorated enforcement of anti-trust laws or subsidies for advocacy by various difficult-to-organize groups. However, these proposals, motivated by economic efficiency concerns, do not require or imply any particular theory of free speech; thus, they are outside the scope of the present paper. Moreover, these reform proposals raise no first amendment issues unless the economic corrective measures involve placing restrictions on activities protected within some first amendment theory.

The assumptions which require guaranteeing adequate, but not equal, presentation of all (serious?) viewpoints are very similar to those of the classic model. In fact, in *On Liberty*, Mill recommended that we search for devices to assure the forceful presentation of viewpoints that, without our positive efforts, would not be adequately presented. Like the classic model, this approach must assume that reason dominates. Only if people use reason to analyze disputes will their conclusions not be controlled by the form and frequency of inputs. This approach assumes that people will use their intellect to find the core of insight, if any, in each message. It merely notes the absence of meaningful access opportunities for certain positions and advocates that these views be guaranteed adequate access to the marketplace. Of course, the practical problem with this position as a constitutional standard rather than as a legislative policy is the difficulty of determining what amounts to an adequate or meaningful presentation opportunity.

This conclusion that an adequate presentation of each view is the constitutional goal points to an interesting fact about, and possibly an objection to, both this market failure theory and the classic market model. Given that some expression of a viewpoint suffices to assure its proper evaluation, a restraint on the speech of some individuals would not obstruct the search for truth as long as others forcefully express the views of those individuals. Unless persuaded by rule utilitarian objections—for example, that it would be costly to prevent or correct predictable misapplications of the power to restrict or censor individuals—government restraints on individuals, as long as the individual's message were adequately presented by others, would be unobjectionable. Despite marketplace rhetoric, a theorist's objection to such restraints often reveals an underlying concern with individual liberty that supersedes the theorist's concern for the workings of the market place.

Equal access for all viewpoints is a quite unusual interpretation of a properly functioning marketplace of ideas. It makes sense, however, if truth (or a best or correct solution) exists but if people's rational faculties are too feeble to avoid or neutralize distortions caused by propagandists' use of quantity or packaging techniques. In other words, this model relies upon the classic model's truth assumption but rejects the second aspect of its rationality assumption, that people are able to sort through the form and frequency of message presentation to evaluate the core notions. Equalizing the presentation opportunities for each potentially true or best viewpoint (in contrast to equalizing the opportunity for each speaker) enables each position to use quantity and packaging to neutralize the other's use. Provision for equal funding of all political candidates attempts, at least in the context of political campaigns, to accomplish that goal. (Or, if passing some threshold level of support provides evidence that a candidate is potentially the best choice, that is, the one who would win if presentation opportunities were equalized, then the state should assure equal resources to those candidates who meet this threshold requirement.)

Equal access for all individuals is the most logical version of the market failure theory. Each of the faulty assumptions of the classic model is replaced with a new one. First, truth is chosen or created not made. Second, reason exists but normally does not control or dominate people's response to debate. Instead, people normally can not divorce their understanding from their experiences in a particular social location; moreover, people respond to packaging, quantity, and context aspects of messages. Third, societal choices must fairly respond to people's different needs and groups' conflicting interests, whether or not the conflict is permanent. Given these assumptions, success in "rational" debate does not provide criteria for judging the merit of particular proposals or perspectives—at least, unless the debate is "fair." Cut adrift from the logic which explained how the marketplace of ideas advances truth, and instead assuming that truth is chosen, at least in part, on the basis of inputs into the marketplace, the democratic notion provides a solution: The marketplace works if and only if all people are equally able to participate in making or influencing the choice. Moreover, providing each person a roughly equal opportunity to generate equal quantities of carefully packaged messages increases the role of reason; the equalization neutralizes the advantage which packaging presently gives to well-financed perspectives. At first, the failure of the classic model's assumptions appeared to make faith in the market place of ideas incoherent. However, once one concludes that the purpose of the market is to provide legitimate scope for differing, often conflicting, interests rather than to promote the discovery of objective truth, and once one accepts a democratic notion that equal individual influence gives legitimate scope for differing interests, then the market place of ideas seems perfectly coherent as long as people have equal opportunities (e.g., equal resources) for participating.

Reliance on this equality standard rather than the existing wealth (market) criterion for determining individual opportunities is not the norm in our basically capitalistic society. The area where we most commonly claim to adopt the equality standard is in the political sphere—"one person, one vote." Thus, the equality standard for individual input will seem most appropriate for speech which relates to what are perceived as political decisions, i.e., collective decisions which will affect the rights as well as the values of the members of the collective. For example, this could explain why the Court has concluded that wealth should not affect one's ability to vote (participate politically) even though generally wealth is, unless the political system concludes otherwise, assumed to be the proper criterion for allocating other goods.

To achieve equality of opportunity for individual input requires either a combination of subsidies and expenditure restrictions or a method of making speech a free good, i.e., making any amount of communication the speaker desires costless to the speaker. Some campaign reform proposals, for example, giving everyone an equal amount of government money to spend on election campaigns, can be interpreted as a *partial* move toward such an egalitarian system.

B. EVALUATION

Some criticisms apply only to specific versions of the market failure theory. For example, the second market failure theory, requiring adequate access for all viewpoints, or the third, requiring equal access for all viewpoints, rely respectively on the classic model's rationality or its truth assumptions. Thus, each of the reformulations is subject to the criticisms of the specific assumption of the classic model upon which it relies. Here, I intend first to develop criticisms which apply to all versions (possibly with differing force). Then, I will note serious practical difficulties with guaranteeing equal access for all individuals. This equal access argument merits special attention since, by reversing each of the classic model's assumptions, it apparently escapes all the theoretical criticisms directed against the classic model.

The most fundamental objection to the market failure theories applies when they require interference with the speech freedom of some people. This objection starkly poses the question whether equalizing "real opportunities" to speak justifies restricting speech or certain other forms of personal liberty....

III. THE LIBERTY MODEL

My thesis is that the first amendment protects a broad realm of nonviolent, noncoercive activity. The method for determining the scope of protection proceeds, first, by determining the purposes or values served by protected speech. These values, however, are also served by violent and coercive activities. Thus, I conclude that constitutional protection of speech is justified not merely because of the values served by speech but because freedom of speech serves these values in a particular, humanly acceptable manner, e.g., nonviolently and noncoercively....

A. First Amendment Values or Purposes

In the marketplace theories, a single value—discovery of truth or reaching the "best" societal or individual decision—justified and defined the scope of protection. This focus is too limited. Professor Emerson, probably the most thoughtful and influential first amendment scholar, finds first amendment freedom essential for four values: (1) individual self-fulfillment, (2) advancement of knowledge and discovery of truth, (3) participation in decision making by all members of the society (which "embraces the right to participate in the building of the whole culture"), and (4) achievement of a "more adaptable and hence stable community."

Emerson's list is acceptable. However, it is informative to see that the first value, self-fulfillment, and the third, participation in change, are key values and to understand why conduct promoting these two values ought to receive constitutional protection. The values of self-fulfillment and participation in change impose somewhat different requirements on a satisfactory theory. The emphasis on "self" in self-fulfillment requires the theory to delineate a realm of liberty for self-determined processes of self-realization. The participation in change value requires the theory to specify and protect activities essential to a democratic, participatory process of change. Emerson's other two values are derivative. Given that truth is chosen or created, not discovered, advancement of knowledge and discovery of truth are merely aspects of participation in change. Also, one apparently achieves a "more flexible and thereby more stable community" by providing for individual self-fulfillment and participation in change. Thus, henceforth, I will refer to individual self-fulfillment and participation in change as the key first amendment values.

Why should these two values receive constitutional protection? I will briefly summarize an answer I have advanced elsewhere. Obligation exists only in relationships of respect. To justify legal obligation, the community must respect individuals as equal, rational and autonomous moral beings. For the community legitimately to expect individuals to respect collective decisions, i.e., legal rules, the community must respect the dignity and equal worth of its members. One can elaborate this core truth of social contract doctrines in order to explain both the propriety of and proper limits on utilitarian policies. And determining the proper limits on utilitarian policies is crucial for identifying constitutional rights because having constitutional protection means that the right prevails over preference maximization policies. The justification for welfare maximization policies is that, in decision making, the state should weight each person's concerns *equally*, thereby respecting the equal worth of each. This required respect for people's equal worth also explains the major limit on adopting welfare maximization policies, i.e., the state's policy must respect people's integrity as rational, equal, autonomous moral beings, it must respect people as ends and not just as means. This requires that people's choices, their definition and development of *themselves*, must be respected—otherwise they become mere objects for manipulation or means for realizing someone else's ideals or desires. This respect for defining, developing or expressing one's self is precisely Emerson's value of self-realization. Moreover, since group decisions significantly influence both one's identity and one's opportunities, respecting people's autonomy as well as people's equal worth requires that people be allowed an equal right to participate in the process of group decision making—which is precisely Emerson's other key value, participation in collective decision making. Without trying to further develop this justification for the centrality of these two values, below I will merely rely on the widely accepted conclusion that *individual self-fulfillment and participation in change are fundamental purposes of the first amendment.* If, however, one accepts the justification offered here, it would help explain why utilitarian balancing does not justify limiting first amendment rights.

*   *   *

THE FIRST AMENDMENT IS AN ABSOLUTE

Alexander Meiklejohn

Forty-two years ago the *Schenck* opinion,[1] written by Mr. Justice Holmes for a unanimous Court, opened a judicial controversy that still rages. It has taken many forms. In recent years it has divided the Supreme Court Justices into two groups which seem unable to understand each other well enough to formulate with clarity the issue about which they differ. Their discussion of that issue, which is indicated by the title of this paper, has been unclear because the contending parties have not been able to agree on the sense in which the word "absolute" shall be used. . . .

I. MR. JUSTICE BLACK'S POSITION

Mr. Justice Black's absolutist thesis is stated by his lecture in one sentence: "I take no law abridging to mean *no law abridging.*" With that general statement in mind, he examined and interpreted, one by one, the ten provisions of the Bill of Rights. And, on historical and philosophical grounds, he found them all to be "absolutes" in the sense that "they mean what they say." . . .

Concerning the Eighth Amendment, Mr. Justice Black said:

From *Supreme Court Review* 245 (1961). Reprinted with permission of the University of Chicago Press.

The Eighth Amendment forbids "excessive bail," "excessive fines," or the infliction of "cruel or unusual punishments." This is one of the less precise provisions. The courts are required to determine the meaning of such general terms as "excessive" and "unusual." But surely that does not mean that admittedly "excessive bail," "excessive fines," or "cruel punishments" could be justified on the ground of "competing" public interest in carrying out some generally granted power like that given Congress to regulate commerce.

And part of his discussion of the Fourth Amendment was as follows:

The use of the word "unreasonable" in this Amendment means, of course, that not *all* searches and seizures are prohibited. Only those which are *unreasonable* are unlawful. There may be much difference of opinion about whether a particular search or seizure is unreasonable and therefore forbidden by this Amendment. But if it *is* unreasonable, it is absolutely prohibited.

About the Fifth Amendment he said: "There has been much controversy about the meaning of 'due process of law.' Whatever its meaning, however, there can be no doubt that it must be granted." And, finally, as he declared the First Amendment to be absolute, Mr. Justice Black supported his assertion by singling out only one phrase of that very complicated statement: "The phrase 'Congress shall make no law' is composed of plain words, easily understood."

With regard to the ambiguity of other phrases of the Amendment, he was not explicit, as he was in dealing with the Eighth and Fourth and Fifth Amendments. But it may, I think, be taken for granted that the words "abridging the freedom of speech, of the press; or the right of the people peaceably to assemble, and to petition the Government for a redress of their grievances" are not "plain words, easily understood." Together with such expressions as "excessive fines" or "cruel or unusual punishments" or "due process of law," they have been subject to "much controversy." We have inherited them from ages of bitter conflict over civil liberties. "The courts are required to determine [their] meaning."

That constitutional effect of a combination of absolutist language with terms of partial ambiguity, Mr. Justice Black summed up in this statement:

To my way of thinking, at least, the history and language of the Constitution and the Bill of Rights, which I have discussed with you, make it plain that one of the primary purposes of the Constitution with its amendments

was to withdraw from the Government *all* power to act in certain areas—
whatever the scope of those areas may be.

It is clear, I think, that Mr. Justice Black, as an absolutist, is here saying,
and is saying only, that the provisions of the Bill of Rights are "universal"
statements. In affirmative form they say "all are"; when negative, they say:
"none are." And such statements are "not open to exceptions." As universals,
they refer, validly or invalidly, clearly or unclearly, to every member of the
class which their terms designate. If you believe that "all are," it is nonsense
to say that "some are not." If you believe that "none are," you thereby believe,
whether you know it or not, that "some are" is false. The "absolute" assertion,
like every other intelligible assertion "means what it says" or, at least, what it
tries to say.

II. MR. JUSTICE HARLAN'S REJECTION
OF THE BLACK POSITION

As one reads the opinions of the "non-absolutists," "balancers," or "opera-
tionalists" who undertake to refute the thesis that Mr. Justice Black advocated
in his lecture, one is amazed at the extent to which they substitute caricature
for refutation. A striking example of this intellectual irrelevance may be found
in the opening words of Mr. Justice Harlan's discussion of the constitutional
issue in his *Konigsberg* opinion:[2]

> At the outset we reject the view that freedom of speech and association . . . ,
> as protected by the First and Fourteenth Amendments are "absolutes," not
> only in the undoubted sense that where the constitutional protection exists
> it must prevail, but also in the sense that the scope of that protection must
> be gathered solely from a literal reading of the First Amendment.
> Throughout its history this Court has consistently recognized at least two
> ways in which constitutionally protected freedom of speech is narrower than
> an unlimited license to talk. . . .

That statement not only flatly rejected the absolutist theory but also gave
two different accounts of what that theory is. The first of these two accounts
might be accepted by any absolutist as a clear and accurate statement of his
belief about the First Amendment. But, in sharp contrast, the second was a

caricature which, for forty-two years since Mr. Justice Holmes, in *Schenck*, initiated and then discarded it, has confused and defeated the intention of the Court to confer reasonably about what the First Amendment means to say.

As he drew the caricature which made possible an easy victory over his opponent, Mr. Justice Harlan claimed the support of Mr. Justice Holmes, who had said of the provisions of the Constitution: "Their significance is vital not formal; it is to be gathered not simply by taking the words and a dictionary, but by considering their origin and the line of their growth." He might also have quoted from Mr. Justice Frankfurter's concurring opinion in *Dennis v. United States*,[3] where the same accusation of historical illiteracy was made: "The language of the First Amendment is to be read not as barren words found in a dictionary but as symbols of historic experience illumined by the presuppositions of those who employed them." But Mr. Justice Harlan's own misunderstanding of his opponent goes further than that of his predecessors. His words misconstrue not only the methods of absolutist thinking but also the conclusion at which such thinking arrives. To the accusation that his opponent relies "solely" on a dictionary, he now adds the charge that he interprets the First Amendment as establishing "an unlimited license to talk."

The absolutist interpretation, when it is thus misstated, is, of course, easily destroyed. The supposed belief in "an unlimited license to talk" is casually refuted by a footnote observation that it "cannot be reconciled with the law relating to libel, slander, misrepresentation, obscenity, perjury, false advertising, solicitation of crime, complicity by encouragement, conspiracy, and the like. But who, among Mr. Justice Harlan's colleagues, believes in "an unlimited license to talk"? Who interprets the words of the First Amendment without "considering their origin or the line of their growth"? Who reads the text as "barren words found in a dictionary" rather than as "symbols of historic experience"?

*   *   *

This section cannot, however, be closed without noting that other "balancers" have similarly caricatured the absolutist contention. This is especially true of Mr. Justice Frankfurter in his *Dennis* opinion, where he referred to my book on free speech. He there described an "absolute" as "a sonorous formula which is in fact only a euphemistic disguise for an unresolved conflict." He also represented it as claiming to be "self-defining and self-enforcing." And he further characterized absolute statements as "dogmas too inflexible for the non-Euclidean problems to be solved."

In relation to these inaccurate characterizations, Mr. Justice Black has said that his "absolutes" are not "self-defining"; they make use of terms whose meanings must be "determined by the courts." Nor are they "self-enforcing." No general principle, whether absolute or not, is enforced except as it is found to "fit the facts." The generalizing and particularizing elements in any intellectual activity must always join forces if they are to be effective. To think without facts is as ineffectual as to think without principles. Again, the absolute provisions are not "inflexible." Mr. Justice Black knows, as well as do his antagonists, that the Constitution did not exist two centuries ago. It provides for its own amendment and, through the courts, for its reinterpretation. How long it will last and how it may be changed no one knows. And, finally, absolute statements are not in themselves "dogmas." They may be either true or false, certain or uncertain, wise or foolish. For example, an assertion that "Congress has unlimited authority to abridge political freedom" is absolute in exactly the same sense as is the assertion that "Congress has no authority to abridge political freedom." Their only relevant difference is that one of these propositions is supported by the Constitution, while the other is repudiated by it.

III. MR. JUSTICE HARLAN'S POSITION

Having refuted an assertion which Mr. Justice Black did not make, Mr. Justice Harlan might next be reasonably expected to attempt to refute the assertion which his opponent did make. But at that point the *Konigsberg* opinion branches off in another direction. It offered a new and more theoretical version of the "balancing" doctrine:

> On the one hand certain forms of speech, or speech in certain contexts, has [*sic*] been considered outside the scope of constitutional protection.... On the other hand, general regulatory statutes, not intended to control the content of speech but incidentally limiting its unfettered exercise, have not been regarded as the type of law the First or Fourteenth Amendment forbade Congress or the States to pass, when they have been found justified by subordinating valid governmental interests, a prerequisite to constitutionality which has necessarily involved a weighing of the governmental interest involved.

These words have interest for this inquiry because in his restatement of the "balancing" doctrine, Mr. Justice Harlan used "contrast" terms which, by implication, suggest the positive meaning of the First Amendment. "Regulatory" suggests, by contrast, "prohibitory"; "not intended to control the content of thought" suggests "intended to control the content of thought"; "incidentally" suggests "by deliberate intention." Here are the elements which, properly fused, might tell us what the First Amendment forbids. But more immediately relevant to the present discussion is the fact that Mr. Justice Harlan here turned from the consideration of "the abridgment of the freedom of speech" to a study of the "regulation of speech." And he did so without determining the relation between "regulation" and "abridgment of freedom." Are these two terms identical? I think not. Nor are freedoms and regulation antithetical. For example, a man may be denied the privilege of speaking at a meeting because someone else "has the floor." But the freedom of discussion is not thereby abridged. Members of Congress are guaranteed freedom "on the floor of either House." But their speaking is regulated under "rules of order." A citizen has authority to "petition" Congress or the Supreme Court. But the time, place, circumstances, and manner of the presentation are determined, not by his own choice, but by carefully prescribed regulations. In 1953 I wrote: "Speech, as a form of human action, is subject to regulation in exactly the same sense as is walking, or lighting a fire, or shooting a gun. To interpret the First Amendment as forbidding such regulation is to so misconceive its meaning as to reduce it to nonsense." In the intervening years I have found no reason to change that assertion.

The freedom that the First Amendment protects is not, then, an absence of regulation. It is the presence of self-government. Our argument now proceeds to define, as clearly as it can, the intention of the Constitutional provision that begins with the words: "Congress shall make no law abridging...."

IV. "RATIONAL PRINCIPLES TO MARK THE LIMITS OF CONSTITUTIONAL PROTECTION"

In his *Free Speech in the United States* Professor Chafee stated the dilemma which confronts our inquiry and which divides the Supreme Court so evenly: "The question whether such perplexing cases are within the First Amendment or not cannot be solved by the multiplication of obvious examples, but only by the development of a rational principle to mark the limits of constitutional protection." Professor Chafee was too much involved in the complexities of balancing to formulate the needed principle of which absolutists speak. But he indicated the goal toward which every interpreter of the First Amendment should now be trying to make his way. We are looking for a principle which is not in conflict with any other provision of the Constitution, a principle which, as it now stands, is "absolute" in the sense of being "not open to exceptions," but a principle which also is subject to interpretation, to change, or to abolition, as the necessities of a precarious world may require.

Apart from the First Amendment itself, the passages of the Constitution which most directly clarify its meaning are the Preamble, the Tenth Amendment, and Section 2 of Article I. All four provisions must be considered in their historical setting, not only in relation to one another but, even more important, in relation to the intention and structure of the Constitution as a whole. Out of such consideration the following principles seem to emerge:

1. All constitutional authority to govern the people of the United States belongs to the people themselves, acting as members of a corporate body politic. . . .

2. By means of the Constitution, the people establish subordinate agencies—such as the legislature, the executive, the judiciary, and delegate to each of them such specific and limited powers as are deemed necessary for the doing of its assigned governing. These agencies have no other powers.

3. The people do not delegate all their sovereign powers. The Tenth Amendment speaks of powers that are reserved "to the people," as well as of powers "reserved to the States."

4. Article I, § 2, speaks of a reserved power which the people have decided to exercise by their own direct activity: "The House of Representatives shall be composed of members chosen every second year by the people of the several States. . . ." Here is established the voting power through which the people, as an electorate, actively participate in governing both themselves, as subjects of the laws, and their agencies, as the makers, administrators, and interpreters of the laws. In

today's government, the scope of direct electoral action is wider than the provisions made when Article I, § 2, was adopted, but the constitutional principle or intention is the same.

5. The revolutionary intent of the First Amendment is, then, to deny to all subordinate agencies' authority to abridge the freedom of the electoral power of the people.

For the understanding of these principles it is essential to keep clear the crucial difference between "the rights" of the governed and "the powers" of the governors. And at this point, the title "Bill of Rights" is lamentably inaccurate as a designation of the first ten amendments. They are not a "Bill of Rights" but a "Bill of Powers and Rights." The Second through the Ninth Amendments limit the powers of the subordinate agencies in order that due regard shall be paid to the private "rights of the governed." The First and Tenth Amendments protect the governing "powers" of the people from abridgment by the agencies which are established as their servants. In the field of our "rights," each one of us can claim "due process of law." In the field of our governing "powers," the notion of "due process" is irrelevant.

V. THE FREEDOM OF THOUGHT AND COMMUNICATION BY WHICH WE GOVERN

The preceding section may be summed up thus: The First Amendment does not protect a "freedom to speak." It protects the freedom of those activities of thought and communication by which we "govern." It is concerned, not with a private right, but with a public power, a governmental responsibility.

In the specific language of the Constitution, the governing activities of the people appear only in terms of casting a ballot. But in the deeper meaning of the Constitution, voting is merely the external expression of a wide and diverse number of activities by means of which citizens attempt to meet the responsibilities of making judgments, which that freedom to govern lays upon them. That freedom implies and requires what we call "the dignity of the individual." Self-government can exist only insofar as the voters acquire the intelligence, integrity, sensitivity, and generous devotion to the general welfare that, in theory, casting a ballot is assumed to express.

The responsibilities mentioned are of three kinds. We, the people who govern, must try to understand the issues which, incident by incident, face the nation. We must pass judgment upon the decisions which our agents make upon those issues. And, further, we must share in devising methods by which those decisions can be made wise and effective or, if need be, supplanted by others which promise greater wisdom and effectiveness. Now it is these activities, in all their diversity, whose freedom fills up "the scope of the First Amendment." These are the activities to whose freedom it gives its unqualified protection. And it must be recognized that the literal text of the Amendment falls far short of expressing the intent and the scope of that protection. I have previously tried to express that inadequacy:

> We must also note that, though the intention of the Amendment is sharp and resolute, the sentence which expresses that intention is awkward and ill-constructed. Evidently, it was hard to write and is, therefore, hard to interpret. Within its meaning are summed up centuries of social passion and intellectual controversy, in this country and in others. As one reads it, one feels that its writers could not agree, either within themselves or with each other, upon a single formula which would define for them the paradoxical relation between free men and their legislative agents. Apparently, all that they could make their words do was to link together five separate demands which had been sharpened by ages of conflict and were being popularly urged in the name of the "Freedom of the People." And yet, those demands were, and were felt to be, varied forms of a single demand. They were attempts to express, each in its own way, the revolutionary idea which, in the slowly advancing fight for freedom, has given to the American experiment in self-government its dominating significance for the modern world.

What I have said is that the First Amendment, as seen in its constitutional setting, forbids Congress to abridge the freedom of a citizen's speech, press, peaceable assembly, or petition, whenever those activities are utilized for the governing of the nation. In these respects, the Constitution gives to all "the people" the same protection of freedom which, in Article I, § 6(1), it provides for their legislative agents: "and for any speech or debate in either House, they shall not be questioned in any other place." Just as our agents must be free in their use of their delegated powers, so the people must be free in the exercise of their reserved powers.

What other activities, then, in addition to speech, press, assembly, and petition, must be included within the scope of the First Amendment? First of all, the freedom to "vote," the official expression of a self-governing man's judgment on issues of public policy, must be absolutely protected. None of his subordinate agencies may bring pressure upon him to drive his balloting this way or that. None of them may require him to tell how he has voted; none may inquire by compulsory process into his political beliefs or associations. In that area, the citizen has constitutional authority and his agents have not.

Second, there are many forms of thought and expression within the range of human communications from which the voter derives the knowledge, intelligence, sensitivity to human values: the capacity for sane and objective judgment which, so far as possible, a ballot should express. These, too, must suffer no abridgment of their freedom. I list four of them below:

1. Education, in all its phases, is the attempt to so inform and cultivate the mind and will of a citizen that he shall have the wisdom, the independence, and, therefore, the dignity of a governing citizen. Freedom of education is, thus, as we all recognize, a basic postulate in the planning of a free society.

2. The achievements of philosophy and the sciences in creating knowledge and understanding of men and their world must be made available, without abridgment, to every citizen.

3. Literature and the arts must be protected by the First Amendment. They lead the way toward sensitive and informed appreciation and response to the values out of which the riches of the general welfare are created.

4. Public discussions of public issues, together with the spreading of information and opinion bearing on those issues, must have a freedom unabridged by our agents. Though they govern us, we, in a deeper sense, govern them. Over our governing, they have no power. Over their governing we have sovereign power.

VI. A PARADOX

Out of the argument thus far stated, two apparently contradictory statements emerge. Congress may, in ways carefully limited, "regulate" the activities by which the citizens govern the nation. But no regulation may abridge the freedom of those governing activities. I am sure that the two statements are not contradictory. But their combination is, to say the least, paradoxical. It is that paradox that I must now face.... As a non-lawyer, I shall not discuss in detail the difficulties and puzzlements with which the courts must deal. I can only suggest that, here and there, seeming contradictions are not real.

First. A distinction must be drawn between belief and communication in their relations to Congressional authority. A citizen may be told when and where and in what manner he may or may not speak, write, assemble, and so on. On the other hand, he may not be told what he shall or shall not believe. In that realm each citizen is sovereign. He exercises powers that the body politic reserves for its own members. In 1953, testifying before the Senate Committee on Constitutional Rights, I said:

> ... our First Amendment freedom forbids that any citizen be required, under threat of penality, to take an oath, or make an affirmation, as to beliefs which he holds or rejects. Every citizen, it is true, may be required and should be required, to pledge loyalty, and to practice loyalty, to the nation. He must agree to support the Constitution. But he may never be required to *believe* in the Constitution. His loyalty may never be tested on grounds of adherence to, or rejection of, any *belief.* Loyalty does not imply conformity of opinion. Every citizen of the United States has Constitutional authority to approve or to condemn any laws enacted by the Legislature, any actions taken by the Executive, any judgments rendered by the judiciary, any principles established by the Constitution. All these enactments which, as men who are governed, we must obey, are subject to our approval or disapproval, as we govern. With respect to all of them we, who are free men, are sovereign. We are "The People." We govern the United States.

*   *   *

Second. We must recognize that there are many forms of communication which, since they are not being used as activities of governing, are wholly outside the scope of the First Amendment. Mr. Justice Holmes has told us about these, giving such vivid illustrations as "persuasion to murder" and "falsely shouting fire in a theatre and causing a panic." And Mr. Justice Harlan, referring to Holmes and following his lead, gave a more extensive list: "libel, slander, misrepresentation, obscenity, perjury, false advertising, solicitation of crime, complicity by encouragement, conspiracy. . . ." Why are these communications not protected by the First Amendment? Mr. Justice Holmes suggested an explanation when he said of the First Amendment in *Schenck*: "It does not even protect a man from an injunction against uttering words that may have all the effect of force."

Now it may be agreed that the uttering of words cannot be forbidden by legislation, nor punished on conviction, unless damage has been done by them to some individual or to the wider society. But that statement does not justify the imputation that all "words that may have all the effect of force" are denied the First Amendment's protection. The man who falsely shouts "Fire!" in a theater is subject to prosecution under validly enacted legislation. But the army officer who, in command of a firing squad, shouts "Fire!" and thus ends a life, cannot be prosecuted for murder. He acts as an agent of the government. And, in fact, all governing communications are intended to have, more or less directly, "the effect of force." When a voter casts his ballot for a tax levy, he intends that someone shall be deprived of property. But his voting is not therefore outside the scope of the First Amendment. His voting must be free.

The principle here at stake can be seen in our libel laws. In cases of private defamation, one individual does damage to another by tongue or pen; the person so injured in reputation or property may sue for damages. But, in that case, the First Amendment gives no protection to the person sued. His verbal attack has no relation to the business of governing. If, however, the same verbal attack is made in order to show the unfitness of a candidate for governmental office, the act is properly regarded as a citizen's participation in government. It is, therefore, protected by the First Amendment. And the same principle holds good if a citizen attacks, by words of disapproval and condemnation, the policies of the government, or even the structure of the Constitution. These are "public" issues concerning which, under our form of government, he has authority, and is assumed to have competence, to judge. Though private libel is subject to legislative control, political or seditious libel is not.

Third. In discussions of the First Amendment too little attention has been given to the regulatory word "peaceable" in relation to "assembly." It suggests principles of limitation which apply also to speech, press, petition, and to the other forms of communication which support them. This limitation is significant in demonstrating that a citizen's governing is often both "regulated" and "free."

Peaceableness in governing may serve either one or both of two purposes. It provides protection for an assembly against external violation of rules of public order. It also seeks to ensure that relations within the assembly shall succeed in serving the governing function which warrants its protection by the First Amendment. The first of these purposes has to do with relations between the assembly and "outsiders" who, disagreeing with its ideas and intentions, may seek to disrupt the discussion and, in various ways, to render it ineffectual. In this situation, both the local authorities which have authority to "regulate" and the police who seek to apply the regulations are held responsible by the intention of the First and Fourteenth Amendments. No ordinance may be based upon disapproval of policies to be discussed or decreed by the assembly. And the police must, to the limit of their power, defend the meeting from interruption or interference by its enemies. But basically more important are the conditions of peaceableness within an assembly itself. It is, of course, impossible that everyone should be allowed to express his point of view whenever and however he chooses. In a meeting for discussion, as contrasted with a lecture, however, no one may be "denied the floor" on the ground of disapproval of what he is saying or would say. And, if the interests of a self-governing society are to be served, vituperation which fixes attention on the defects of an opponent's character or intelligence and thereby distracts attention from the question of policy under discussion may be forbidden as a deadly enemy of peaceable assembly. Anyone who persists in it should be expelled from the meeting, and, if need be, the police should give help in getting it done.

I cannot, however, leave those words on record without noting how inadequate, to the degree of non-existence, are our public provisions for active discussions among the members of our self-governing society. As we create and enlarge freedom, such universal discussion is imperative. In every village, in every district of every town or city, there should be established at public expense cultural centers inviting all citizens, as they may choose, to meet together for the consideration of public policy. And conditions must be provided under which such meetings could be happily and successfully conducted. I am not thinking of such lunatic-fringe activities as those in Hyde Park in London. I am thinking of a self-governing body politic, whose freedom of individual expression should be cultivated, not merely because it serves to prevent outbursts of violence which would result from suppression, but for the positive purpose of bringing every citizen into active and intelligent sharing in the government of his country.

Fourth. Largely because of our failure to make adequate provision for free and unhindered public discussion, the courts are called upon to judge the constitutionality of local ordinances which forbid or limit the holding of public meetings in public places. Such ordinances come into effect when individuals or groups assemble in such a way as to interfere with other interests of the community or of its members. The most striking and perplexing cases of this kind occur when meetings are held on the public streets or in parks whose primary use is, in the opinion of the authorities, blocked or hindered to a degree demanding action. Now if such ordinances are based upon official disapproval of the ideas to be presented at the meeting, they clearly violate the First Amendment. But if no such abridgment of freedom is expressed or implied, regulation or prohibition on other grounds may be enacted and enforced.

It must not be assumed that every governmental regulation of a public meeting is, under current conditions, destructive of political freedom. Conditions of traffic on a city street are very different from those in the relatively open spaces of a country village. Parks may be needed for rest, quiet, and release from excitement and strain. Just as an individual, seeking to advocate some public policy may not do so, without consent, by interrupting a church service, or a classroom, or a sickroom, or a session of Congress or of the Supreme Court, or by ringing a doorbell and demanding to be heard, so meetings must conform to the necessities of the community, with respect to time, place, circumstance, and manner of procedure. And, unless those considerations are dishonestly used as a cover for unconstitutional discrimination against this idea or that, there is no First Amendment complaint against the ordinances which express them. The Amendment, I repeat, does not establish an "unlimited right to talk."

It must further be noted that in "emergency" situations, when something must be said and no other time, place, circumstance, or manner of speech will serve for the saying of it, a citizen may be justified in "taking the law into his own hands." In the famous example of Mr. Justice Holmes, a man is not allowed to shout "Fire!" *falsely* in a theater. But, if, during a performance in a theater, a person sees a fire which threatens to spread, he is not only allowed, he is duty-bound, to try to find some way of informing others so that a panic may not ensue with its disastrous consequences. The distinction between "falsely" and "truly" is here fundamental to an understanding of what freedom is.

Fifth. In the current discussions as to whether or not "obscenity" in literature and the arts is protected by the First Amendment, the basic principle is, I think, that literature and the arts are protected because they have a "social importance" which I have called a "governing" importance. For example, the novel is at present a powerful determinative of our views of what human beings are, how they can be influenced, in what directions they should be influenced by many forces, including, especially, their own judgments and appreciations. But the novel, like all the other creations of literature and the arts, may be produced wisely or unwisely, sensitively or coarsely, for the building up of a way of life which we treasure or for tearing it down. Shall the government establish a censorship to distinguish between "good" novels and "bad" ones? And, more specifically, shall it forbid the publication of novels which portray sexual experiences with a frankness that, to the prevailing conventions of our society, seems "obscene"?

The First Amendment seems to me to answer that question with an unequivocal "no." Here, as elsewhere, the authority of citizens to decide what they shall write and, more fundamental, what they shall read and see, has not been delegated to any of the subordinate branches of government. It is "reserved to the people," each deciding for himself to whom he will listen, whom he will read, what portrayal of the human scene he finds worthy of his attention. And at this point I feel compelled to disagree with Professor Kalven's interpretation of what I have tried to say. In his recent article on obscenity, he wrote:

> The classic defense of John Stuart Mill and the modern defense of Alexander Meiklejohn do not help much when the question is why the novel, the poem, the painting, the drama, or the piece of sculpture falls within the protection of the First Amendment. Nor do the famous opinions of Hand, Holmes, and Brandeis. The emphasis is all on truth winning out in a fair fight between competing ideas. The emphasis is clearest in Meiklejohn's argument that free speech is indispensable to the informed citizenry required to make democratic self-government work. The people need free speech because they vote. As a result his argument distinguishes sharply between public and private speech. Not all communications are relevant to the political process. The people do not need novels or dramas or paintings or poems because they will be called upon to vote. Art and belles-lettres do not deal in such ideas—at least not good art or belles-lettres....

In reply to that friendly interpretation, I must, at two points, record a friendly disavowal. I have never been able to share the Miltonian faith that in a fair fight between truth and error, truth is sure to win. And if one had that faith, it would be hard to reconcile it with the sheer stupidity of the policies of this nation—and of other nations—now driving humanity to the very edge of final destruction. In my view, "the people need free speech" because they have decided, in adopting, maintaining and interpreting their Constitution, to govern themselves rather than to be governed by others. And, in order to make that self-government a reality rather than an illusion, in order that it may become as wise and efficient as its responsibilities require, the judgment-making of the people must be self-educated in the ways of freedom. That is, I think, the positive purpose to which the negative words of the First Amendment gave a constitutional expression. Moreover, as against Professor Kalven's interpretation, I believe, as a teacher, that the people do need novels and dramas and paintings and poems, "because they will be called upon to vote." The primary social fact which blocks and hinders the success of our experiment in self-government is that our citizens are not educated for self-government. We are terrified by ideas, rather than challenged and stimulated by them. Our dominant mood is not the courage of people who dare to think. It is the timidity of those who fear and hate whenever conventions are questioned.

*   *   *

NOTES

1. *Schenck v. United States*, 249 U.S. 47 (1919).
2. *Konigsberg v. State Bar of California*, 353 U.S. 252 (1957).
3. 341 U.S.494 (1951).

EQUALITY AS A CENTRAL PRINCIPLE IN THE FIRST AMENDMENT

Kenneth L. Karst

*   *   *

The ideal of equality runs deep in the American tradition. A just society, we believe, must offer "equal liberties" in the realm of political participation. Within the past generation, this tradition has flowered into a number of new constitutional doctrines, aimed at effectuating the ideal of political equality. In the aggregate, these doctrines mark the emergence of a principle of equal liberty of expression, not merely in the political arena, but throughout all the interdependent "decisionmaking" processes of a complex society.

A natural doctrinal vehicle for promoting the principle of equal liberty of expression is the guarantee of equal protection of the laws. In a number of recent cases involving first amendment interests, the Supreme Court has used the framework of equal protection analysis to limit government's power to restrict free expression. This approach has met with the objection, both within and outside the Court, that the first amendment itself would have been a more appropriate ground for decision. Framing the problem of free expression in equal protection terms, it is said, misses the basic purpose of the first amendment, which is not equality but liberty. By emphasizing the equality

From *University of Chicago Law Review* 43 (1975). Reprinted with permission.

principle, the Court may invite government to equalize not by lifting restrictions from some but by suppressing the expression of all. The principle of equality may have its uses in ensuring the freedom of expression, the critics argue, but those uses are marginal to the first amendment's main goals.

This line of argument is misleading. Although the critics' preference for the first amendment as a ground for decision is perfectly sound, their argument gives life to a false assumption about the amendment's meaning. The principle of equality, when understood to mean equal liberty, is not just a peripheral support for the freedom of expression, but rather part of the "central meaning of the First Amendment."

Although the Supreme Court has only recently recognized the centrality of the equality principle in the first amendment, the principle was implicit in the Supreme Court's "public forum" decisions as well as in its decisions protecting the associational rights of political minorities. More fundamentally, the principle of equal liberty lies at the heart of the first amendment's protections against government regulation of the content of speech. Proper appreciation of the importance of the equality principle in the first amendment suggests the need for a reconsideration of the results reached by the Supreme Court in several doctrinal subspheres.

Just such a reconsideration is the aim of this article. When the equality principle is applied to content regulation, it demands a rethinking of several lines of decision. In the "public forum" area, where the equality principle made its first appearances, a clear understanding of the principle should encourage the Court to abandon inconsistent precedents. The principle of equal liberty of expression also calls for a new look at the problem of access to the communications media. Finally, the first amendment's equality principle implies further constitutional progress toward equalization of the electoral process.

Exploring these doctrinal areas in light of the principle of equal liberty of expression will necessarily raise ancillary questions long familiar in equal protection analysis: the problem of inequalities resulting from hidden or inexplicit "classifications," the relation between formal and substantive equality, the "stopping-place" problem, and analogies to the "state action" limitation.

*   *   *

I. EQUALITY AND THE PURPOSES OF THE FIRST AMENDMENT

The principle of equal liberty of expression underlies important purposes of the first amendment. Three such purposes, not always distinct in practice, are commonly identified: (1) to permit informed choices by citizens in a self-governing democracy, (2) to aid in the search for truth, and (3) to permit each person to develop and exercise his or her capacities, thus promoting the sense of individual self-worth. As a practical matter, realization of these goals implies realization of the first amendment's equality principle.

A. SELF-GOVERNMENT

It was logical for the Declaration of Independence to link the ideal of political equality with the affirmation that governments derive their just powers from the consent of the governed. Contract theorists from Locke to Rawls have drawn a similar connection, giving political content to Luther's doctrine of the priesthood of all believers. If persons are equal, then legitimate government must be based on the consent of the governed. And if equals consent to be governed, rational self-interest dictates that each can preserve his or her own liberty only by agreeing to the equal liberty of all. Consent is thus conditioned on the preservation of equality under law. In Rousseau's words,

> [t]he social compact establishes among the citizens such an equality that they all pledge themselves under the same conditions and ought all to enjoy the same rights... [T]he sovereign never has a right to burden one subject more than another, because then the matter becomes particular and his power is no longer competent.

The principle invoked by Rousseau is not limited to political rights, but logically extends into the argument advanced by Justice Jackson in his justly celebrated concurrence in *Railway Express Agency v. New York*.[1]

> There is no more effective practical guaranty against arbitrary and unreasonable government than to require that the principles of law which officials would impose upon a minority must be imposed generally. Conversely, nothing opens the door to arbitrary action so effectively as to allow those officials to pick and choose only a few to whom they will apply legislation

and thus to escape the political retribution that might be visited upon them if larger numbers were affected. Courts can take no better measure to assure that laws will be just than to require that laws be equal in operation.

A general theory of equal protection is thus derived from the contract rationale that earlier generated a theory of equal political participation.

Alexander Meiklejohn based his eloquent defense of the freedom of political expression on similar reasoning. In *Free Speech and Its Relation to Self-Government*, Meiklejohn argued that a government deriving its legitimacy from the consent of the governed is based upon "a voluntary compact among political equals" and depends for its success on the wisdom of the voters. This wisdom is to be found "only in the minds of [the self-governing community's] individual citizens." The government, Meiklejohn contended, must not prevent the community from hearing any ideas relevant to their task of self-government:

> Citizens…may not be barred [from speaking] because their views are thought to be false or dangerous.…And the reason for this equality of status in the field of ideas lies deep in the very foundations of the self-governing process. When [people] govern themselves, it is they—and no one else—who must pass judgment upon unwisdom and unfairness and danger.

Insofar as a guarantee of free speech rests on a theory of self-government, then, the principle of equal liberty of expression is inherent in that guarantee.

B. The Search for Truth

The suppression of speech necessarily retards society's search for knowledge. The argument on behalf of the need for unfettered speech has been stated most eloquently by John Stuart Mill:

> Complete liberty of contradicting and disproving our opinion is the very condition which justifies us in assuming its truth for purposes of action; and on no other terms can a being with human faculties have any rational assurance of being right.

Mill was not only a political philosopher, but also a pioneer of modern social science. His quoted statement reflects the essence of the scientific method: no hypothesis can be taken as proved in the absence of attempts to disprove it.

The widest freedom to contradict prevailing opinion is thus implicit in any serious search for truth.

The advancement of knowledge depends on unfettered competition between today's prevailing opinions and those opinions that may come to prevail tomorrow. Preserving competition among ideas demands protecting the expression of all views, including minority views, and all speakers, including unpopular ones.

C. SELF-EXPRESSION AND INDIVIDUAL DIGNITY

The interest in voting is fundamental, it is sometimes said, because it is "preservative of all rights." But irrespective of any tangible benefits to be obtained from government through the ballot, voting remains a crucial symbol of citizenship, of membership in the community. In this sense, racial discrimination in voting inflicted the same harm as denial of service to blacks at lunch counters; both served to degrade and humiliate a racial minority.

Seen in this perspective, the principle of equal liberty of expression serves the same ends as equality in the right to vote. Each is necessary not only for the development of the individual's capacities, but also for the sense of self-respect that comes from being treated as a fully participating citizen.

It is no accident that strains on the system of freedom of expression typically come from the disadvantaged. The boisterous assertiveness of much of the civil rights movement, for example, is traceable not only to a need to use the streets and parks as a "public forum," but more fundamentally to a need for self-assertion simply as a way of staking a claim to equal citizenship. Equality of expression is indispensable to a society committed to the dignity of the individual.

II. THE CRYSTALLIZATION OF THE EQUALITY PRINCIPLE

Although the principle of equal liberty of expression is inherent in the first amendment, it has only recently received full and explicit articulation in an opinion of the Supreme Court. Fleeting pronouncements are to be found in some opinions of a generation ago, and more recently the principle was the basis of an oft-cited concurring opinion. But it was not until 1972, in *Police Department of the City of Chicago v. Mosely*,[2] that the Court enunciated the principle fully. In *Mosley*, a man who had been picketing peacefully near a school,

carrying a sign protesting "black discrimination," sought to enjoin enforcement of a new city ordinance prohibiting picketing within 150 feet of a school
during school hours; he had been advised by the police that he would be
arrested if he continued to picket. The ordinance contained an exception for
"peaceful picketing of any school involved in a labor dispute." The Seventh
Circuit held the ordinance invalid as an overly broad restriction of first
amendment rights. The Supreme Court affirmed but rested its decision on the
ground that the ordinance violated the fourteenth amendment's guarantee of
equal protection of the laws.

   Mosley squarely addresses the relationship between the equality principle
and the first amendment. Despite the Court's choice of an equal protection
ground for decision, its opinion speaks chiefly to first amendment values and
primarily cites first amendment cases as authority. In discussing the question
of equal opportunity to be heard, Justice Marshall, writing for the Court,
observes that the main problem with the ordinance

> is that it describes permissible picketing in terms of its subject matter....
> [A]bove all else, the First Amendment means that government has no power
> to restrict expression because of its message, its ideas, its subject matter, or
> its content.... To permit the continued building of our politics and culture,
> and to assure self-fulfillment for each individual, our people are guaranteed
> the right to express any thought, free from government censorship. The
> essence of the forbidden censorship is content control....
>
> Necessarily, then, under the Equal Protection Clause, not to mention the
> First Amendment itself, government may not grant the use of a forum to
> people whose views it finds acceptable, but deny use to those wishing to
> express less favored or more controversial views. And it may not select which
> issues are worth discussing or debating in public facilities. There is an
> "equality of status in the field of ideas" [quoting Meiklejohn] and govern-
> ment must afford all points of view an equal opportunity to be heard.

Justice Marshall then discusses the level of judicial scrutiny to be applied
when first amendment interests are adversely affected by an unequal opportunity to be heard:

> We have continually recognized that reasonable "time, place and manner"
> regulations of picketing may be necessary to further significant govern-

mental interests.... Similarly, under an equal protection analysis, there may
be sufficient regulatory interests justifying selective exclusions or distinctions among pickets.... But these justifications for selective exclusions from
a public forum must be carefully scrutinized. Because picketing plainly
involves expressive conduct within the protection of the First Amendment
...discriminations among pickets must be tailored to serve a substantial governmental interest....

In this case, the ordinance itself describes impermissible picketing not in
terms of time, place, and manner, but in terms of subject matter. The regulation "thus slip[s] from the neutrality of time, place and circumstances into
a concern about content" [quoting Kalven]. This is never permitted.

Largely ignored by the law reviews, *Mosley* is a landmark first amendment
decision. It makes two principal points: (1) the essence of the first amendment
is its denial to government of the power to determine which messages shall be
heard and which suppressed; "government must afford all points of view an
equal opportunity to be heard." (2) Any "time, place and manner" restriction
that selectively excludes speakers from a public forum must survive careful
judicial scrutiny to ensure that the exclusion is the minimum necessary to further a significant government interest. Taken together, these statements
declare a principle of major importance. The Court has explicitly adopted the
principle of equal liberty of expression.

Adherence to the principle of equal liberty of expression will have far-
reaching implications even though absolute equality is a practical impossi-
bility. The principle requires courts to start from the assumption that all
speakers and all points of view are entitled to a hearing, and permits deviation from this basic assumption only upon a showing of substantial necessity.
The emergence of the equality principle compels a critical re-examination of
several lines of first amendment decisions. We begin at the heart of the first
amendment, with its prohibition on censorship of speech content.

III. THE EQUALITY PRINCIPLE
AND CONTENT DISCRIMINATION

The absence of a clear articulation of the principle of equal liberty of expression in Supreme Court decisions before *Mosley* may be attributable to a belief

that the principle is so obviously central among first amendment values that it requires no explanation. In *Schacht v. United States*,[3] for example, a participant in an antiwar skit was prosecuted under a statute that prohibited wearing an Army uniform without authorization. The statute contained an exception allowing the uniform to be worn in a theatrical performance "if the portrayal does not tend to discredit" the armed forces. Justice Black, speaking for the Court, found it unnecessary to cite any authority or offer any explanation for holding that the statutory exception, "which leaves Americans free to praise the war in Vietnam but can send persons like Schacht to prison for opposing it, cannot survive in a country which has the First Amendment." There is a sense in which we have always known that "unless we protect [freedom of speech] for all, we will have it for none."

The equality principle, viewed as a barrier against content censorship, also implicitly underlies the elaborate first amendment doctrines that prohibit giving officials discretion to decide when speech shall be permitted and when it shall be punished or the speaker denied a license. The danger of delegating such discretionary authority is that a vague licensing or criminal statute would enable the prosecutor or censor to enforce the law selectively, tolerating orthodox views while suppressing unpopular ones. The same concern underlies decisions imposing rigorous limits on the seizure of obscene literature. It is not accidental that these first amendment doctrines serve equality not only at the level of principle but also at a practical level, defending nonconformists, dissenters, and the disadvantaged. The principle of equal liberty of expression, like the equal protection clause, has special relevance for protecting the downtrodden.

Given the centrality of the equality principle as a protection against content censorship, it seems likely that the Supreme Court will eventually complete the job of dismantling what Harry Kalven termed the "two-level" theory of speech. According to this theory, which sprang from an unguarded dictum in *Chaplinsky v. New Hampshire*,[4] certain kinds of speech content, such as obscenity, libel, or "fighting words," lie outside the protection of the first amendment and may be banned without judicial scrutiny of the state's justification. Kalven destroyed the intellectual foundations of the two-level theory as early as 1960, in his classic analysis of the law of obscenity. He argued that the two-level theory not only begged the crucial question of formulating a constitutional test for obscenity, but made judicial categorization dispositive without defining the categories adequately. More importantly, he observed that the two-level theory, by reading obscenity out of the first amendment because it lacks "redeeming social importance," violates the first amendment principle that prohibits weighing the social utility of speech.

The two-level theory is radically inconsistent with the principle of equal liberty of expression. While the equality principle in the first amendment does not prohibit all content regulation, it does require that courts start with a presumptive prohibition against governmental control of the content of speech. A showing of high probability of serious harm might justify regulation of a particular kind of speech content, but the two-level theory evades the question of justification by placing certain types of speech outside the scope of the first amendment. In other words, the two-level theory rejects the principle of equality in the marketplace of ideas.

In the field of defamation, the Court has already gone far toward abandoning the two-level theory. No one would suggest that *New York Times Co. v. Sullivan*[5] and its diverse offspring leave libel outside the boundaries of protected speech. And even the "fighting words" cases have fought their way out of the confines of the two-level theory, coming to rest on a variety of the clear-and-present-danger test....

*   *   *

NOTES

1. 336 U.S. 106 (1949).
2. 408 U.S. 92 (1972).
3. 398 U.S. 58 (1970).
4. 315 U.S. 568 (1942).
5. 376 U.S.254 (1964).

Part III

SELECTED DOCTRINAL
BATTLEGROUNDS

CONTENT REGULATION AND THE FIRST AMENDMENT

Geoffrey R. Stone

INTRODUCTION

Perhaps the most intriguing feature of contemporary first amendment doctrine is the increasingly invoked distinction between content-based and content-neutral restrictions on expression. Although the distinction has its roots in decisions of the 1930s and 1940s, and began gradually to emerge as a central premise of the Court's analysis in the 1950s and 1960s, it was not until the last decade that the distinction attained its present prominence. It is, indeed, the Burger Court's foremost contribution to first amendment analysis, and it is, today, the most pervasively employed doctrine in the jurisprudence of free expression.

Content-neutral restrictions limit communication without regard to the message conveyed. Laws that prohibit noisy speeches near a hospital, ban billboards in residential communities, impose license fees for parades and demonstrations, or forbid the distribution of leaflets in public places are examples of content-neutral restrictions. Content-based restrictions, on the other hand, limit communication because of the message conveyed. Laws that prohibit seditious libel, ban the publication of confidential information, forbid

---

From *William and Mary Law Review* 25, no. 2 (Winter 1983). Reprinted with permission.

the hiring of teachers who advocate the violent overthrow of government, or outlaw the display of the swastika in certain neighborhoods illustrate this type of restriction. The Court employs two quite distinct modes of analysis to assess the constitutionality of content-based and content-neutral restrictions. This dichotomy has come under attack in recent years. In this article, I will explore the merits and limitations of the content-based/content-neutral distinction.

I. CONTENT-NEUTRAL ANALYSIS

The Supreme Court tests the constitutionality of content-neutral restrictions with an essentially open-ended form of balancing. That is, in each case the Court considers the extent to which the restriction limits communication, "the substantiality of the government interests" served by the restriction, and "whether those interests could be served by means that would be less intrusive on activity protected by the First Amendment." The burden on government to demonstrate the substantiality of its interests and the absence of less restrictive alternatives varies from case to case, depending upon the extent to which the restriction actually interferes with the opportunities for effective communication. The greater the interference with effective communication, the greater the burden on government to justify the restriction.

The Court's primary concern in the content-neutral realm is that such restrictions, by limiting the availability of particular means of communication, can significantly impair the ability of individuals to communicate their views to others. This is, of course, a central first amendment concern, for to the extent that content-neutral restrictions actually reduce the total quantity of expression, they necessarily undermine the "search for truth," impede meaningful participation in "self-governance," and frustrate individual "self-fulfillment."

The Court's content-neutral balancing is a sensible response to this concern. Unlike a consistently deferential approach, which would uphold every content-neutral restriction that rationally furthers legitimate governmental interests, the Court's approach critically examines restrictions that seriously threaten significant first amendment interests. And unlike a rigid "clear and present danger" or "compelling interest" approach, which would invalidate almost all content-neutral restrictions, the Court's analysis does not sacrifice legitimate governmental interests when significant first amendment interests are not at issue. Thus, by assuring the availability of ample opportunities and outlets for expression, without needlessly undermining competing governmental interests, the Court has achieved a reasonable accommodation. One might quarrel with some of the Court's results, but the overall mode of analysis is defensible.

II. CONTENT-BASED ANALYSIS

In the content-based realm, the Court employs a markedly different mode of analysis. At the outset, the Court determines whether the restricted speech is of only "low" first amendment value, and thus deserving of only limited constitutional protection. The "low" value theory first appeared in the famous dictum of *Chaplinsky v. New Hampshire*,[1] in which the Court observed that "certain well-defined and narrowly limited classes of speech . . . are no essential part of any exposition of ideas, and are of such slight social value as a step to truth that any benefit that may be derived from them is clearly outweighed by the social interest in order and morality."

The precise factors that the Court considers in determining whether a particular class of speech occupies only a "subordinate position in the scale of First Amendment values" remain somewhat obscure. The Court apparently focuses, however, on the extent to which the speech furthers the historical, political, and philosophical purposes that underlie the first amendment. In making this determination, the Court applies a "defining out" approach. That is, the Court begins with the presumption that the first amendment protects all communication and then creates areas of nonprotection only after it affirmatively finds that a particular class of speech does not sufficiently further the underlying purposes of the first amendment. The Court, applying this approach, has held that several classes of speech have only low first amendment value, including express incitement, false statements of fact, obscenity, commercial speech, fighting words, and child pornography.

The conclusion that a particular class of speech has only low first amendment value does not mean that the speech is wholly without constitutional protection or that the government may suppress it at will. Rather, the low value determination is merely the first step in the Court's analysis, for once the Court concludes that a particular class of speech is deserving of only limited first amendment protection, it then employs a form of categorical balancing, through which it defines the precise circumstances in which the speech may be restricted. In attempting to strike an appropriate "balance" for each class of low value speech, the Court considers a number of factors, including the relative value of the speech and the risk of inadvertently chilling "high" value expression. Applying this approach, the Court has articulated quite different standards for different classes of low value speech. Express incitement, for example, may be suppressed only if it is "directed to inciting or producing imminent lawless action and is likely to incite or produce such action." Commercial speech, on the other hand, may be suppressed if it is false or misleading, or if the restriction "directly advances a substantial" governmental interest and is "not more extensive than is necessary" to achieve that interest. And obscenity, which is perhaps the least protected class of low value expression, may be suppressed whenever a relatively undemanding scienter requirement is satisfied.

Whatever the merits of the low value theory, this theory is not the focus of the content-based/content-neutral distinction. The puzzling quality of the distinction arises not from the Court's analysis of low value speech, but from its treatment of high value expression. For in dealing with high value speech, the Court employs, not a balancing approach akin to its content-neutral balancing, but a far more speech-protective analysis. Indeed, in assessing the constitutionality of content-based restrictions on high value expression, the Court employs a standard that approaches absolute protection. In an oft-quoted declaration, for example, the Court announced in *Police Department v. Mosley*[2] that, "above all else, the First Amendment means that government has no power to restrict expression because of its message, its ideas, its subject matter, or its content." Although this declaration has proved to be somewhat overstated, the Court has been remarkably true to its word, for except when low value speech is at issue, the Court has invalidated almost every content-based restriction that it has considered in the past quarter-century. Thus, whether the Court evaluates such restrictions by an "absolute protection" approach, a "clear-and-present-danger" test, a "compelling government interest" standard, or some other formulation, it clearly applies a different and more stringent standard to content-based than to content-neutral restrictions.

It has been suggested that the "most puzzling aspect of the distinction between content-based and content-neutral restrictions is that either restriction reduces the sum total of information or opinion disseminated." Indeed, in many instances a content-neutral restriction may more substantially reduce "the sum total of information or opinion disseminated" than a related con-tent-based restriction. For example, a law banning all billboards restricts more speech than a law banning Nazi billboards, and a law limiting the political activities of public employees restricts more speech than a law limiting the Socialist political activities of public employees. Under current doctrine, however, the Court subjects the content-based restrictions to a more stringent standard of justification than the more suppressive content-neutral restric-tions. Why?

In addressing this question, I shall focus first…on viewpoint-based restrictions—that is, laws that expressly restrict the communication of partic-ular ideas, viewpoints, or items of information—for such restrictions are at the very core of the content-based/content-neutral distinction. I shall then turn, in Part V, to more peripheral forms of content-based restrictions, such as laws that are neutral on their face but are applied on the basis of "commu-nicative impact," laws that restrict speech because of its "subject matter," and other laws that restrict expression in a "viewpoint-neutral" manner.

III. VIEWPOINT-BASED RESTRICTIONS

Consider two hypothetical statutes. First, suppose State X enacts a law pro-hibiting all billboards. Second, suppose State X enacts a law prohibiting all criticism of the antibillboard law. From the standpoint of total reduction in expression, the two statutes appear quite similar. The antibillboard law is con-tent-neutral, however, and thus will be tested by a relatively moderate stan-dard of review; the anticriticism law is content-based, and thus will be tested by a more stringent standard of justification.

The explanation is that the first amendment is concerned, not only with the extent to which a law reduces the total quantity of communication, but also—and perhaps even more fundamentally—with the extent to which the law distorts public debate. Although the anticriticism statute may produce only a small reduction in the total quantity of communication, the reduction falls entirely on one side of the debate. Moreover, the potential distorting effect of the statute is dramatic, for it subjects critics of the antibillboard law not to a mere marginal competitive disadvantage, but to an effective prohibi-tion on the expression of their view. Any law that substantially prevents the communication of a particular idea, viewpoint, or item of information violates the first amendment except, perhaps, in the most extraordinary of circumstances. This is so, not because such a law restricts "a lot" of speech, but because by effectively excising a specific message from public debate, it mutilates "the thinking process of the community" and is thus incompatible with the central precepts of the first amendment.

*   *   *

It is true, of course, that content-neutral restrictions may also have content-differential effects, for such restrictions may impair the communication of some messages more than others. For example, the antibillboard statute may have a disproportionate impact upon those groups or individuals who tended previously to use billboards. By their very nature, however, content-neutral restrictions limit the availability of only *particular* means of communication. They thus leave speakers free to shift to other means of expression. As a result, content-neutral restrictions do not distort public debate to the same degree as content-based restrictions that substantially prevent the communication of particular ideas, viewpoints, or items of information by *all* means. The uniquely powerful distorting effect of such content-based restrictions thus goes a long way towards explaining the content-based/content-neutral distinction.

IV. MODEST VIEWPOINT-BASED RESTRICTIONS

The distorting effect, however, does not explain the distinction in its entirety, for not every law that restricts the communication of a particular idea, viewpoint, or item of information *substantially* prevents the message from being communicated. To the contrary, such restrictions are often limited in scope, restricting expression in only narrowly defined circumstances. For example, laws that prohibit the public destruction of a draft card as an expression of opposition to the draft, the display of the swastika within 100 feet of a synagogue on Yom Kippur, or the advocacy of homosexuality on any billboard are viewpoint-based, but restrict expression only in terms of time, place, or manner. They are thus unlikely to distort public debate to the same degree as viewpoint-based restrictions that more pervasively restrict the communication of particular messages. One might expect, therefore, that the Court would test these more modest viewpoint-based restrictions by less stringent standards, similar to the standards applied in the content-neutral context. The Court, however, has applied the content-based/content-neutral distinction, and the stringent standards of content-based analysis, even to these more modest viewpoint-based restrictions.

Consider, for example, *Schacht v. United States*,[3] *Linmark Associates v. Township of Willingboro*,[4] and *Nebraska Press Association v. Stuart*.[5] In *Schacht*, the Court held unconstitutional a federal statute permitting actors to wear the uniform of an armed force of the United States in a theatrical or motion-picture production only "if the portrayal does not tend to discredit that armed force." Although the statute imposed only a modest restriction on the ability of individuals to oppose governmental policy, and although the government could constitutionally make "it an offense to wear our military uniforms without authority," the Court held the statute invalid because it restricted expression on the basis of content. In *Linmark*, the Court held unconstitutional an ordinance that attempted to stem the flight of white homeowners from racially integrated neighborhoods by prohibiting the posting of real estate "For Sale" signs. Although conceding that the ordinance "restricted only one method of communication," the Court emphasized that the ordinance "proscribed particular types of signs based on their content" and thus held that it must be tested, not as a content-neutral "time, place, or manner" restriction, but "on the basis of the township's interest in regulating the content of the communication." In *Nebraska Press Association*, the Court held unconstitutional a state court order restraining the press from publishing or broadcasting accounts of confessions or other facts strongly implicative of a murder defendant. Although noting that the order expired by its own terms when the jury was impaneled, and that it thus merely postponed and did not prohibit publication, the Court nonetheless employed the demanding standards of content-based analysis.

Thus, in these and other decisions, the Court has consistently applied the stringent standards of content-based analysis even to relatively modest viewpoint-based restrictions. Why? At least four possible explanations come to mind.

A. EQUALITY

It has been suggested that the concept of equality "lies at the heart of the first amendment's protections against government regulation of the content of speech." Indeed, it has been argued that, "just as the prohibition of government-imposed discrimination on the basis of race is central to equal protection analysis, protection against governmental discrimination on the basis of speech content is central among first amendment values." There is, indeed, a seemingly obvious connection between the content-based/content-neutral distinction and the concept of equality. When government restricts only certain ideas, viewpoints, or items of information, people wishing to express the restricted messages receive "unequal" treatment. When government restricts speech in a content-neutral manner, however, everyone is treated "equally." Moreover, an equality-based theory of the content-based/content-neutral distinction might explain the Court's use of the same standards of justification for *all* viewpoint-based restrictions, regardless of their potential to distort public debate. For just as we "strictly scrutinize" any law that discriminates on the basis of race, whether it denies an important or trivial benefit, so too must we "strictly scrutinize" any law that discriminates on the basis of content, whether it has a substantial or only a modest impact on public debate. It is the fact of discrimination, not the impact on public debate, that warrants "strict scrutiny."

It is not, however, that simple. In fact, the Court employs at least two quite distinct modes of content-based analysis, only one of which focuses explicitly on "equality." In the more traditional mode of analysis, the Court asks only whether the restricted speech is sufficiently harmful to justify the restriction. The Court does not concern itself with whether *other* speech is similarly restricted. In *Schenck v. United States*,[6] for example, the Court asked whether the restricted speech created a "clear and present danger." The Court did not ask whether the Espionage Act embodied an impermissible "inequality" because it failed to restrict other, perhaps equally dangerous, messages. Similarly, in *Whitney v. California*,[7] the Court, in upholding California's criminal syndicalism statute, focused only on the dangers of the restricted speech and rather cavalierly rejected an assertion that the Act unconstitutionally distinguished between those who advocated "a resort to violent and unlawful methods as a means of changing industrial and political conditions" and those who advocated "a resort to those methods as a means of maintaining such conditions." More recently, ... the Court has routinely applied the "compelling interest" and "clear and present danger" standards without asking the logically preliminary question whether the challenged restrictions embodied impermissible "inequalities" because they prohibited the publication of only specific types of "confidential" information. What these cases suggest, then, is that although a concern with inequality may underlie the content-based/content-neutral distinction, the concern is often submerged, and there exists a traditional and well-founded mode of content-based analysis that pays no explicit attention to the equality issue.

The second mode of content-based analysis focuses explicitly on "equality." This mode of analysis, which has come to the fore only recently, emphasizes underinclusion as a basis for invalidation. The key issue is not whether the restricted speech is sufficiently harmful to justify its restriction, but whether the government may constitutionally restrict only the speech restricted. *Police Department v. Mosley, Erznoznik v. Jacksonville*,[8] and *Widmar v. Vincent*[9] are illustrative.

In *Mosley*, the Court considered the constitutionality of a Chicago ordinance that prohibited picketing or demonstrating on a public way within 150 feet of a school building while the school was in session. The ordinance was not content-neutral, however, for it expressly exempted "peaceful picketing of any school involved in a labor dispute." Without deciding whether the ordinance, absent the labor-picketing exemption, would be a permissible content-neutral restriction, the Court invalidated the ordinance because it described prohibited picketing, "not in terms of time, place, and manner," but in terms of content. Although conceding that cities may have a substantial interest in prohibiting picketing that disrupts a school, the Court held that Chicago may not ban nonlabor picketing "unless that picketing is clearly more disruptive than the picketing Chicago...permits."

In *Erznoznik*, the Court held unconstitutional an ordinance that prohibited the exhibition of films containing nudity by drive-in movie theaters if the screen was visible from a public street or public place. Without deciding whether "a narrowly drawn non-discriminatory traffic regulation" requiring the screening of all drive-in theaters from the view of motorists would "be a reasonable exercise of police power," the Court held that "even a traffic regulation cannot discriminate on the basis of content unless there are clear reasons for the distinctions." The ordinance, the Court held, was "strikingly underinclusive," for there was "no reason to think that a wide variety of other scenes in the customary screen diet, ranging from soap opera to violence, would be any less distracting to the passing motorist."

And in *Widmar*, the Court held unconstitutional a policy of the University of Missouri that allowed registered student groups to use university facilities, but that prohibited such groups from using the facilities "for purposes of religious worship or religious teaching." The Court explained that the "Constitution forbids a State to enforce certain exclusions from a forum generally open to the public, even if it was not required to create the forum in the first place." Here, the Court reasoned, the university had voluntarily created such a forum, and to justify "discriminatory exclusion" because of the "content of a group's intended speech," the university would have to "show that its regulation was necessary to serve a compelling state interest and that it was narrowly drawn to achieve that end." The Court held that the university had not met that standard.

The Court's express recognition in the *Mosley* line of cases of the nexus between free expression and equality has had a generally salutary effect, for as Justice Jackson recognized in [earlier cases], there is no more effective way "to assure that laws will be just than to require that laws be equal in operation." There are dangers in the emphasis on equality, however, and those dangers should not be overlooked. By focusing on equality, the Court may invite government to "equalize," not by permitting more speech, but by adopting even more "suppressive" content-neutral restrictions. This result, one might argue, is hardly consistent with the first amendment. As Justice Rehnquist has observed, under the Court's approach, "the State would fare better by adopting *more* restrictive means, a judicial incentive I had thought this Court would hesitate to afford." Moreover, an undue emphasis on equality may lead the Court to sustain "equal" restrictions on expression without sufficient consideration of the other dangers such restrictions might pose. This tendency is evident in several recent decisions in which the Court, in upholding a number of potentially troublesome content-neutral restrictions, stressed repeatedly that the restrictions were, after all, "content-neutral." Finally, in several recent decisions, the Court has relied explicitly on the equal protection clause as well as, and even instead of, the first amendment. The degree of scrutiny that is appropriate in testing the constitutionality of content-based restrictions, however, is fundamentally a first amendment issue. Invocation of the equal protection clause adds nothing constructive to the analysis. It may, however, by appearing to "simplify" matters, deflect attention from the central constitutional issue.

*   *   *

B. COMMUNICATIVE IMPACT

A second possible explanation for the content-based/content-neutral distinction derives from the notion that the government ordinarily may not restrict speech because of its communicative impact—that is, because of "a fear of how people will react to what the speaker is saying."

Most laws that are content-neutral on their face do not turn on communicative impact. For example, the government may restrict the distribution of leaflets to reduce litter, the use of loudspeakers to reduce noise, and the size and location of billboards to improve the aesthetics of the community. Most content-based laws, on the other hand, do turn on communicative impact. For example, the government may ban the advocacy of the violent overthrow of government because such advocacy might persuade individuals to engage in unlawful acts, it may restrict the display of the swastika in predominantly Jewish communities because such displays might offend the sensibilities of residents and trigger a violent response, and it may prohibit the wearing of "Ban the Bomb" buttons in schools because such buttons might distract students from their schoolwork.

The content-neutral and content-based concepts do not, however, coincide perfectly with communicative impact. Some laws that are content-neutral on their face are applied on the basis of communicative impact. For example, a law prohibiting any person from making any speech that may provoke a breach of the peace is content-neutral on its face, but turns in application on the reaction of individuals "to what the speaker is saying." Similarly, some laws are content-based on their face but do not turn in application on communicative impact. For example, a law excluding communists from employment in defense facilities might be based on a concern that communists would perform their duties in an undesirable manner, and a law prohibiting the display of partisan political messages in certain public facilities might be based on a concern that the display of such messages would involve the government in especially troublesome "administrative" problems.

To what extent, if any, does the communicative impact concept explain the content-based/content-neutral distinction? There are several formulations of the communicative impact theory. The first formulation treats as content-based any law that is either content-based on its face or turns in application on communicative impact. This formulation assumes that laws that are content-based on their face require strict scrutiny whether they turn on communicative impact and thus employs the communicative impact concept to expand the class of content-based restrictions. Although I shall return later to this formulation, it is of no concern here, for it does not rely on communicative impact to justify the use of stringent standards of review for laws that are content-based on their face.

The second formulation also treats as content-based any law that is either content-based on its face or turns in application on communicative impact but, unlike the first formulation, assumes that the communicative impact concept justifies the use of stringent standards of review for all restrictions that it treats as content-based. This formulation is obviously unsatisfactory, for as we have already seen, not all laws that are content-based on their face turn on communicative impact. This formulation thus puts more weight on the communicative impact concept than it can logically bear.

The third formulation treats as content-based any restriction that turns on communicative impact. This formulation uses communicative impact to define the category of content-based restrictions, and thus excludes from this category all laws that do not turn on communicative impact, even if they are content-based on their face. Whatever the merits of this formulation, it does not comport with the Court's own understanding of the content-based/content-neutral distinction. There are, quite simply, too many decisions to the contrary. To cite just three of many possible examples, in *Police Department v. Mosley*, perhaps the seminal content-based/content-neutral decision, the Court treated as content-based an ordinance prohibiting all picketing within 150 feet of a school, except peaceful picketing of any school involved in a labor dispute, even though the city sought to defend the ordinance, not in terms of communicative impact, but on the ground that nonlabor picketers were themselves more prone to violence than labor picketers....

The final formulation of the communicative impact theory provides that any governmental effort to justify a restriction on speech in terms of the communicative impact of the restricted expression must be tested by stringent standards of review. This formulation treats communicative impact as a sufficient, but not a necessary, condition for the invocation of content-based analysis. This formulation does not explain the content-based/content-neutral distinction in its entirety, for as we have seen, some content-based restrictions are not based on communicative impact. Most content-based restrictions are based on communicative impact, however, and if this formulation is supportable it would explain much of the distinction.

Of course, the question remains: should a law that is content-based on its face be tested by stringent standards of review, even if it will not substantially distort public debate, because the government attempts to justify it on the basis of "a fear of how people will react to what the speaker is saying"? Should government efforts to justify restrictions of speech in terms of communicative impact be viewed differently from other justifications for restricting expression? To explore this line of inquiry, we must examine the dynamic of communicative impact. That is, we must determine what we mean when we say "how people will react to what the speaker is saying." As we shall see, there are essentially three such "reactions," and an analysis of these reactions sheds considerable light on the nature of the communicative impact concern.

In the most common communicative impact situation, the government attempts to restrict expression because the expression may persuade individuals to act in an undesirable or unlawful manner. For example, the government might prohibit any person from distributing antiwar leaflets within 100 feet of an enlistment center in order to prevent persons from being persuaded not to enlist in the armed forces. Is such a law, despite its modest suppressive effect, unconstitutional? May government legitimately restrict speech for this reason?

The Court has long embraced an "antipaternalistic" understanding of the first amendment. It has observed, for example, that the first amendment assumes that ideas and information are not in themselves "harmful, that people will perceive their own best interests if only they are well enough informed, and that the best means to that end is to open the channels of communication rather than to close them." "The people in our democracy," the Court has explained, "are entrusted with the responsibility for judging and evaluating the relative merits of conflicting arguments," and "if there be any danger that the people cannot evaluate the information and arguments advanced during the course of public debate, it is a danger contemplated by the Framers of the First Amendment."

*   *   *

This antipaternalistic understanding of the first amendment explains, at least in part, the Court's use of stringent standards of review to test the constitutionality of content-based restrictions that the government attempts to justify in paternalistic terms. Because paternalistic justifications are constitutionally disfavored, the government may restrict expression for paternalistic reasons in only the most compelling circumstances, if ever. And this is so even if the restriction does not substantially prevent the communication of a particular idea, viewpoint, or item of information, for the Court's use of stringent standards of review in such cases derives, not from a concern about the potential distorting effects of the restriction, but from the disfavored status of the government's justification.

*   *   *

The Court has long maintained that the first amendment does not permit government to prohibit the public expression of views merely because they are offensive or unpopular. As the Court has observed, "it is firmly settled that under our Constitution the public expression of ideas may not be prohibited merely because the ideas are themselves offensive to some of their hearers." Indeed, the Court has consistently held that "the ability of government, consonant with the Constitution, to shut off discourse solely to protect others from hearing it is … dependent upon a showing that substantial privacy interests are being invaded in an essentially intolerable manner." "Any broader view of this authority," the Court has explained, "would effectively empower a majority to silence dissidents simply as a matter of personal predilections." Moreover, the Court has embraced a similarly critical view of governmental efforts to restrict speech because the ideas or information expressed might trigger a hostile audience response. . . .

The Court's reluctance to accept the "heckler's veto," and its refusal to permit one group of citizens effectively to "censor" the expression of others because they dislike or are prepared violently to oppose their ideas, seem well-grounded in the central precepts of the first amendment. Thus, "intolerance-based" justifications for restricting expression, like paternalistic justifications, are constitutionally disfavored, even if the restriction does not substantially prevent the communication of a particular idea, viewpoint, or item of information.

*   *   *

What, then, has this inquiry into the "dynamic of communicative impact" accomplished? For one thing, we have discovered why communicative impact matters. We care about communicative impact, not because government is attempting to restrict speech because of "a fear of how people will react to what the speaker is saying," but because, when government does so, it almost invariably relies upon constitutionally disfavored justifications to support the restriction. Moreover, we have identified an explanation for at least part of the content-based/content-neutral distinction. For when government attempts to justify a content-based restriction on paternalistic or intolerance-based grounds, the restriction must be tested by stringent standards of review, whether or not it significantly distorts public debate. This does not, of course, explain the content-based/content-neutral distinction in its entirety. It does, however, unravel at least part of the puzzle.

C. DISTORTION OF PUBLIC DEBATE

A third possible explanation for the content-based/content-neutral distinction derives from the fact that content-based restrictions, by their very nature, restrict the communication of only some messages and thus affect public debate in a content-differential manner. Indeed, as we have seen, some content-based restrictions so substantially impair the communication of particular ideas, viewpoints, or items of information that, for that reason alone, they are presumptively invalid. We are concerned here, however, with viewpoint-based restrictions that do not *substantially* impair the communication of particular messages. Because these more modest viewpoint-based restrictions leave open alternative channels of communication, they do not as dramatically skew the thought processes of the community. The question, then, is whether the disparate effects of these more modest viewpoint-based restrictions can explain the content-based/content-neutral distinction.

There are two elements to this inquiry. First, do the relatively limited content-differential effects of modest viewpoint-based restrictions distinguish them from content-neutral restrictions? And second, is the difference, if one exists, sufficiently important to explain the doctrinal distinction?

Although neutral on their face, content-neutral restrictions often have "unequal effects on various types of messages." For example, a law banning all street demonstrations may have a disproportionate impact upon those who rely on such demonstrations to communicate their views; a law banning the distribution of leaflets in welfare offices may have a disproportionate impact upon those who rely on leaflets to communicate with welfare recipients; and a content-neutral disclosure requirement may have a disproportionate impact upon those with controversial or unpopular views. Indeed, most content-neutral restrictions have at least some de facto content-differential effects, and although such effects may be less severe than those associated with content-based restrictions that *substantially* prevent the communication of particular ideas, viewpoints, or items of information, they are at least arguably analogous to the content-differential effects associated with more modest viewpoint-based restrictions. Thus, in assessing the extent to which the content-differential effects of modest viewpoint-based restrictions might explain the Court's use of stringent standards of justification to test the constitutionality of such restrictions, it may be useful to examine the Court's analysis of the content-differential effects of content-neutral restrictions. For if the Court considers the content-differential effects of content-neutral restrictions to be a serious first amendment problem, that would help explain the Court's approach to viewpoint-based restrictions.

There are two means by which the Court might manifest a concern with the de facto content-differential effects of content-neutral restrictions. First, the Court might use an especially stringent standard of review for content-neutral restrictions that have content-differential effects. Second, it might hold that groups or individuals who are disproportionately disadvantaged by a particular content-neutral restriction are constitutionally entitled to an exemption from the ordinary operation of that restriction.

In two quite distinct situations, the Court has demonstrated a concern with the de facto content-differential effects of content-neutral restrictions. First, in the public forum context, the Court has recognized that restrictions on the distribution of leaflets and similar means of communication may have a disproportionate effect upon those who, for reasons of finances or ideology, do not have ready access to more conventional means of communication. In such circumstances, the Court has reviewed restrictions on such traditional but unconventional means of communication by a more stringent standard than other content-neutral restrictions. Indeed, the public forum doctrine is in part a reflection of this concern.

Second, in the disclosure context, the Court has recognized that content-neutral disclosure requirements may have especially harsh consequences for groups or individuals with controversial or unpopular views and that such requirements may thus be unconstitutional as applied to such groups or individuals.…

Although the Court's concern with the de facto content-differential effects of content-neutral restrictions in the public forum and disclosure contexts might suggest that such content-differential effects play a significant role in the Court's analysis of content-neutral restrictions, this is not in fact the case. Indeed, these are the only situations in which the Court has emphasized the content-differential effects of content-neutral restrictions. In other situations, it has essentially ignored the issue.

*   *   *

D. MOTIVATION

A fourth possible explanation for the content-based/content-neutral distinction derives from the notion, apparently embraced by the Court, that "when regulation is based on the content of speech, governmental action must be scrutinized more carefully to ensure that communication has not been prohibited 'merely because public officials disapprove the speaker's views.'" This concern with ferreting out "improper" motivation reflects a general shift in constitutional jurisprudence, for although the Warren Court tended to shy away from motivation as a central feature of constitutional analysis, the Burger Court has tended increasingly to emphasize motivation as a paramount constitutional concern.

In the first amendment context, the concept of improper governmental motivation consists chiefly of the precept that the government may not restrict expression simply because it disagrees with the speaker's views. This precept has two significant corollaries: the government may not exempt expression from an otherwise general restriction because it agrees with the speaker's views; and the government may not restrict expression because it might be embarrassed by publication of the information disclosed. This precept and its corollaries are central to our first amendment jurisprudence, for any effort of government to restrict speech because it conveys a "false" or "bad" idea is inconsistent with the three basic first amendment assumptions: in the long run, the best test of truth is "the power of the thought to get itself accepted in the competition of the market"; in a self-governing system, the people, not the government "are entrusted with the responsibility for judging and evaluating the relative merits of conflicting arguments"; and, in our constitutional system, the protection of free expression is designed to enhance personal growth, self-realization, and the development of individual autonomy.

To clarify the precise role of improper governmental motivation in first amendment theory, it may be useful to contrast the improper motive of restricting expression because government disagrees with the speaker's views with the related problem of paternalistic justifications. In examining the communicative impact concept, we saw that governmental efforts to restrict the expression of particular ideas, viewpoints, or items of information because the government does not trust its citizens to make wise or desirable decisions if they are exposed to such expression are "constitutionally disfavored," and that the government may thus restrict expression for such paternalistic reasons in only the most compelling of circumstances.

Although the improper motivation and paternalistic justification concepts are in many respects similar, there are important and enlightening differences. First, the improper motivation concept focuses on the government's *disagreement* with the speaker's views, whereas the paternalistic justification concept focuses on the government's concern with the *consequences* that might result if others accept the speaker's views. In many instances, both concerns will be present. For example, if the government restricts expression advocating that one's moral duty is to refuse induction into the army, the government may have both an improper motive—a desire to suppress the "bad" idea that people have a moral duty to refuse induction—and a paternalistic justification—concern that people will be persuaded to refuse induction. In other instances, only one of the concerns may be present. For example, if the government restricts expression deploring the brutality of war because such speech might cause people to refuse induction, the government will have a paternalistic justification—concern that people will be induced to refuse induction—but not necessarily an improper motive—it may agree that war is deplorably brutal. Alternatively, if the government refuses to employ in its defense plants people who oppose the war, it may have an improper motivation—a desire to suppress the "bad" idea that the war is unjust—but a nonpaternalistic justification. Moreover, as this last example illustrates, the concept of improper motivation is wholly independent of communicative impact, for there may be an improper motivation whether or not the restriction involves communicative impact.

Second, although paternalistic justifications are constitutionally disfavored, they are not per se illegitimate. In compelling circumstances, as where there is a clear and present danger of some serious evil, a paternalistic justification may be sufficient to sustain a restriction on expression. An improper motivation, however, is by definition per se illegitimate. The government can never justify a restriction on otherwise protected expression merely because it disagrees with the speaker's views.

Third, although the paternalistic justification concept ordinarily precludes the government from justifying content-based restrictions on paternalistic grounds, the existence of a possible paternalistic justification does not preclude the government from justifying such restrictions on alternative, non-paternalistic grounds. The existence of a possible paternalistic justification, in other words, does not taint the restriction. The improper motivation concept, however, clearly operates as a taint. That is, if an improper motivation played a substantial role in the government's decision to restrict expression, the restriction must be invalidated even if alternative, proper justifications are available. The improper motivation concept thus demands an effort to ferret out improper motivations and to eliminate their impact on governmental decisions to restrict expression.

The problem, of course, is to devise some effective means to ferret out these improper motivations. It is at this point that the content-based/content-neutral distinction enters the picture, for the probability that an improper motivation has tainted a decision to restrict expression is far greater when the restriction is directed at a particular idea, viewpoint, or item of information than when it is content-neutral. Indeed, in the content-neutral context the risk of improper motivation is quite low, for such restrictions necessarily apply to all ideas, viewpoints, and items of information, and are thus unlikely to reflect a specific intent on the part of those who adopted the restriction to suppress any particular message. In such circumstances, it seems sensible to presume the absence of improper motivation and to put the burden of proving such a motivation on the party challenging the restriction on motivational grounds.

When a restriction is directed at a particular idea, viewpoint, or item of information, however, the risk of improper motivation is quite high, for government officials considering the adoption of such a restriction will almost invariably have their own opinions about the merits of the restricted speech and there is thus a substantial risk that, in deciding whether to adopt the restriction, they will be affected, either consciously or unconsciously, by an improper motive. The officials, in other words, may be more inclined to adopt the restriction, and to pursue the competing governmental interest at the expense of "free speech," when they disapprove, rather than approve, of the ideas expressed. In such circumstances, the most sensible course might be simply to presume improper

motivation and to put the burden of proving the absence of improper motivation on the government. The government could meet this burden by proving, for
example, that the challenged restriction was the least restrictive means of
achieving a compelling governmental interest, for such proof would effectively
demonstrate that the government would have adopted the restriction even in
the absence of improper motivation. Thus, the need to ferret out improper
motivations may help to explain both the content-based/content-neutral distinction and the Court's use of stringent standards of review to test the constitutionality of even modest viewpoint-based restrictions.

But is all this really persuasive? Can the concern with improper motivation fairly support the doctrinal structure? After all, even proof of an actual
improper motive requires the invalidation of an otherwise constitutional
restriction; the need to guard against the mere possibility of improper motivation does not necessarily justify the invalidation of *all* viewpoint-based
restrictions that are not demonstrably necessary to further compelling governmental interests. Although such a standard may ensure that the government would have adopted the viewpoint-based restrictions even in the
absence of improper motivation, this standard also has substantial costs, for it
would invalidate not only viewpoint-based restrictions that were in fact
improperly motivated, but also those viewpoint-based restrictions that further
significant governmental interests, and that the government might reasonably
have adopted even in the absence of improper motivation. One might question, then, whether the need to assure motivational purity is sufficiently
weighty to justify so substantial a sacrifice of legitimate governmental interests. Indeed, one might argue that a more sensible approach would be to presume proper motivation, in the absence of specific proof to the contrary,
whenever a viewpoint-based restriction reasonably furthers a significant governmental interest.

The answer, I think, is that the critical motivational inquiry is not whether
the government officials would have adopted the restriction even if they did
not disfavor the restricted speech, but whether they would have adopted it
even if it had been directed at speech that they themselves supported. The
concern, in other words, is not only that government officials should not affirmatively attempt to suppress ideas with which they disagree, but also that they
should act in an even-handed manner and thus treat disfavored ideas with the
same respect they would accord to the ideas that they support. Viewed in this
light, the more stringent standard of review seems sensible, for government

officials are unlikely to disadvantage the ideas that they themselves support except in the most compelling circumstances.

Another aspect of the improper motivation issue lends further support to the content-based/content-neutral distinction. For just as there is a danger of improper motivation in the formulation and adoption of viewpoint-based restrictions in the legislative and administrative processes, so too is there a danger of improper motivation in the interpretation and application of such restrictions in the judicial process. Indeed, as noted earlier, ideological predispositions may influence judges and jurors called upon to implement content-based restrictions directed at specific ideas, viewpoints, or items of information. To minimize the impact of such biases, and to protect against potential manipulation of the judicial process, it may be sensible to test such restrictions with especially stringent standards of review, thus leaving little room for ideological distortion.

Content-neutral restrictions, on the other hand, do not pose these dangers to the same degree. There is, of course, a risk of distortion whenever judges and jurors are called upon to determine, as a matter of fact, whether a particular speaker actually violated a restriction on expression, for the biases of the fact finder inherently threaten the integrity of the fact finding process. But there is likely to be relatively little distortion in the more fundamental determination of whether the content-neutral restriction is itself constitutional, for this determination will necessarily affect, not only the particular speaker involved in the litigation, but other speakers as well, regardless of their viewpoint or message. The very breadth of application of the determination will thus tend to reduce the incentive for manipulation.

In light of these four considerations—equality, communicative impact, distortion, and motivation—there is, I think, a sound basis for the Court's content-based/content-neutral distinction and for its use of especially stringent standards of review to test the constitutionality of even modest viewpoint-based restrictions. Although particular content-neutral restrictions may limit as much or even more total expression than particular viewpoint-based restrictions, the latter pose special, quite distinct dangers to the system of free expression. And although no one of these four considerations may independently explain the distinction in its entirety, in combination they both explain and justify the Court's heightened scrutiny of viewpoint-based restrictions.

V. AMBIGUOUS RESTRICTIONS: CONTENT-NEUTRAL OR VIEWPOINT-BASED?

This does not end our inquiry, however, for up to this point, I have focused on only those content-based restrictions that are directed at the communication of particular ideas, viewpoints, or items of information. As we have seen, there are sensible reasons for distinguishing such viewpoint-based restrictions from content-neutral restrictions and for testing such viewpoint-based restrictions by especially stringent standards of review. In this part, I shall consider four types of restrictions that cannot clearly be characterized as either content-neutral or viewpoint-based: restrictions that are content-neutral on their face, but are justified in terms of communicative impact; restrictions that are directed at a particular subject-matter; restrictions that are directed at the use of profanity, nudity, or other arguably viewpoint-neutral forms of "content"; and "speaker-based" restrictions.

A. CONTENT-NEUTRAL RESTRICTIONS THAT TURN ON COMMUNICATIVE IMPACT

In most instances, the government defends content-neutral restrictions in terms that are unrelated to the communicative impact of the particular ideas expressed. For example, the government might defend a restriction on the distribution of leaflets on the ground that such distribution produces litter; it might defend a restriction on loudspeakers on the ground that loudspeakers create noise; and it might defend a restriction on parades on the ground that parades obstruct traffic. In some instances, however, the government defends content-neutral restrictions in terms of communicative impact. To what extent, if any, should the Court treat such restrictions as content-based? There are several variations.

First, suppose that, to protect its citizens against unwanted exposure to "offensive" messages, the government bans all billboards. In effect, the government argues that billboards are especially obtrusive and that it should be permitted to protect the interests of the "captive audience" in this situation so long as it acts in a content-neutral manner. Because this restriction is facially content-neutral, it would not seem to pose appreciably greater risks of inequality, distortion, or improper motivation than other content-neutral restrictions. But the restriction is designed to limit expression because ideas may be offensive and, as we have seen, such intolerance-based justifications for restricting expression are constitutionally disfavored and, hence, presumptively invalid. How, then, should we analyze this restriction—by content-neutral balancing, the more stringent standards of content-based review, or some other standard?

At the outset, it should be noted that, for the reasons discussed earlier, any effort of the government to defend a restriction on expression in terms of a constitutionally disfavored justification automatically triggers a stringent standard of review, and this is so even in the absence of any concern about equality, distortion, or motivation. It is not clear, however, that this situation implicates a constitutionally disfavored justification, for the government's interest in protecting its citizens against exposure to offensive messages does not seem as threatening to first amendment concerns when government restricts all messages equally as when it restricts only those messages that give the greatest "offense." Indeed, the censorial and "heckler's veto" aspects of intolerance-based justifications seem much reduced when the government attempts to protect this interest in a content-neutral manner.

This suggests, then, that this type of restriction should be tested by less stringent standards than viewpoint-based restrictions, such as, for example, a law banning only Nazi messages from billboards, but perhaps by more stringent standards than content-neutral restrictions that are defended on grounds unrelated to communicative impact. Indeed, the Court appears to have embraced precisely this analysis, for the Court has held that the "ability of government . . . to shut off discourse solely to protect others from hearing it," even in the form of a viewpoint-neutral restriction, is "dependent upon a showing that substantial privacy interests are being invaded in an essentially intolerable manner," a standard that falls somewhere between content-neutral balancing and the more demanding standards of content-based review.

*   *   *

A[nother] variation on the communicative impact issue is illustrated by the problem of the hostile audience. Suppose, for example, that a soapbox orator's speech triggers a hostile audience response and that the orator thereafter is charged with provoking a breach of the peace. Breach of the peace statutes do not usually single-out particular messages for restriction. Rather, such laws usually define prohibited speech in terms of prohibited effects. They are facially content-neutral. One might think, therefore, that such laws should be treated no differently than any other content-neutral law that regulates the time, place, and manner of expression. Such laws turn in application on communicative impact, however, and are closely analogous to the second variation. Indeed, like the second variation, breach of the peace statutes have distinct viewpoint-differential effects, raise serious concerns about governmental motivation, and are defended in terms of a clearly intolerance-based justification.

There is, however, at least one difference between the second and third variations. In the second variation, opposition to a particular message results in continued restriction, whereas in the third variation, opposition results in restriction only at the particular time and place of opposition. That is, in the second variation, the law bans future expression once a threshold of past opposition has been attained; in the third variation, the law bans future expression only when the expression may trigger a further breach of the peace. The third variation would thus seem to have a less severe suppressive effect. This distinction, however, is more apparent than real, for unless stringent standards of review are applied to the third variation, the mere possibility of opposition might be sufficient to restrict even future expression, thus merging the second and third variations. In any event, this difference, although perhaps relevant to the degree of potential distortion of public debate, does not affect the motivational and intolerance-based concerns.

Thus, although the hostile audience issue may not pose all the problems of expressly viewpoint-based restrictions, the concerns are quite similar, and the hostile audience issue, like the second variation, should be governed by the standards of content-based review.

As a final variation, suppose the managers of a state fair enact a rule prohibiting all peripatetic distributions of leaflets on the grounds of [a] fair, and a court upholds the rule as a reasonable content-neutral restriction designed to prevent interference with the movement of persons within the fair. Suppose also, however, that an extreme political group can prove that it was the only group engaged in peripatetic distribution of leaflets on a regular basis prior to the enactment of the rule, and that the managers adopted the rule in substantial part because of their hostility to the group's views. In such circumstances, the rule presumably would be invalidated as the product of improper motivation.

Suppose now, however, that the group can prove that the managers were affected not by a personal desire to suppress the group's views, but by a flood of complaints from fairgoers who were "offended" by the group's leaflets.

How should we deal with this situation? Because we are concerned here with a disfavored justification rather than an improper motivation, at least three resolutions exist. First, we might treat the rule as viewpoint-based. Second, we might treat the rule like the first variation, and test it by an intermediate standard because, like the first variation, it restricts all messages without regard to the communicative impact of any particular message. And third, we might treat the rule as content-neutral.

The answer, I think, lies in the notion, explored earlier, that a critical factor differentiating an improper motive from a disfavored justification is that the presence of the former requires automatic invalidation, whereas the presence of the latter does not affect the analysis if alternative, nondisfavored justifications are available. Here, the rule is defended as a reasonable means of protecting the free movement of people within the fair, as well as on the ground that it protects fairgoers from offensive messages. Because the free movement rationale is an available, nondisfavored justification, the rule should be analyzed as an ordinary content-neutral restriction. The existence of an alternative, disfavored justification does not affect the analysis.

*   *   *

VI. CONCLUSION

Properly defined and understood, the content-based/content-neutral distinction makes sense. The distinction has powerful intuitive appeal and is consistent with core first amendment values. Although criticism of the distinction is not wholly without merit, it is not persuasive. An understanding of the first amendment that fails to distinguish between content-neutral and viewpoint-based restrictions would treat problems that are different as if they were alike. It would meld existing first amendment standards into a single, unified approach. This would have a leveling effect. It would unduly enhance the protection accorded to content-neutral restrictions, at the expense of competing governmental interests, and it would dilute the protection accorded to viewpoint-based restrictions, at the expense of core first amendment values.

The distinction, however, is more subtle and complex than might at first appear. The content-based and content-neutral concepts are not self-defining. Taken literally, they do not comport precisely with the concerns underlying the distinction. Moreover, several types of ambiguous restrictions do not fit neatly within either the content-based or the content-neutral category. Careful scrutiny of these ambiguous restrictions reveals an almost bewildering array of easily masked analytic refinements and distinctions. These ambiguous restrictions pose a central jurisprudential conflict between precision of analysis and clarity of doctrine. To what extent should we tolerate miscategorization for the sake of clarity? To what extent should we sacrifice clarity for the sake of analytic consistency? I have attempted in this article, less to resolve this conflict, than to expose the puzzles and to bring the conflict to light. Only by understanding the nature of the problems can we begin thoughtfully to seek solutions.

NOTES

1. 315 U.S. 568 (1942).
2. 408 U.S. 92 (1972).
3. 398 U.S. 58 (1970).
4. 431 U.S. 85 (1977).
5. 427 U.S. 539 (1976).
6. 249 U.S. 47 (1919).
7. 274 U.S. 357 (1927).
8. 422 U.S. 205 (1975).
9. 454 U.S. 263 (1981).

RULES OF ENGAGEMENT FOR CULTURAL WARS
REGULATING CONDUCT, UNPROTECTED SPEECH, AND PROTECTED EXPRESSION IN ANTI-ABORTION PROTESTS

Alan E. Brownstein

*   *   *

A. JUSTIFYING THE RIGOROUS REVIEW OF DISCRIMINATORY SPEECH REGULATIONS

Why do content- and viewpoint-discriminatory laws receive such rigorous scrutiny? All regulations of speech, whether they are viewpoint-discriminatory, content-discriminatory, or content-neutral, have the effect of suppressing ideas and information. They all make it more difficult for individuals to communicate their messages. If we think about the issue solely in conventional, quantitative terms, viewpoint- and content-discriminatory regulations, because of their more precise and limited scope, probably restrict *less* speech than content-neutral laws, which may often extend far more broadly and interfere with many more messages.

Nonetheless, despite the narrowness of the burdens they impose, viewpoint-and content-discriminatory regulations of speech are recognized to be particularly hazardous to First Amendment guarantees. The danger inherent in such laws is not based on the magnitude of the burden they place on speech. Rather, it is the nature of the impact and the purpose of such laws that explains the rigorous scrutiny they receive under current doctrine.

1. The Danger of Distortion in Public Discourse

Content- and viewpoint-discriminatory regulations are constitutionally pernicious, in the words of Geoffrey Stone, primarily because they "distort public debate" in our society. They "excise" particular information or messages from the marketplace of ideas and in doing so manipulate the discussion and resolution of public policy issues by the polity.

While both content- and viewpoint-discriminatory regulations of protected expression receive strict scrutiny, it is generally recognized that viewpoint discrimination represents the greater constitutional evil. Thus, for example, in particular circumstances such as the regulation of speech in a non-public forum, viewpoint-discriminatory restrictions will still receive strict scrutiny while content-discriminatory limits on speech in the same location will be upheld as long as they are reasonable.

This distinction cannot be explained by reference to the diminishing effect of excising information or messages from the marketplace of ideas because both forms of regulation produce that result. Indeed, a content-discriminatory ban on all political speech excises even more information and messages than a viewpoint-discriminatory ban on left-wing or right-wing speech. Thus, whatever makes viewpoint-discriminatory laws particularly distorting and inconsistent with First Amendment principles, it must be something other than the fact that these laws make the marketplace of ideas substantively smaller than it would otherwise be.

Viewpoint-discriminatory laws are uniquely violative of the First Amendment because they directly empower one side of a debate with weapons that are denied to the proponents of the other side. This distorts the ability of the participants to fairly compete on the merits of their ideas. Justice Scalia recognizes this distinguishing quality of viewpoint-discriminatory laws in *R.A.V.*[1] when he argues that the state has no authority "to license one side of a debate to fight freestyle, while requiring the other to follow Marquis of Queensbury Rules."

Content-discriminatory laws do not create the same kind of distortion in public discourse because the regulatory classification that the government employs does not distinguish directly between competing ideas or perspectives. It is ludicrous to suggest, for example, that the proponents of non-political speech are unfairly empowered when political speech alone is prohibited. There is simply no conflict between political and non-political speech that will be skewed by government intervention.

It is true that content-discriminatory laws may be the result of deliberate manipulation that is intended to distort the marketplace of ideas and skew debate in favor of one side or the other. That is also true of content-neutral laws, however, and it is by no means clear that content-discriminatory laws are always substantially more vulnerable to such abuses than content-neutral ones. Indeed, both content-neutral and content-discriminatory laws can be used to indirectly influence debate in a similar manner that can be easily contrasted with the direct distortion created by viewpoint-discriminatory laws.

If we consider the abortion debate, for example, it is obviously unconstitutional to prohibit only anti-abortion messages in traditional public fora, while allowing speech supporting the right of women to have an abortion to be expressed in those same fora. The unequal impact of that law on the ability of the two sides of the abortion debate to influence public opinion is flagrant. If a law is passed prohibiting the expression of all speech relating to reproductive health issues in traditional public fora, however, it is far less clear that this law empowers one side of the abortion debate and disables the other. Both sides use traditional public fora for expressive purposes and are disabled by this law.

If we narrow the content-discriminatory law so that it prohibits only speech relating to reproductive health issues in traditional public fora adjacent to reproductive health clinics, the impact of the law changes again. Now, the alleged even-handedness of the law can be forcefully challenged. The new law arguably disables anti-abortion protestors more severely than it does supporters of the right to have an abortion, since the former group finds the sidewalks adjacent to clinics to be a particularly advantageous and valuable site for their expression. This is the same kind of unfair distortion in effect that renders viewpoint-discriminatory laws so problematic.

The arguable unfairness created by this law, however, is not a result of content discrimination alone. It results at least as much from the location specific nature of the law. A content-neutral law that prohibited all expressive activity adjacent to reproductive health clinics would produce almost the exact same kind of unequal impact. Both the content-discriminatory law and the content-neutral law are problematic because the two sides of the abortion debate have different needs and assign different values to particular opportunities for expression. The fact that only the former law is directed on its face at the communicative impact of speech does not necessarily mean that it contributes to greater inequality and distortion of the marketplace of ideas.

In one sense, the argument just presented seems counter-intuitive. Content-discriminatory laws *seem* so much more problematic than content-neutral laws. A law banning all political speech, for example, surely has a greater distorting effect on public debate than a law prohibiting the use of loudspeakers. Indeed, it does, but the reason for the obviously greater distortion resulting from a law banning political speech is not grounded entirely on its content-discriminatory nature. A law banning speech related to Mother Goose Rhymes, for example, is far less distorting than a law prohibiting all leafletting, rallies, and demonstrations in traditional public fora despite the content-discriminatory nature of the former law.

Many of the arguments suggesting that content-discriminatory laws are more dangerous and distorting than content-neutral laws seem to involve a comparison of apples and oranges. When a broad prohibition against the expression of some valued subject of speech is compared to a narrow prohibition limiting some relatively marginal method of communicating, it is hardly surprising that the content-discriminatory law is found to be more dangerous than the content-neutral one. It is important to remember, however, that if the variables are reversed, the result will be reversed as well. A broad prohibition restricting the use of effective and important means of communicating will distort public debate much more than a narrow restriction of a trivial subject of discourse.

If the breadth and value of what is being regulated is held constant, the two types of regulation may be equally distorting. I am not at all certain, for example, that a ban on all political speech in traditional public fora is substantially more distorting than a ban on all leafletting, loudspeakers, signs, rallies, and picketing in traditional public fora. At least the case for greater distortion in the above example remains to be made. Similarly, it is not clear that a content-discriminatory ban on all political speech in city parks between the hours of five o'clock and seven o'clock in the evening on Sundays is more distorting than a content-neutral ban on all public expression of any kind in the park during the same period.

Also, it is important to recognize that a skeptical examination of the "special" risks associated with content-discriminatory laws need not deny the conclusion that such laws have a greater distorting effect on public debate than content-neutral laws. The arguments presented above do not depend on the premise that there is *no* difference between content-discriminatory and content-neutral laws with regard to their propensity to cause the same kind of effects as, or to mask, viewpoint discrimination. It is sufficient to establish that whatever difference exists is not so substantial that this distinction alone can explain and justify the varying standards of review that the courts apply.

A content-discriminatory law, such as a law banning picketing related to labor disputes, may distort public debate to a greater extent than a law banning picketing at certain times and in specific locations. But this distinction should not be overstated. A law banning picketing of any kind in front of a manufacturing establishment is content-neutral, but probably almost as disadvantageous to union speech as a similar law prohibiting only picketing related to labor disputes. Indeed, a law prohibiting only pro-union picketing in front of manufacturing establishments may be only marginally more distorting than the content-neutral law. Not many anti-union activists, after all, spend their time picketing in front of manufacturing establishments.

Thus, we see yet again that a narrow, underinclusive content-discriminatory law may create a real risk of hidden viewpoint discrimination, but it is the time, place, and manner limitations that do the lion's share of the viewpoint-discriminatory work in such laws. It is these time, place, and manner constraints in conjunction with content discrimination that narrow the scope of these laws and make them underinclusive in a way that disadvantages one side of a dispute but not the other. Standing alone, carefully crafted but facially neutral time, place, and manner restrictions may be almost as effective as narrowly stated content-discriminatory laws in unfairly influencing public debate.

If the above analysis is correct, and the distorting effect of content-discriminatory laws may be closer in kind and magnitude to the impact of content-neutral laws than it is to the impact of viewpoint-discriminatory laws, then what accounts for the courts' commitment to the rigorous scrutiny of content-discriminatory regulations of protected speech? There are several parts to the answer.

2. Other Hazards of Content Discrimination

a. The Not-So-Special Nature of Content-Discriminatory Laws

To begin with, it is important to recognize that the constitutional prohibition against content discrimination is much more porous than the almost impenetrable barrier raised by the First Amendment against viewpoint discrimination. Content-discriminatory laws regulating most public property, virtually all public land other than streets and parks, will be upheld under low level "reasonableness" review. Regulations restricting the content of what is popularly described as lesser protected speech, such as commercial speech or indecent speech, receive relatively deferential review. Content-discriminatory laws regulating speech that creates "secondary effects" may be upheld without rigorous scrutiny. In brief, in many cases in which the value of the speech at issue seems to be particularly low or the government's rationale for regulating speech seems particularly plausible or justified, the rigor of the review provided content-discriminatory laws is reduced. Thus, one explanation for the courts' allegedly special concern about content-discriminatory regulations suggests that this concern is really not as special as it may seem at first glance.

b. The Risks of Improper Motive and Directing Laws at the Communicative Impact of Speech

If content-discriminatory laws do not involve a sufficiently increased propensity for indirect viewpoint discrimination to justify the heightened review they receive, there must be other concerns with these kinds of regulations that explain why courts subject them to rigorous scrutiny. Professor Stone's analysis of the justifications for rigorously reviewing content-discriminatory laws probably remains the most definitive discussion of this issue. I have already alluded to one of the justifications Stone identifies, the propensity of content-discriminatory laws to distort public debate by excising certain information and perspectives from public discourse.

Stone also describes two other concerns that help to explain the rigor of the review applied to content-discriminatory regulations of protected speech. First, content- and viewpoint-discriminatory regulations often reflect an improper motive on the part of the government adopting such laws. The government is trying to suppress speech because it disagrees with the ideas being expressed. That objective, of course, is starkly inconsistent with First Amendment values.

Second, content- and viewpoint-discriminatory laws are directed at the communicative impact of speech. This concern overlaps the risk that discriminatory regulations reflect an improper motive. Government directs laws at the communicative impact of speech for either of two reasons. The government may fear how people will react to the speech at issue. It fears, for example, that people will believe and be influenced by bad ideas. Alternatively, the government believes that people will be offended or angered by what a speaker says and it acts to silence the speaker on the listeners' behalf. Both objectives, again, directly contradict accepted First Amendment principles.

3. FACTORING OUT VIEWPOINT DISCRIMINATION

Professor Stone's analyses of the justifications for rigorously reviewing discriminatory speech regulations, astute as they are, are only of limited utility in resolving the problems that *R.A.V.* presents. Stone, for the most part, examines content- and viewpoint-discriminatory laws together as if they represented one form of problematic speech regulation. The thesis of this article, however, is that the content-discriminatory regulation of unprotected speech should be reviewed differently than viewpoint-discriminatory regulations. Thus, Stone's discussion represents a good starting place for trying to understand why content-discriminatory regulations require careful scrutiny. The justifications he cites, however, will have to be re-examined to determine how well they work when viewpoint-discriminatory restrictions on speech are factored out of the analysis.

The primary problem with discriminatory speech regulations, as noted previously, is that they distort public debate. We have seen that content-discriminatory regulations do not have the same directly unequal impact as viewpoint-discriminatory regulations in this regard. Content-discriminatory regulations do not excise one perspective or point of view from the debate leaving the opposing position unchallenged the way that viewpoint-discriminatory regulations do. If the concerns about debate distortion do not justify the rigorous review of content-discriminatory laws, what alternative explanation supports this result?

a. Secondary Distortion—Diminishing the Marketplace of Ideas

Content-discriminatory regulations *do* directly manipulate public debate, but they do so in a different way than viewpoint-discriminatory regulations. Content discrimination excises information and entire subjects of discussion from public discourse. While one side of a debate is not unfairly debilitated, the entire marketplace of ideas is weakened. The scope and richness of public discussion is artificially restricted. All else being equal, for First Amendment purposes, more speech, wider discussion, and new topics of analysis are always preferable to a restricted world of expression in which part of the domain of thought and speech has been placed off limits to the polity. Content-discriminatory laws are problematic for First Amendment purposes because they substantively diminish the marketplace of ideas. In essence, content discrimination threatens to shrink the unregulated, information supermarket that provides abundant consumer choices into a mismanaged convenience store that offers minimal, stale, and colorless selections.

b. Revisiting Improper Motives—The State's Role in Valuing Speech

With regard to the second justification for rigorously reviewing discriminatory speech regulations, Stone's suggestion that such laws reflect improper motives of the government, content-discriminatory regulations must also be distinguished from those that are viewpoint-discriminatory. By enacting content-discriminatory laws that are not viewpoint-discriminatory, the government does not directly and precisely suppress those ideas with which it disagrees. The shift from viewpoint to content discrimination generalizes the law's scope and mitigates its utility for punishing unacceptable ideas. To be sure, content discrimination can mask viewpoint discrimination and can produce viewpoint-discriminatory effects. We have seen, however, that the same can be said of content-neutral laws that receive significantly more deferential scrutiny. Once we are focusing on indirect effects, content-discriminatory laws do not uniquely skew public debate. Nor are they uniquely intended to serve debate distorting purposes.

Content-discriminatory laws do suggest a different and independently inappropriate motivation of government, the state's belief that it has some special role or expertise in determining the value of speech. To the contrary, as a people, we mistrust the government's evaluation of the worth of speech and its willingness to substitute its judgment for that of individuals in deciding whether speech has merit and utility. We do not trust the government to conclude for us what subjects of speech are particularly valuable or worth our attention. Moreover, we demand respect for our own choices and for our capacity to make those choices. What we say, and what we choose to see and hear, determines in an important sense who we are. That decision belongs to the individual, not the state. Determining the subjects of our discourse and the audiences we will join is part of our basic autonomy. By enacting content-discriminatory laws, the government impermissibly intrudes into the process by which people define themselves. Thus, the distinctive improper purpose motivating content-discriminatory laws is not the goal of suppressing bad ideas, but rather a paternalistic vision of the state in which citizens are reduced to the status of children.

This same argument can be made regarding the instrumental value of speech for the resolution of public policy debates. We reject content-discriminatory laws because we do not trust the government to correctly evaluate what people need to know to decide how our society should be governed. The government's perspective may be biased, even if officials are not consciously aware of their own predispositions, and therefore its vision will often be more limited than the choices of an unrestrained market.

A broad ban on political speech, for example, reduces sources of information available to the public and opportunities for subjecting ideas to the crucible of public discussion. While not directly viewpoint-discriminatory, a ban of this kind would have the effect of protecting the status quo by dampening political discussion in general. The problem is not so much that a ban on private political speech leaves the government free to pursue its own expressive agenda while private critics are silenced. Even if the state did not promote its own policies through government speech, prohibiting political expression would be intolerable. Expression is the primary tool that connects isolated people experiencing discontent and enables them to organize around mutual interests. A content-discriminatory ban on political expression, or political expression on a particular subject such as civil rights, blatantly interferes with and disrupts such possibilities.

c. Revisiting Communicative Impact—The Overly Protective State

The final justification Stone posits turns on the fact that content-discriminatory laws are directed at the communicative impact of speech. The state fears how people will react if they are allowed to hear suppressed speech. When it enacts content-discriminatory laws, however, the state is not directly concerned that people will be influenced by the kind of "bad ideas" that would be silenced through viewpoint discrimination. First Amendment doctrine aside, there is no reason for the state to suppress all speech on a subject, including messages it supports, in order to eliminate a dangerous point of view. Rather, in deciding to enact a content-discriminatory regulation, the state presumably fears that people will misinterpret, be confused by, or make inappropriate use of most information expressed on some subject of discussion. The disrespect directed at the citizenry by laws intended to keep people ignorant and uninformed to counter that risk, while different from the disparagement of the polity communicated by viewpoint discrimination, is also blatantly inconsistent with First Amendment values.

Stone's second concern with laws directed at the communicative impact of speech is more complicated and requires further discussion. Stone suggests that there is something problematic about the state's objective of protecting people from speech that they find offensive, or allowing the majority to use the state to protect most citizens from being confronted with speech they do not want to hear. This concern makes some sense when the government engages in viewpoint discrimination because only one side of a debate is protected against offensive speech. It is difficult to explain, however, why this objective is inconsistent with the First Amendment when content-discriminatory laws are at issue. Presumably, there is nothing inherently valuable or positive about expression that offends people or the experience of being offended. Nor is it likely that the Constitution empowers speakers to conscript unconsenting individuals into joining their audience. Further, the same autonomy concerns that prevent the state from prohibiting speakers from expressing their views and audiences from hearing them ought to allow the state to facilitate listeners in escaping from expression they do not want to hear. In some limited circumstances that may require permitting the state to force a speaker to end a conversation in order to protect a "captive audience's" autonomy.

Restrictions on offensive speech are problematic under the First Amendment when the state attempts to prevent a speaker from talking to someone who wants to hear the speaker's views in order to protect the sensibilities of third parties to the conversation. The state cannot prevent A from talking to B, who wants to hear A's message, in order to protect the sensibilities of C, who is deeply offended by what A has to say. The problem with content-discriminatory laws of this kind is not that they protect C from hearing a message she wants to avoid. It is that in many cases such a law not only insulates C from speech that offends her, but in doing so the law interferes with A's speech to B as well.

4. The Need for Additional Justifications

As modified in the above discussion, Stone's justifications explain why content-discriminatory laws raise serious First Amendment concerns that are distinct from the problems associated with viewpoint-discriminatory laws. Do these concerns also adequately justify the heightened review that content-discriminatory laws receive in comparison to the scrutiny directed at content-neutral laws? I think they do with regard to the problem of government substituting its conclusions as to the value of speech for that of citizens. Content-neutral laws do not raise the same autonomy concerns or reflect the same disrespect for the judgment of citizens as content-discriminatory laws.

It is less clear, however, that content-discriminatory laws diminish the scope and richness of the marketplace of ideas in comparison with content-neutral laws. Again we are confronted with the problem of comparing laws of varying scope regulating subjects of speech, or the means and location of speech, of differing value. A content-neutral law that limits public debate to a barely audible whisper but allows all subjects of interest to be discussed may diminish the marketplace of ideas as much as a law prohibiting certain subjects of discourse while allowing permitted subjects of discussion to be shouted from the rooftops.

a. Increasing the Difficulty of Regulating Speech

In the end, examining the purpose of content-discriminatory regulations and the effect of such regulations on public debate does not provide us an adequate justification for regulating content-discriminatory laws much more rigorously than content-neutral laws. An additional piece needs to be added to the puzzle to make this argument fully persuasive. A constitutional regime that permits content-discriminatory regulations of speech makes it too easy for government to restrict expression. The issue here is one of process, not substance. The breadth and general applicability of content-neutral laws may make them difficult to enact because they impair the expressive activities of politically powerful groups within society. A general ban on picketing outside commercial or medical establishments may provoke sufficient political resistance from unions, for example, that the law will not be adopted. A law that prohibits picketing at medical facilities only when the picketing is motivated by opposition to the health services the facilities provide, on the other hand, will be contested by a more limited constituency. Thus, by rigorously reviewing content-discriminatory laws, we prevent government from excluding politically powerful groups from the coverage of its neutral speech restrictions and, thereby, increase the political difficulty of burdening expression in general.

The process argument suggested here is widely accepted. As is true of legislation on virtually any subject, the more widespread the burdens imposed by a law, the more difficult it is to obtain support for the passage of the law. Generality requirements constrain government from regulating unfairly, but in doing so, they also constrain government from regulating at all. Thus, by limiting the government's ability to restrict expression precisely, judicial intolerance of content-discriminatory laws reduces the likelihood that *any* speech regulation will be adopted. Since almost all laws restricting protected speech by their nature reduce the scope and richness of public debate, we further First Amendment values by making it more difficult for government to restrict speech.

b. The Value of Content-Neutral Laws

There is a second, related, process-based argument that supports the courts' constitutional preference for content-neutral laws. The broader coverage of the content-neutral law not only makes it more difficult to enact, it also suggests that the legislature's evaluation of the costs and benefits that allegedly justify the law's enactment are more worthy of respect. If a law burdens the very citizens who support its enactment, by depriving them of valuable interests, the contention that the law's benefits outweigh its burdens seems plausible on its face. Certainly, we can be more confident of that conclusion than the alternative. We are rightfully dubious of the value of a law that exacts no cost from the many for the privilege of burdening the few.

Moreover, we review content-neutral laws more deferentially than content-discriminatory laws, not only because we are more trusting of content-neutral laws due to their generality, but because we recognize that some content-neutral laws are necessary to the organization of an orderly society. It is almost impossible to imagine how a society committed to freedom of speech could avoid chaos of Babel-like proportions without being able to adopt some meaningful time, place, and manner regulations. The utility of content-discriminatory laws seems less obvious and, thus, more open to dispute.

B. THE INAPPLICABILITY OF THE JUSTIFICATIONS FOR RIGOROUSLY REVIEWING CONTENT-DISCRIMINATORY LAWS TO THE REGULATION OF UNPROTECTED SPEECH

The arguments that support strict scrutiny of content-discriminatory laws, discussed above, are varied. No single explanation is persuasive by itself, but cumulatively a strong case can be made for rigorous review. Justifying the rigorous review of content-discriminatory regulations restricting protected speech in comparison to the more deferential scrutiny applied to content-neutral laws, however, is only half of the battle. Standing alone, this conclusion does little to support or undermine the Court's holding in *R.A.V.* The remaining critical question is whether any of the justifications that persuade courts to carefully evaluate content-discriminatory regulations of protected speech apply with significant force to the regulation of unprotected speech. Virtually none of them do! Almost all of the concerns about content-discriminatory laws pertain primarily, if not exclusively, to the regulation of protected speech.

* * *

NOTE

1. *R.A.V. v. St. Paul*, 505 U.S. 377 (1992).

THE CONCEPT OF THE PUBLIC FORUM

Harry Kalven Jr.

* * *

III. TOWARD A THEORY OF THE PUBLIC FORUM

* * *

A. THE PRINCIPLE AND TWO DICTA

The initial questions are whether the citizen using the street as a forum and not as a passageway is making an anomalous use of it, and whether he is, in a sense, always out of place and out of order when he chooses the streets for his meeting place. Certainly it is easy to think of public places, swimming pools, for example, so clearly dedicated to recreational use that talk of their use as a public forum would in general be totally unpersuasive. Is the street, however, a kind of public hall, a public communication facility?

One would have thought the theoretical issue had been put to rest a generation ago by the collision of dicta in *Davis v. Massachusetts*[1] and *Hague v.*

From *Supreme Court Review* 1 (1965). Reprinted with permission of the University of Chicago Press.

C.I.O.[2] *Davis*, it will be recalled, was one of the less admired efforts of Justice Holmes, then still on the Massachusetts Supreme Judicial Court. In reviewing a conviction for speaking on the Boston Common without a permit, in violation of an ordinance inhibiting many varieties of uses of the Common including "the discharge of cannon" thereon, Justice Holmes observed: "For the Legislature absolutely or conditionally to forbid public speaking in a highway or public park is no more an infringement of rights of a member of the public than for the owner of a private house to forbid it in the house."

When the case reached the United States Supreme Court, the Court endorsed the Holmes decision and its rationale. Said Chief Justice White: "The right to absolutely exclude all right to use, necessarily includes the authority to determine under what circumstances such use may be availed of, as the greater power contains the lesser." This position has at least the virtue of clarity. The citizen uses the streets for political purposes at the sufferance of the state; his use is anomalous and marginal and can be terminated whenever and for whatever reason the state decides.

This view survived until 1937 when Mayor Hague of Jersey City got into an argument, not with Jehovah's Witnesses, but with the CIO, then seeking energetically to organize New Jersey labor. In a complicated lawsuit, the Court passed on the city's claim that its ordinance requiring a permit for an open air meeting was justified by the plenary power rationale of the *Davis* case. In rejecting the point, Mr. Justice Roberts uttered the counter dictum:

Wherever the title of street and parks may rest, they have immemorially been held in trust for the use of the public and time out of mind, have been used for purposes of assembly, communicating thoughts between citizens, and discussing public questions. Such use of the streets and public places has from ancient times, been a part of the privileges, immunities, rights, and liberties of citizens.

On this view the matter is perhaps not quite so clear, but there is the aura of a large democratic principle. When the citizen goes to the street, he is exercising an immemorial right of a free man, a kind of First-Amendment easement. If so generous a statement of principle does not tell us exactly when his privileges may be curtailed in the interest of other speech or other uses of the street, it does give us a good starting point for the argument.

*   *   *

In [a number of important] cases, all involving leaflet distribution, *Schneider*,[3] ... *Valentine*,[4] and *Talley*,[5] the Court has given impressive content to the Roberts dictum.

In *Schneider*, Mr. Justice Roberts got the first chance to put his own dictum into operation. The case combined four separate controversies over municipal ordinances, three of which are relevant for our immediate purposes. Each invoked a flat prohibition against the distribution of handbills, circulars, dodgers, etc., in public places. The defendants, Jehovah's Witnesses, were convicted for violation of the ordinances, and in an 8 to 1 decision, Mr. Justice McReynolds dissenting, the Court upset the convictions. What is important here is that the state did not argue its plenary power but argued rather that the purpose of the restraint was to prevent littering in the streets. There was, therefore, no need to go back to *Davis*.

At the outset Mr. Justice Roberts made clear that although "pamphlets had become historic weapons in the defense of liberty," the right to distribute leaflets was subject to certain obvious regulations: "For example, a person could not exercise this liberty by taking his stand in the middle of a crowded street contrary to traffic regulations and maintain his position to the stoppage of all traffic."

What was called for was a balancing of the conflicting interests, but with a weight of enthusiasm for the personal rights involved. "This court," Mr. Justice Roberts paused to note, "has characterized the freedom of speech and that of the press as fundamental personal rights and liberties. The phrase is not an empty one and was not lightly used." He continued:

> In every case, therefore, where legislative abridgement of the rights is asserted, the courts should be astute to examine the effect of the challenged legislation. Mere legislative preference or beliefs respecting matters of public convenience may well support regulation directed at other personal activities but be insufficient to justify such as diminishes the exercise of rights so vital to the maintenance of democratic institutions. And so, as the cases arise, the delicate and difficult task falls upon the courts to weigh the circumstances and to appraise the substantiality of the reasons advanced in support of the regulation of the free enjoyment of the rights.

He then moved swiftly and surely to the evaluation of the contested ordinances:

We are of the opinion that the purpose to keep the streets clean and of good appearance is insufficient to justify an ordinance which prohibits a person rightfully on a public street from handing literature to one willing to receive it. Any burden imposed upon the city authorities in cleaning and caring for the streets as an indirect consequence of such distribution results from the constitutional protection of the freedom of speech and press.

The Milwaukee ordinance could not be saved by the argument that in actual practice prosecutions under it were limited to cases where the recipients throw it into the streets. The answer was still that "public convenience in respect to cleanliness of the streets" did not justify an interference with free communication. Nor could the Los Angeles and Worcester ordinances be saved by the circumstance that they were limited to streets and alleys, leaving other public places open. Here the point was met in language with echoes from the *Hague* dictum: "[A]s we have said, the streets are natural and proper places for the dissemination of information and opinion; and one is not to have the exercise of his liberty of expression in appropriate places abridged on the plea that it may be exercised in some other place."

The result, whether or not one likes it as a policy, had an impressive bite. Leaflet distribution in public places in a city is a method of communication that carries as an inextricable and expected consequence substantial littering of the streets, which the city has an obligation to keep clean. It is also a method of communication of some annoyance to a majority of people so addressed; that its impact on its audience is very high is doubtful. Yet the constitutional balance in *Schneider* was struck emphatically in favor of keeping the public forum open for this mode of communication.

Two years later Mr. Justice Roberts etched in his point still more firmly in *Valentine v. Chrestensen*. Once again there was an ordinance prohibiting discrimination of handbills and circulars. The one distinguishing feature of this ordinance was its limitation to commercial and advertising matter. The defendant was the owner of a former United States submarine that he sought to exhibit for profit. Accordingly he prepared handbills advertising the ship and soliciting visitors for a stated admission fee. Advised by the police that only handbills on public issues would be lawful, the defendant resourcefully attempted to alchemize his leaflet into a message of social significance by printing a protest against the police and the ordinance on one side and his advertisement on the other. He then proceeded to distribute his double-edged leaflet. Threatened further by police displeasure, he brought suit to enjoin the police from interfering with his distribution. He won in the lower courts, but the Supreme Court reversed in a unanimous decision, and in so doing added measurably to the point made by *Schneider* and the *Hague* dictum.

Mr. Justice Roberts began with a sturdy reaffirmation of the dictum:

> This court has unequivocally held that the streets are proper places for the exercise of the freedom of communicating information and disseminating opinion and that though the states and municipalities may appropriately regulate the privilege in the public interest, they may not unduly burden or proscribe its employment in these public thoroughfares.

He then made short shrift of the distributor's claim. The stratagem was transparent; this was still advertising matter. The issue is a different one where distribution of commercial advertising is at stake. Here the judgment of the legislature concerning the appropriate accommodation of interests is final. There was clear recognition of the principle of public use that was urged in *Schneider.* "The question is not whether the legislative body may interfere with the harmless pursuit of a lawful business, but whether it must permit such pursuit by what it deems an undesirable invasion of, or interference with, the full and free use of the highways by the people in fulfillment of the public use to which streets are dedicated."

*   *   *

The handbill sequence may be brought to a close for my purposes with consideration of *Talley v. California*, a 1960 decision related only obliquely to the previous cases. It represents, however, the high-water mark of the Court's protection of speech by handbill. The case is set apart by the fact that the ordinance banned, not all handbills, but only those that did not carry the name and address of the author, printer, and sponsor. It is a key precedent, therefore, for problems of compulsory disclosure. The defendants were arrested for distributing handbills, without the required identification, urging boycotts of certain merchants for discriminating in employment against "Negroes, Mexicans, and Orientals."

The Court upset the convictions, but this time there was disagreement within the ranks. Mr. Justice Harlan filed a separate concurrence and there were dissents from Justices Clark, Whittaker, and Frankfurter. The majority opinion of Mr. Justice Black framed the issue in a curious manner. The ban on leaflet distribution, we were told, fell under the rulings in *Schneider* and *Jamison*, "unless the ordinance is saved by the qualification that handbills can be distributed if they carry the appropriate identification." In an interesting and important passage, the Court then analyzed the virtues of anonymity in the fight for freedom, and concluded that the qualification did not save the ordinance. Nor was the state's interest in preventing fraud sufficiently related to the identification requirement to justify the ordinance.

At the very least the decision can be read as saying that leaflet distribution cannot be barred except for very good reasons and that anonymity of the leaflets is not a good enough reason, whatever its connection with preventing fraud. More generously, the case can be read as treating the distribution of leaflets in the public forum as so basic a right that it cannot be burdened with even the modest sanction of compulsory disclosure of sponsorship.

*   *   *

NOTES

1. 167 U.S. 43 (1897).
2. 307 U.S. 496 (1939).
3. *Schneider v. New Jersey*, 308 U.S. 147 (1939).
4. *Valentine v. Chrestensen*, 316 U.S. 52 (1942).
5. *Talley v. California*, 362 U.S. 60 (1960).

THE CASE OF THE MISSING AMENDMENTS

R.A.V. v. CITY OF ST. PAUL

Akhil Reed Amar

In *R.A.V. v. City of St. Paul*,[1] the Justices claimed to disagree about a good many things, but they seemed to stand unanimous on [a number of] points. First, the 1989 flag burning case, *Texas v. Johnson*[2]—itself an extraordinarily controversial decision—remains good law and indeed serves as an important font of First Amendment first principles....

*   *   *

...*R.A.V.*'s first point of apparent consensus—*Johnson* lives!—is nothing less than an "occasion for dancing in the streets." *R.A.V.*'s second point of seeming unanimity, however, is more sobering. All nine Justices analyzed cross burning and other forms of racial hate speech by focusing almost exclusively on the First Amendment. They all seemed to have forgotten that it is a *Constitution* they are expounding, and that the Constitution contains not just the First Amendment, but the Thirteenth and Fourteenth Amendments as well.

The issues lurking beneath *R.A.V.* are far more difficult than those that *Johnson* presented. May government treat racial hate speech differently from other forms of hate-filled expression? Within the category of racial hate

---

From *Harvard Law Review* 106 (1992). Reprinted with permission.

speech, can government treat words such as—and I apologize in advance—
"nigger" differently from words such as "racist," "redneck," "honky," or
"cracker"? Although not posing and answering these questions in so many
words, the *R.A.V.* majority strongly implied that nothing in the First Amendment authorizes such differential treatment. However, the majority failed to
consider whether the Reconstruction Amendments might provide a principled basis for such distinctions. The minority in *R.A.V.* seemed more willing to
allow hate-speech regulations specifically tailored to protect "groups that
have long been the targets of discrimination." Yet the minority also failed to
organize its analysis and intuitions around the Reconstruction Amendments.

Thus, none of the Justices forcefully framed and engaged the most difficult question hiding behind *R.A.V.*: whether, and under what circumstances,
words such as "nigger" and symbols such as burning crosses cease to be part
of the freedom of speech protected by the First and Fourteenth Amendments,
and instead constitute badges of servitude that may be prohibited under the
Thirteenth and Fourteenth Amendments.

[T]his Comment focuses on [among other things] what all the Justices saw
in *R.A.V.*: the importance of *Texas v. Johnson* and its underlying principles....

I. THE CASE OF THE FIRST AMENDMENT

A. OVERVIEW: WHAT THE JUSTICES SAID

The Court's opinion in *R.A.V.* opened with a crisp, if bloodless, statement of
the facts:

> In the predawn hours of June 21, 1990, petitioner and several other
> teenagers allegedly assembled a crudely-made cross by taping together
> broken chair legs. They then allegedly burned the cross inside the fenced
> yard of a black family that lived across the street from the house where peti-
> tioner was staying.

This conduct, if proved, might well have violated various Minnesota laws
against arson, criminal damage to property, and terroristic threats. But the city
of St. Paul chose instead to prosecute R.A.V. (Robert A. Viktora—then a juve-
nile) under a St. Paul ordinance that made it a misdemeanor to:

place[] on public or private property a symbol, object, appellation, characteri-
zation or graffiti, including, but not limited to, a burning cross or Nazi swastika,
which one knows or has reasonable grounds to know arouses anger, alarm or
resentment in others on the basis of race, color, creed, religion or gender.

The ordinance was sloppily drafted and, taken literally, obviously overbroad. It would seem to criminalize the display of swastikas, burning crosses,
and other emblems of white supremacy at, say, a political rally in support of
David Duke's presidential campaign. The Minnesota Supreme Court, however,
slapped a judicial gloss on the ordinance in an effort to salvage its constitutionality. The state's high court, in effect, rewrote the ordinance, purporting to
limit its application to "fighting words." Such fighting words, claimed the Minnesota court, had already been held by the United States Supreme Court in
1942 in *Chaplinsky v. New Hampshire*[3] to be unprotected by the First Amendment. The state high court went on to uphold the city ordinance as glossed,
even though the rewritten ordinance prohibited not all fighting words but only
those fighting words based on race, color, gender, and religion.

The United States Supreme Court unanimously struck down the ordi-
nance but splintered over the rationale. In an opinion for the Court, Justice
Scalia, joined by Chief Justice Rehnquist and Justices Kennedy, Souter, and
Thomas, offered an ambitious reconceptualization and synthesis of First
Amendment doctrine. Justice Scalia pointedly declined to decide whether the
Minnesota Supreme Court's gloss had indeed been true to *Chaplinsky* and, if
so, whether *Chaplinsky's* precise formulation of the fighting words doctrine
remains good law. Instead, the majority assumed, arguendo, the continued
vitality of *Chaplinsky's* formulation and the Minnesota Supreme Court's
fidelity to *Chaplinsky*, but held that even "fighting words" are not "entirely
invisible" to the First Amendment. Although entitled to much less protection
than other speech, fighting words and other disfavored doctrinal categories
(for example, obscenity and defamation) are not—contrary to the overenthu-
siastic rhetoric of earlier cases—wholly unprotected "nonspeech." Even
fighting words are sometimes "quite expressive indeed," said Justice Scalia.

Although he allowed that less favored categories of speech might be altogether prohibited (putting to one side the precise formulation of the boundaries of fighting words), Justice Scalia resisted the facile idea that the power
to prohibit entirely necessarily subsumes the power to prohibit selectively—
in other words, to discriminate. Government could prohibit all intentional

libel, but not only intentional libel of Republicans or incumbents. Government could prohibit all obscenity (even obscenity with some tiny political content), but not "only those legally obscene works that contain criticism of the city government." So too with fighting words. Government could prohibit all fighting words, but not only those fighting words deemed politically incorrect. In a nutshell, "government may not regulate use based on hostility—or favoritism—towards the underlying message expressed."

With this refurbished doctrinal framework in place, the Scalia Five turned to the glossed ordinance and found it wanting. On its face, the ordinance "discriminated" on the basis of content, treating race-based fighting words ("Nigger!") differently from other fighting words ("Bastard!"). Even more ominous, in "its practical operation" the ordinance discriminated on the basis of viewpoint, according to Justice Scalia:

> One could hold up a sign saying, for example, that all "anti-Catholic bigots" are misbegotten; but not that all "papists" are, for that would insult and provoke violence "on the basis of religion." St. Paul has no such authority to license one side of a debate to fight freestyle, while requiring the other to follow Marquis of Queensbury Rules.

When considered along with various statements made by St. Paul officials during the *R.A.V.* litigation, the ordinance, said the Scalia Five, presented a "realistic possibility that official suppression of ideas is afoot."

Justice Scalia conceded that the government might regulate certain messages in certain contexts if those messages are "swept up incidentally within the reach of a statute directed at conduct rather than speech." He acknowledged, for example, that "sexually derogatory 'fighting words,' among other words, may produce a violation of Title VII's general prohibition against sexual discrimination in employment practices." Justice Scalia also cited a federal anti-housing-discrimination statute, section 1982, which proscribes certain messages in certain contexts, such as the words "For Whites Only" on a residential "For Sale" sign. Yet when he later analyzed the St. Paul ordinance, Justice Scalia all but ignored this concession and offered no detailed explanation of how the St. Paul ordinance differed from the "incidental" regulation of speech under Title VII or section 1982. Apparently the Scalia Five thought it obvious that, unlike the federal statutes, the local ordinance targeted only "speech" and not "conduct."

In a sharply worded separate opinion, Justice White—joined by Justices Blackmun and O'Connor, and in large part by Justice Stevens—concurred in "the judgment, but not the folly of the [Scalia] opinion." The minority began its challenge of the Court's opinion by questioning the Court's decision to break new doctrinal ground and to decide the case on a theory that, Justice White insisted, "was never presented to the Minnesota Supreme Court" and was not "briefed by the parties before this Court."

Focusing their analysis on the main theory presented by the parties, the White Four voted to strike down the St. Paul ordinance not because it discriminated among fighting words, but because it reached beyond fighting words. The limiting gloss of the Minnesota Supreme Court, said the White Four, was a failure. The state judges had misread *Chaplinsky*; thus, their *Chaplinsky*-inspired surgery had not been probing enough—it failed to excise the ordinance's threat to speech outside the category of fighting words, properly defined. In doctrinal terms, the ordinance was "overbroad"; it fell not because its application to R.A.V. would violate his First Amendment rights—for he had none, Justice White said—but because its application to other speakers might violate *their* First Amendment rights, rights that R.A.V. could assert under special third-party standing rules in First Amendment cases.

At times, Justice White insisted that fighting words are simply not "speech" at all for First Amendment purposes and that the Amendment "does not apply" to such "worthless" words. The language from earlier cases describing fighting words as "unprotected" meant just that, Justice White said, contrary to Justice Scalia's revisionist effort to dismiss these dicta as not "literally true." Yet the minority conceded that even within unprotected categories such as fighting words and intentional libel, government power is limited: the state could not, for example, enforce a "defamation statute that drew distinctions on the basis of political affiliation." The minority's real break with the majority, then, was that the White Four simply did not believe that the St. Paul ordinance, had it truly been limited to fighting words, would present a "'realistic possibility that official suppression of ideas is afoot.'" To the extent the ordinance discriminated on the basis of content—by prohibiting only hate speech involving racial, gender, and religious bias—it was nonetheless legitimate:

This selective regulation reflects the City's judgment that harms based on race, color, creed, religion, or gender are more pressing public concerns than the harms caused by other fighting words. In light of our Nation's long and

painful experience with discrimination, this determination is plainly reasonable.... [Fighting words are] at [their] ugliest when directed against groups
that have long been the targets of discrimination.

The minority pointed to Title VII, which, like the St. Paul ordinance, targets only certain words. For example, a personnel officer with the sign "No Niggers" on his desk would violate Title VII, but not if he instead had a sign that
read "No Bastards." Under what theory, Justice White asked, could Title VII be
distinguished from the St. Paul ordinance (as applied only to fighting words)?

Although willing to countenance certain *content*-based discriminations,
the minority stopped short of giving the government carte blanche to engage
in *viewpoint*-based discrimination, even within "unprotected" categories.
Indeed, in a separate opinion, Justice Stevens (writing only for himself on this
point) challenged head on Justice Scalia's claim that the St. Paul ordinance
was in fact viewpoint-discriminatory. Justice Scalia's claim that St. Paul had
rigged the rules of verbal boxing was itself rigged, Justice Stevens argued:

> The response to a sign saying that "all [religious] bigots are misbegotten" is
> a sign saying that "all advocates of religious tolerance are misbegotten."
> Assuming such signs could be fighting words (which seems to me extremely
> unlikely), neither sign would be banned by the ordinance for the attacks
> were not "based on...religion" but rather on one's beliefs about tolerance.
> Conversely (and again assuming such signs are fighting words), just as the
> ordinance would prohibit a Muslim from hoisting a sign claiming that all
> Catholics were misbegotten, so the ordinance would bar a Catholic from
> hoisting a similar sign attacking Muslims.

> The St. Paul ordinance is evenhanded.... [It] does not prevent either side
> from hurling fighting words at the other on the basis of their conflicting
> ideas, but it does bar *both* sides from hurling such words on the basis of the
> target's "race, color, creed, rligion or gender." To extend the Court's
> pugilistic metaphor, the St. Paul ordinance simply bans punches "below the
> belt"—*by either party*. It does not, therefore, favor one side of any debate.

Writing only for himself, Justice Stevens proposed a more multifactored,
contextual First Amendment approach than that proposed by either Justice
Scalia or Justice White. Other portions of his concurrence echoed Justice
White's view that the St. Paul ordinance would have posed a minimal threat

to free expression if indeed it had been limited to fighting words; these portions were joined by Justices White and Blackmun.

Justice Blackmun also wrote a short separate statement expressing sympathy for racial minorities victimized by cross burnings and concern about Justice Scalia's reconceptualization of First Amendment doctrine. The Court's approach so troubled Justice Blackmun that he wondered aloud whether the Court could really have meant what it said. Perhaps, he darkly suggested, in the future the case will be seen as a sport—"a case where the Court manipulated doctrine to strike down an ordinance whose premise it opposed, namely, that racial threats and verbal assaults are of greater harm than other fighting words."

B. Analysis: Finding the First Amendment . . .

1. Common Ground: The Reaffirmation of Texas v. Johnson.—It is tempting, in light of the close vote and the sharp rhetoric in *R.A.V.*, to begin analysis with the issues that divided the Court. The temptation grows stronger when one notices the interesting way in which the Court split—no other major case has yielded the particular 5-4 line up so visible in *R.A.V.*

But we should resist this temptation. Notwithstanding the high-pitched rhetoric, the Justices share more common ground than they openly acknowledged in the heat of battle. Despite their disagreement at doctrinal margins, all of the Justices share a common First Amendment Tradition and a commitment to basic First Amendment principles. Only after we understand these principles—the hard core of a hard-won tradition—can we appreciate the modesty of marginal disagreement in *R.A.V.* The deep issues underlying *R.A.V.* make it in many ways a difficult case, and the best way to see this is to reconsider an easy case: *Texas v. Johnson.* For in spite of their heated disagreements about how to treat the First Amendment periphery, all nine Justices in *R.A.V.* now pledge allegiance to the flag-burning case.

My choice of *Johnson* as the best window into *R.A.V.* reflects more than the obvious surface similarities between cross burning and flag burning and between the particular voting alignments in the two cases. It also reflects my belief that *Johnson* illuminates with exceptional clarity, and in a way that few other cases do, much of the hard core of the First Amendment. To understand *Johnson* and its main antecedents—the court of history's repudiation of the Sedition Act of 1798, and the Warren Court's seminal opinions in *New York*

Times v. Sullivan[4] and *United States v. O'Brien*[5]—is, I believe, to understand the heart of our First Amendment Tradition. Conversely, to fail to see that *Johnson* is an easy case is, quite bluntly, to misunderstand First Amendment first principles.

In *Johnson*, the Court recognized a First Amendment right to criticize, dishonor, heap contempt on, shout words about, scribble words and symbols on, mutilate, decorate, "desecrate," or disrespectfully burn the American flag. In so doing, the Court reaffirmed at least five basic First Amendment principles, each of which (with one possible exception) was unanimously endorsed in *R.A.V.*

Principle One: Symbolic Expression Is Fully Embraced by the First Amendment.— The flag is a symbol. So is the cross. The right to wield and manipulate these symbols is fully protected by "the freedom of speech, [and] of the press." The First Amendment does not speak of protecting only "words." The Amendment vests Americans with a broad right to communicate with each other. This communication takes place through *symbols* that represent ideas, events, persons, places, objects, and so on. In fact, words are themselves symbols. In English, words are made by combining 26 standard letters, but surely the Amendment protects communication in languages that rely on unique word-pictures, pictograms, or hieroglyphics. Surely there is no First Amendment difference between the word "cross" and the pictographic symbol "+"; between the letters "NAZI" and the crooked cross swastika hieroglyph that represents the same ugly ideas; or between the words "American flag" and the unique red, white, and blue, star-spangled symbol impressed upon banners.

Nor is it relevant for First Amendment purposes that one does not orally "speak" a flag or a cross the way one orally speaks words. Is a deaf citizen's communication by sign language unprotected because it is not oral? Does the flag not "speak" to us, in every relevant and nontrivial sense? Does not the cross in a worship service? Does not the written Constitution? In any event, even the most willful and stubborn literalist must recognize that the First Amendment yokes the freedom of speech to the freedom of the press and thereby signals an intent to embrace all communication, regardless of the precise medium of transmission. Quite literally, the unique ink marks *printed and pressed* upon a cloth are what make the cloth a *flag* in exactly the same way that the unique ink marks *printed and pressed* upon a sheet of paper make it the *New York Times*. And if thin slivers of processed wood pulp—papers—are obviously protected when crafted to carry a message, why are thicker pieces of wood that carry messages—crosses—any different? Of course, if the wooden cross is used as other than an expressive symbol—say, to clobber someone over the head—then the cross loses its First Amendment protection. It becomes a physical weapon, not an ideational symbol. But the same is true of the Sunday *New York Times*.

If all of this seems to belabor the obvious, I hasten to point out that many of the participants in the flag-burning debate failed to understand these simple points. Again and again, they confused the physical and the symbolic in speaking of their desires to protect the "physical integrity" of the flag. But *the* flag is, in its deepest sense, not physical. Like a word, it is a symbol, an idea. It cannot be destroyed; it is fireproof. One can destroy only single manifestations, iterations, or copies of the symbol.

Justice Stevens, dissenting in *Johnson*, tried to analogize flag mutilation to "spray[ing] paint...on the facade of the Lincoln Memorial." The proper analogy, however, is to mutilating a toy model—a replica, a copy, a *symbol*—of the Lincoln Memorial. And of course, *that* expression is wholly protected. Chief Justice Rehnquist's dissent in *Johnson* was even more embarrassing. He repeated the Lincoln Memorial canard and bubbled on about the "physical integrity" of the flag. At one point he even put the phrase "symbolic speech" in quotation marks, apparently to rhetorically distance such speech from the real speech protected by the First Amendment. The implied distinction is bankrupt; all speech is symbolic in the sense of being conducted through symbols. As the *Johnson* majority put it, the First Amendment's "protection does not end at the spoken or written word....Pregnant with expressive content, the flag as readily signifies that is, symbolizes this Nation as does the combination of letters found in 'America.'"

Most important for our purposes here, this principle underlying *Johnson* received new life in *R.A.V.*, in which the facts, of course, involved not words, but the symbol of the cross. Citing *Johnson*, the *R.A.V.* majority began its substantive First Amendment analysis by equating laws "proscribing speech" with laws "proscribing...expressive conduct, because of disapproval of the ideas expressed." Later, the majority spoke explicitly about the need to protect "symbols that communicate a message." The White Four also reaffirmed the protection of "expressive activity," and elsewhere, Justice White made clear that the First Amendment would fully protect "burning a cross at a political rally." On both occasions, Justice White cited *Texas v. Johnson*.

*   *   *

Principle Two: Government May Not Regulate the Physical Medium with the Purpose of Suppressing the Ideological Message.—The presence of a flame does not somehow cause the First Amendment to evaporate. The founding generation was well aware of—and presumably meant to protect—a venerable political practice in which the flame was itself an intrinsic part of the message: burning one's political opponents in effigy. (Unlike the *Johnson* dissenters, the Founders understood the obvious difference between burning a real person, and burning a *symbol*—an effigy.) Chief Justice Rehnquist's *Johnson* dissent described flag burning as akin to "an inarticulate grunt" and thus unworthy of serious protection. However, few political expressions in American history have been more eloquent than abolitionist William Lloyd Garrison's 1854 burning of the Constitution to protest its original pro-slavery bias.

Of course, involvement in First Amendment activity provides no automatic exemption from generally applicable laws unrelated to the suppression of expression: the *New York Times* has no First Amendment license to ignore air pollution regulations. For this point, the *Johnson* Court cited the famous *O'Brien* case, in which the Court upheld the prosecution of a Vietnam War protester who intentionally burned his government-issued official draft card. Although the Court, in an opinion authored by Chief Justice Warren, claimed that the law under which O'Brien was prosecuted was unrelated to the suppression of expression, skeptics remain unconvinced. Did the Court not wink at the obvious censorial purpose underlying O'Brien's prosecution? And isn't the holding of *O'Brien*—that draft-card burning can be criminalized—almost fatal for those who would claim the right to burn flags and crosses?

In fact, a closer look reveals that *O'Brien* dramatically supports the *Johnson* holding. The government had issued official draft cards for legitimate identification purposes. Tampering with such cards implicated genuine concerns about "false identification," "counterfeit[ing]," "forgery," and "deceptive misuse." Thus, Congress passed a law punishing anyone "who forges, alters, knowingly destroys, knowingly mutilates, or in any manner changes his official card...." But how can a judge tell whether the claimed purpose of the law is the real purpose, rather than a smokescreen for censorship? One way is to closely parse the law itself and examine its operation, to test whether the legitimate purpose can fully account for the law's sweep—both what it includes and what it omits. The draft-card law meets this test because it was perfectly tailored to fit the government's claimed and legitimate purpose of preventing draft fraud. The law criminalized even *non*expressive intentional tampering with official draft cards, and it did not touch wholly expressive burnings of unofficial draft card replicas. A key tipoff here was that it would have been no crime to make a lifesize or postersize copy, a replica—a symbol—of the draft card and burn *the symbol* as a purely ideological protest. Yet in *Johnson*, the government was trying to do just that: criminalize the mutilation of any *symbol* of government authority (that is, a flag) that a citizen might make or buy. Unlike a draft card, every replica of a flag is itself a flag.

*   *   *

R.A.V.'s endorsement of the *O'Brien-Johnson* line calls for judicial vigilance to flush out unconstitutional motivations that hide behind a seemingly neutral law. Thus, truly neutral anti-burning ordinances must apply evenhandedly to speakers and nonspeakers alike. If the government allows ordinary cloth to be burned, it cannot invoke environmental protection as a reason to ban flag burning. The only difference between the flag and any other cloth is the ideological symbol printed on the former, and that is, of course, wholly unrelated to the claimed environmental purpose. The same principles apply, of course, to wood and crosses.

Both the majority and the minority in *R.A.V.* agreed that laws that restrict speech must be scrutinized to flush out illegitimate motivation. They simply disagreed about whether the lines St. Paul had drawn were rooted in a legitimate minority protection policy akin to Title VII and housing discrimination laws, or in an illegitimate desire to suppress ideas.

Principle Three: Political Expression—Especially Expression Critical of Government—Lies at the Core of the First Amendment.—Freedom of speech means both more and less than freedom of words. Merely because words are used to communicate a threat—"your money or your life!"—does not mean that government may not punish the threat. Thus, even the Scalia Five conceded that burning a cross in the dead of night on the yard of a black family might be punishable as a terroristic threat—in the same way as would the explicit words: "Move out niggers, or we will kill you or torch your house!"

If freedom of speech, then, means both more and less than freedom of words, exactly what does it mean? Is there any unifying principle of inclusion and exclusion? Two prominent candidates exist. The first focuses on freedom of speech as a guarantee of individual self-expression and autonomy. Under this theory, threats of imminent illegal physical violence, even if communicated through words, may be prohibited precisely because they undermine the autonomy of others and thus betray the very reason for generally protecting words. Although the Supreme Court has protected self-expressive speech in many contexts, its case law stops short of enshrining autonomy and self-expression as the centerpiece of the First Amendment. Nude dancing, for example, even if remarkably self-expressive, is "only marginally" within "the outer perimeters of the First Amendment."

A more promising descriptive theory of Supreme Court case law, and one rooted in the history and popular sovereignty ideology behind the First Amendment, builds on the work of Alexander Meiklejohn. As with its explicit textual counterpart in Article I, Section 6, which guarantees freedom of "Speech or Debate" in Congress, the Freedom of Speech Clause was designed, at a minimum, to safeguard the necessary preconditions of collective, democratic self-government. In order to vote and deliberate on public policy, citizens must be free to exchange political opinions and information with each other. Threats of imminent unlawful violence play no part in legitimate political persuasion and may be punished, as may offers to buy votes with money. Such threats and bribes—even if made with words—are a corruption of the democratic self-governance ideal that underlies the First Amendment.

The Supreme Court embraced this underlying vision in the landmark First Amendment case of *New York Times v. Sullivan*, and reaffirmed it in *Texas v. Johnson*. In *Sullivan*, the Court, per Justice Brennan, spoke

> of a profound national commitment to the principle that debate on public issues should be uninhibited, robust, and wide-open, and that it may well include vehement, caustic, and sometimes unpleasantly sharp attacks on government and public officials.
>
> ....
>
> ...It is as much [the citizen's] duty to criticize as it is the official's duty to administer. As Madison said, "the censorial power is in the people over the Government, and not in the Government over the people."

In *Johnson*, Justice Brennan again delivered the opinion of the Court: "Johnson was not, we add, prosecuted for the expression of just any idea; he was prosecuted for his expression of dissatisfaction with the policies of this country, expression situated at the core of our First Amendment values."

This theme also resounded through the *R.A.V.* opinions. We have already noted that Justice White, although deeming *R.A.V.*'s arguable self-expression "evil and worthless" and "unprotected," explicitly recognized that cross-burning at a "*political rally*" would almost certainly be protected expression." Why? Because "political discourse...enjoys the greatest social value." Justice Stevens was even more emphatic: "Speech about public officials or matters of public concern receives greater protection than speech about other topics.... Core political speech occupies the highest, most protected position...." Although the minority accused the majority of disrupting this doctrinal hierarchy, the Scalia Five did no such thing. The majority did not explicitly speak of "political speech" as such, but again and again used examples of citizen criticism of government officials as the epitome of core First Amendment activity.

Principle Four: Courts Must Guard Vigilantly Against De Jure and De Facto Discrimination Against Disfavored Viewpoints.—"If there is a bedrock principle underlying the First Amendment, it is that the government may not prohibit the expression of an idea simply because society finds the idea itself offensive or disagreeable."

So wrote the Court in *Johnson*. And so said the Justices in *R.A.V.* Indeed, Justice Stevens quoted this "bedrock principle" language in its entirety and then added: "'[V]iewpoint discrimination is censorship in its purest form'...." The Scalia Five were no less insistent that "the government may not regulate use based on hostility or favoritism towards the underlying message expressed." Nor did Justice White's opinion really take issue with any of this. As we have seen, the minority simply disagreed with the Scalia Five about whether the ordinance truly did rig the verbal boxing match. In the minority's view, the ordinance was no different from Title VII and housing discrimination laws and had nothing to do with "official suppression of ideas."

How can judges tell whether a law is indeed designed to penalize disfavored ideas? Sometimes the illegitimate purpose will be prominent on the face of the law. Flag-burning ordinances, for example, typically outlawed "contempt" or "desecration" of the flag, but not "respect" or "reverence" for it. So too, the infamous Sedition Act of 1798 made it a crime to criticize federal officials, but not to praise them; a crime for challengers to heap contempt on incumbents, but not vice-versa. Conveniently (and suspiciously), the Act was written to expire after the next election.

Often, however, judges must go beyond the formal words of a law and consider its real-life effect. A Federalist administration predictably used the Sedition Act to punish Republican critics of Federalists, but not Federalist critics of Republicans. (The office of the Vice-Presidency—held by the Republican Thomas Jefferson—was revealingly gerrymandered out of the Act's protection of federal officeholders.) A hippie radical with a flag rump patch would more likely be prosecuted under flag mutilation laws than would a suburban grandmother with a flag-inspired scarf. In *Johnson*, the Chief Justice expressed genuine pain and outrage over Leftist disrespect for the flag that our brave soldiers fought and died for, and were buried with. But his pain was selective. What about the Reactionaries who show disrespect for the stars and stripes by prancing around with Confederate and Nazi flags—flags literally used to wage war against Old Glory, flags that actually led to the death of many of our soldiers? Why did flag protection laws not treat Confederate flag waving as a desecration of Old Glory?

Even a law that is applied evenhandedly can be designed to disadvantage one side of the public debate. In the 1960s, for example, a law that banned *anyone* from using the words "baby-killing" or "napalm" in public discourse would, of course, have disadvantaged critics of the government. So would a ban on even a crude, filthy word like "motherfucker," given its prominence in various Leftist slogans (as in "Up Against the Wall....").

*   *   *

Principle Five: Exceptions to These Principles Must Not Be Ad Hoc.—In the end, one searches the *Johnson* dissents in vain for any plausible legal argument. Apart from those we have already canvassed (which simply will not wash) and scraps of dicta from earlier cases (none of which contains even a plausible argument, as opposed to an assertion or intuition), the Chief Justice's dissent consisted mostly of references to, and quotations from, hymns, anthems, poems, marches, pledges, and the like, celebrating Old Glory. To borrow John Hart Ely's words about another famous case, the problem is not so much that the dissent "is *bad* constitutional law" but that "it is *not* constitutional law and gives almost no sense of an obligation to try to be."

Indeed, the most interesting rhetorical move in the *Johnson* dissents came close to throwing down the mask, abandoning all pretense, and openly admitting the weakness of the dissenters' legal analysis. The flag, the dissenters passionately and urgently insisted, is *different.* It is "unique." Therefore (the implicit argument whispered), ordinary First Amendment rules don't apply. The call was seductive, but almost literally lawless. The *Johnson* majority virtuously resisted seduction:

> We have not recognized an exception to [bedrock First Amendment principles] even where our flag has been involved.
>
> ....
>
> ...There is, moreover, no indication—either in the text of the Constitution or in our cases interpreting it—that a separate juridical category exists for the American flag alone....We decline, therefore, to create for the flag an exception to the joust of principles protected by the First Amendment.

The problem was not that the First Amendment and the Republic for which it stands are so fragile that they would crumble under the tiniest deviation from principle. Nor was it that it would be impossible to craft a narrow and self-contained exception for the flag. Thus, if a narrow flag exception to the First Amendment had been ratified in 1990 as the Twenty-Seventh Amendment, the Republic would have survived. Such an explicit amendment, if expressly limited to the flag, would not necessarily have exerted a downward gravitational pull on the rest of First Amendment doctrine. It merely would have made clear "in the text of the Constitution...that a separate juridical category exists for the American flag alone," in keeping with the *Johnson* test.

The creation by the Supreme Court of such an exception, however, would be a different matter. The *Johnson* dissenters, to their credit, were uncomfortable with the knowledge that they were simply making up—out of whole cloth, as it were—a flag exception. They felt compelled to at least go through the motions of standard doctrinal argument. But in the process they said things that utterly warped the basic framework of the First Amendment Tradition; they made implicit and explicit arguments that might indeed have spilled over into non-flag First Amendment cases.

All the members of the *R.A.V.* Court claimed to reject the legitimacy of *ad hoc* exceptions to bedrock principles of the First Amendment. In fact, the majority tried to reconceptualize First Amendment doctrine to lend it greater coherence and rationalize the profusion of First Amendment categories. And just as the *Johnson* Court resisted the idea that "the flag is different, so all bets are off," the *R.A.V.* majority was skeptical of the naked policy claims that "race, gender and religion are different" and that "the burning cross is different." ...

* * *

NOTES

1. 505 U.S. 733 (1992).
2. 491 U.S. 397 (1989).
3. 315 U.S. 568 (1942).
4. 376 U.S. 254 (1964).
5. 319 U.S. 367 (1968).

PUBLIC RESPONSE TO RACIST SPEECH

CONSIDERING THE VICTIM'S STORY

Mari J. Matsuda

I. INTRODUCTION

A black family enters a coffee shop in a small Texas town. A white man places a card on their table. The card reads, "You have just been paid a visit by the Ku Klux Klan." The family stands and leaves.

A law student goes to her dorm and finds an anonymous message posted on the door, a caricature image of her race, with a red line slashed through it.

A Japanese-American professor arrives in an Australian city and finds a proliferation of posters stating "Asians Out or Racial War" displayed on telephone poles. She uses her best, educated inflection in speaking with clerks and cab drivers, and decides not to complain when she is overcharged.

These unheralded stories share company with the more notorious provocation of swastikas at Skokie and burning crosses on suburban lawns. The threat of hate groups like the Ku Klux Klan and the neo-Nazi skinheads goes beyond their repeated acts of illegal violence. Their presence and the active dissemi-

From *Michigan Law Review* 87 (1989). Reprinted with permission of Mari J. Matsuda.

nation of racist propaganda means that citizens are denied personal security and liberty as they go about their daily lives. Professor Richard Delgado recognized the harm of racist speech in his breakthrough article, *Words That Wound*, in which he suggested a tort remedy for injury from racist words. This article takes inspiration from Professor Delgado's position, and makes the further suggestion that formal criminal and administrative sanction—public as opposed to private prosecution—is also an appropriate response to racist speech.

In making this suggestion, this article moves between two stories. The first is the victim's story of the effects of racist hate messages. The second is the first amendment's story of free speech. The intent is to respect and value both stories. This bipolar discourse uses as method what many outsider intellectuals do in silence: it mediates between different ways of knowing in order to determine what is true and what is just.

In calling for legal sanctions for racist speech, this article rejects an absolutist first amendment position. It calls for movement of the societal response to racist speech from the private to the public realm. The choice of public sanction, enforced by the state, is a significant one. The kinds of injuries and harms historically left to private individuals to absorb and resist through private means is no accident. The places where the law does not go to redress harm have tended to be the places where women, children, people of color, and poor people live. This absence of law is itself another story with a message, perhaps unintended, about the relative value of different human lives. A legal response to racist speech is a statement that victims of racism are valued members of our polity.

The call for a formal, legal-structural response to racist speech goes against the long-standing and healthy American distrust of government power. It goes against an American tradition of tolerance that is precious in the sense of being both valuable and fragile.

Dean Lee Bollinger has concluded that a primary reason for the legal protection of hate speech is to reinforce our commitment to tolerance as a value. If we can shore up our commitment to free speech in the hard and public cases, like [Nazis marching in the town of Skokie, Illinois, where many holocaust survivors live], perhaps we will internalize the need for tolerance and spare ourselves from regrettable error in times of stress. Given the real historical costs of state intolerance of minority views, the first amendment purpose identified by Dean Bollinger is not one lightly set aside.

Recognizing both the real harm of racist speech and the need to strengthen our dangerously fickle collective commitment to freedom of discourse, this writer intends to feel and to work within the first amendment tension armed with stories from human lives. This article suggests... that outsider jurisprudence—jurisprudence derived from considering stories from the bottom—will help resolve the seemingly irresolvable conflicts of value and doctrine that characterize liberal thought.... [This essay] calls for doctrinal change, and concludes that an absolutist first amendment response to hate speech has the effect of perpetuating racism: Tolerance of hate speech is not tolerance borne by the community at large. Rather, it is a psychic tax imposed on those least able to pay.

II. OUTSIDER JURISPRUDENCE

If we cannot understand this pain that women, that Indian women, that Black women, that Hawaiian women, that Chicano women go through, we are never going to understand anything. All the mega-theory will not get us anywhere because without that of understanding, mega-theory does not mean anything, does not reflect social reality, does not reflect people's experience.
—Patricia Monture

There is an outsider's jurisprudence growing and thriving alongside mainstream jurisprudence in American law schools. The new feminist jurisprudence is a lively example of this. A related, and less-celebrated, outsider jurisprudence is that belonging to people of color.

What is it that characterizes the new jurisprudence of people of color? First is a methodology grounded in the particulars of their social reality and experience. This method is consciously both historical and revisionist, attempting to know history from the bottom. From the fear and namelessness of the slave, from the broken treaties of the indigenous Americans, the desire to know history from the bottom has forced these scholars to sources often ignored: journals, poems, oral histories, and stories from their own experiences of life in a hierarchically arranged world.

This methodology, which rejects presentist, androcentric, Eurocentric, and false-universalist descriptions of social phenomena, offers a unique description of law. The description is realist, but not necessarily nihilist. It accepts the standard teaching of street wisdom: law is essentially political. It accepts as well the pragmatic use of law as a tool of social change, and the aspirational core of law as the human dream of peaceable existence. If these views seem contradictory, that is consistent with another component of jurisprudence of color: it is jurisprudence recognizing, struggling within, and utilizing contradiction, dualism, and ambiguity.

Dean Derrick Bell's book *And We Are Not Saved* is an example of this. In a lyrical style Dean Bell describes a world infused with racism. This description ties law to racism, showing that law is both a product and a promoter of racism. Like the feminists who have shown that patriarchy has had its own march through history, related to but distinct from the march of class struggle, scholars of color have shown how racism is a separate, distinct, and central phenomenon in American life.

The hopeful part of the description offered by theorists such as Bell is the occasional recognition of the vulnerability of racist structures. The few who have managed to subject the many to conditions of degradation have used a variety of devices, from genocide to liberal doublespeak, that reveal the deep contradictions and instability inherent in any organization of social life dependent upon subordination. The sorrow songs of the jurisprudence of color are thus tempered by an underlying descriptive message of the inevitability of humane social progress.

This progress can lead to a just world free of existing conditions of domination. The prescriptive message of outsider jurisprudence offers signposts to guide our way there: the focus on effects. The need to attack the effects of racism and patriarchy in order to attack the deep, hidden, tangled roots characterizes outsider thinking about law. Outsiders thus search for what Anne Scales has called the rachet—legal tools that have progressive effect, defying the habit of neutral principles to entrench existing power. They have derived rachet-like measures to eliminate effects of oppression, including affirmative action, reparations, desegregation, and the criminalization of racist and misogynist propaganda. Such measures are best implemented through formal rules, formal procedures, and formal concepts of rights, for informality and oppression are frequent fellow-travelers. While cognizant of the limits of law reform, outsider scholars have emphasized the instrumental uses of formal legal rules to achieve substantive justice.

Using the descriptive and prescriptive messages of the emerging outsider jurisprudence to confront the problem of racist hate messages provides new insights into the longstanding neutral-principle dilemma of liberal jurisprudence. The following section will show how the victim's story illuminates particular values and suggests particular solutions to the problem of racist hate messages.

III. RACIST HATE MESSAGES: THE VICTIM'S STORY

> The attempt to split bias from violence has been this society's most enduring rationalization.
>
> —Patricia Williams

A. WHO SEES WHAT: SOME INITIAL STORIES

In writing this article I am forced to ask why the world looks so different to me from how it looks to many of the civil libertarians whom I consider my allies. Classical thought labels *ad hominem* analysis a logical fallacy. The identity of the person doing the analysis often seems to make the difference, however, in responding to racist speech. In advocating legal restriction of hate speech, I have found my most sympathetic audience in people who identify with target groups, while I have encountered incredulity, skepticism, and even hostility from others.

This split in reaction is also evident in case studies of hate speech. The typical reaction of target-group members to an incident of racist propaganda is alarm and immediate calls for redress. The typical reaction of non-target-group members is to consider the incidents isolated pranks, the product of sick-but-harmless minds. This is in part a defensive reaction: a refusal to believe that real people, people just like us, are racists. This disassociation leads logically to the claim that there is no institutional or state responsibility to respond to the incident. It is not the kind of real and pervasive threat that requires the state's power to quell.

Here are some true "just kidding" stories:

An African-American worker found himself repeatedly subjected to racist speech when he came to work. A noose was hanging one day in his work area. "KKK" references were directed at him, as well as other unfortunately typical racist slurs and death threats. His employer discouraged him from calling the police, attributing the incidents to "horseplay."

In San Francisco, a swastika was placed near the desks of Asian-American and African-American inspectors in the newly integrated fire department. The official explanation for the presence of the swastika at the fire department was that it was presented several years earlier as a "joke" gift to the battalion chief, and that it was unclear why or how it ended up at the work stations of the minority employees.

In Jackson, Mississippi, African-American employees of Frito-Lay found their cars sprayed with "KKK" inscriptions, and were the targets of racist notes and threats. Local African Americans and Jews were concerned, but officials said the problem was attributable to children.

An African-American FBI agent was subject to a campaign of racist taunts by white co-workers. A picture of an ape was pasted over his child's photograph, and racial slurs were used. Such incidents were called "healthy" by his supervisor.

In Seattle, a middle-management Japanese American was disturbed by his employer's new anti-Japanese campaign. As the employer's use of slurs and racist slogans in the workplace increased, so did the employee's discomfort. His objections were viewed as overly sensitive and uncooperative. He finally quit his job, and he was denied unemployment insurance benefits because his departure was "without cause."

In Contra Costa, California, Ku Klux Klan symbols were used to turn families looking for homes away from certain neighborhoods. The local sheriff said there was "nothing . . . to indicate this is Klan activity."

Similarly, a Hmong family in Eureka, California, was twice victimized by four-foot-high crosses burning on their lawn. Local police dismissed this as "a prank."

Why might anti-Japanese racial slurs mean something different to Asian and white managers? Here is a story of mine:

As a young child I was told never to let anyone call me a J—p. My parents, normally peaceable and indulgent folk, told me this in the tone reserved for dead-serious warnings. Don't accept rides from strangers. Don't play with matches. Don't let anyone call you that name. In their tone they transmitted a message of danger, that the word was a dangerous one, tied to violence.

Just as I grew up to learn the facts about the unspoken danger my parents saw in the stranger in the car, I learned how they connected the violence of California lynch mobs and Hiroshima atom bombs to racist slurs against Japanese Americans.

This early training in vigilance was reinforced by what I later learned about violence and Asian Americans: that people with features like mine are regular victims of violence tied to a wave of anti-Asian propaganda that stretches from Boston to San Francisco, from Galveston to Detroit.

The white managers who considered Mr. O. (the Japanese-American manager) an overly sensitive troublemaker, and the unemployment board that determined there was no good cause for him to quit his job, came from a different experience. They probably never heard of Vincent Chin. They do not know about the Southeast-Asian-American children spat upon and taunted as they walk home from school in Boston; about the vigilante patrols harassing Vietnamese shrimpers in Texas. Nor do they know that the violence in all these cases is preceded by propaganda similar to that used in Mr. O's workplace: that those [racist slur for Asian groups] are taking over "our" country.

Stories of anti-Asian violence are regularly reported in the Asian-American press, just as stories of synagogue vandalism are regularly reported in the Jewish-American press, and anti-African-American violence, including the all-too-common phenomenon of "move-in" violence, is regularly reported in the African-American press. Members of target-group communities tend to know that racial violence and harassment is widespread, common, and life-threatening; that "the youngsters who paint a swastika today may throw a bomb tomorrow."

The mainstream press often ignores these stories, giving rise to the view of racist and anti-Semitic incidents as random and isolated, and the corollary that isolated incidents are inconsequential. For informed members of these victim communities, however, it is logical to link together several thousand real life stories into one tale of caution.

B. The Structure of Racism

While this article focuses on the phenomenology of racism, it includes discussion of the closely related phenomenon of anti-Semitism. The same groups, using many of the same techniques, and operating from many of the same motivations and dysfunctions typically produce racist and anti-Semitic speech. The serious problems of violent pornography and anti-gay and anti-lesbian hate speech are not discussed in this article. While I believe these forms of hate speech require public restriction, these forms also require a sep-

arate analysis because of the complex and violent nature of gender subordination, and the different way in which sex operates as a locus of oppression.
They are, therefore, beyond the scope of this piece.

The claim that a legal response to racist speech is required stems from a
recognition of the structural reality of racism in America. Racism, as used
here, comprises the ideology of racial supremacy and the mechanisms for
keeping selected victim groups in subordinated positions. The implements of
racism include:

1. Violence and genocide;
2. Racial hate messages, disparagement, and threats;
3. Overt disparate treatment; and
4. Covert disparate treatment and sanitized racist comments.

In addition to physical violence, there is the violence of the word. Racist
hate messages, threats, slurs, epithets, and disparagement all hit the gut of
those in the target group. The spoken message of hatred and inferiority is conveyed on the street, in schoolyards, in popular culture, and in the propaganda
of hate widely distributed in this country. Our college campuses have seen an
epidemic of racist incidents in the 1980s. The hate speech flaring up in our
midst includes insulting nouns for racial groups, degrading caricatures, threats
of violence, and literature portraying Jews and people of color as animal-like
and requiring extermination.

While violence and hate propaganda are officially renounced by elites,
other forms of racism are not. Jim Crow, which persists today in the form of
private clubs and de facto segregated schools and neighborhoods, is seen as
less offensive than cross burnings. Covert disparate treatment and sanitized
racist comments are commonplace and socially acceptable in many settings.
The various implements of racism find their way into the hands of different
dominant-group members. Lower- and middle-class white men might use
violence against people of color, while upper-class whites might resort to private clubs or righteous indignation against "diversity" and "reverse discrimination." Institutions—government bodies, schools, corporations—also per-
petuate racism through a variety of overt and covert means.

From the victim's perspective, all of these implements inflict wounds,
wounds that are neither random nor isolated. Gutter racism, parlor racism,
corporate racism, and government racism work in coordination, reinforcing

existing conditions of domination. Less egregious forms of racism degenerate easily into more serious forms.

The Japanese-American executive who resigns in protest when his employer starts publishing anti-Japanese slogans to improve sales knows that there is a connection between racist words and racist deeds. The racially motivated beating death of Vincent Chin by unemployed white auto workers in Detroit, during a time of widespread anti-Asian propaganda in the auto industry, was no accident. Nor was the murder of the Davis, California, high school student Thong Hy Huynh, after months of anti-Asian racial slurs.

Violence is a necessary and inevitable part of the structure of racism. It is the final solution, as fascists know, barely held at bay while the tactical weapons of segregation, disparagement, and hate propaganda do their work. The historical connection of all the tools of racism is a record against which to consider a legal response to racist speech.

C. The Specific Negative Effects of Racist Hate Messages

everywhere the crosses are burning,
sharp-shooting goose-steppers around every corner,
here are snipers in the schools...
(I know you don't believe this.
You think this is nothing
but faddish exaggeration. But they
are not shooting at you.)
—Lorna Dee Cervantes

Racist hate messages are rapidly increasing and are widely distributed in this country using a variety of low and high technologies. The negative effects of hate messages are real and immediate for the victims. Victims of vicious hate propaganda have experienced physiological symptoms and emotional distress ranging from fear in the gut, rapid pulse rate and difficulty in breathing, nightmares, post-traumatic stress disorder, hypertension, psychosis, and suicide. Professor Patricia Williams has called the blow of racist messages "spirit murder" in recognition of the psychic destruction victims experience.

Victims are restricted in their personal freedom. In order to avoid receiving hate messages, victims have had to quit jobs, forgo education, leave their homes, avoid certain public places, curtail their own exercise of speech rights, and otherwise modify their behavior and demeanor. The recipient of hate messages struggles with inner turmoil. One subconscious response is to reject one's own identity as a victim-group member. As writers portraying the African-American experience have noted, the price of disassociating from one's own race is often sanity itself.

As much as one may try to resist a piece of hate propaganda, the effect on one's self-esteem and sense of personal security is devastating. To be hated, despised, and alone is the ultimate fear of all human beings. However irrational racist speech may be, it hits right at the emotional place where we feel the most pain. The aloneness comes not only from the hate message itself, but also from the government response of tolerance. When hundreds of police officers are called out to protect racist marchers, when the courts refuse redress for racial insult, and when racist attacks are officially dismissed as pranks, the victim becomes a stateless person. Target-group members can either identify with a community that promotes racist speech, or they can admit that the community does not include them.

The effect on non-target-group members is also of constitutional dimension. Associational and other liberty interests of whites are curtailed by an atmosphere rife with racial hatred. In addition, the process of dissociation can affect their mental health. Dominant-group members who rightfully, and often angrily, object to hate propaganda share a guilty secret: their relief that they are not themselves the target of the racist attack. While they reject the Ku Klux Klan, they may feel ambivalent relief that they are not African-American, Asian, or Jewish. Thus they are drawn into unwilling complacency with the Klan, spared from being the feared and degraded thing.

Just as when we confront human tragedy—a natural disaster, a plane crash—we feel the blessing of the fortunate that distances us from the victims, the presence of racist hate propaganda distances right-thinking dominant-group members from the victims, making it harder to achieve a sense of common humanity. Similarly, racist propaganda forces victim-group members to view all dominant-group members with suspicion. It forces well-meaning dominant-group members to use kid-glove care in dealing with outsiders. This is one reason why social relations across racial lines are so rare in America.

Research in psychosocial and psycholinguistic analysis of racism suggests a related effect of racist hate propaganda: at some level, no matter how much both victims and well-meaning dominant-group members resist it, racial inferiority is planted in our minds as an idea that may hold some truth. The idea is improbable and abhorrent, but it is there before us, because it is presented repeatedly. "Those people" are lazy, dirty, sexualized, money-grubbing, dishonest, inscrutable, we are told. We reject the idea, but the next time we sit next to one of "those people" the dirt message, the sex message, is triggered. We stifle it, reject it as wrong, but it is there, interfering with our perception and interaction with the person next to us. For the victim, similarly, the angry rejection of the message of inferiority is coupled with absorption of the message. When a dominant-group member responds favorably, there is a moment of relief—the victims of hate messages do not always believe in their insides that they deserve decent treatment. This obsequious moment is degrading and dispiriting when the self-aware victim acknowledges it.

Psychologists and sociologists have done much to document the effects of racist messages on both victims and dominant-group members. Writers of color have given us graphic portrayals of what life is like for victims of racist propaganda. From the victim's perspective racist hate messages cause real damage.

If the harm of racist hate messages is significant, and the truth value marginal, the doctrinal space for regulation of such speech is a possibility. An emerging international standard seizes this possibility.

*   *   *

V. THE UNIQUELY AMERICAN APPROACH OF PROTECTION OF RACIST HATE PROPAGANDA: THE CIVIL LIBERTARIAN'S STORY

Many foreign lawyers, including those from countries close to the United States in ideology, are perplexed by the uniquely American approach of protection of racist hate organizations. American citizens themselves express frustration when they find that the Klan and the Nazis are free to march in public places, with publicly financed police protection. This section will state the American position, and attempt to make its strongest case. This is a starting point for exploring the dominant story of racism in American social life, and for showing that the American position is neither inevitable nor sound as a matter of democratic theory, constitutional doctrine, or value.

By the American position, I refer to the position that would require reservation to article 4 and forbearance from other efforts to control racist speech, on the ground that restriction of racist hate propaganda and hate organizations is incompatible with the first amendment. There is no single authoritative assertion of this position. The discussion here thus addresses a composite of mainstream first amendment thinking.

Getting a clear statement of the American position is not easy. First amendment doctrine is notably confused, but a reading of the cases reveals the following core ideas. Freedom of expression, the argument goes, is the most fundamental right protected under the Constitution. Democratic, representative government presumes that people are free to think and say whatever they might, even the unthinkable. They can advocate the end of democracy. We risk the chance that they will prevail because to give government the power to control expression is an even greater threat. Power is jealous, and the temptation to stifle legitimate opposition is too great. Thus under our system, there is "no such thing as a false idea." All ideas deserve a public forum, and the way to combat anti-democratic ideas is through counter-expression. When all ideas are voiced freely, we have the greatest chance that the right results will obtain.

We have no way of knowing what the right results are in advance. Ideas that were once accepted as truth we now reject. Because our ideas about what we want as a society are changing and emergent, we cannot say that certain ideas are unacceptable. New ideas often meet opposition, and we have seen new ideas, including major advances in civil rights, eventually become the majority position. We have no basis for distinguishing good from bad ideas, and the only logical choice is to protect all ideas.

If the state feels threatened by certain ideas, it is not without recourse. It can use education and counter-speech to combat those ideas. It can control conduct or action arising from those ideas. Thus while the state cannot outlaw a militaristic political party, it can control the stockpiling of weaponry and punish any acts of violence. Incitement to imminent violence is a related and acceptable point of intervention. Such control is admittedly less effective than direct and preventive repression, but we have made the commitment to a free society, and we will not become un-free even in self-defense. To do otherwise abandons the basic foundation of democracy, rendering nonsensical any claim to necessity. Furthermore, if we accept that ours is a racist society, that is all the more reason to give primacy to the first amendment. The best means to combat racist oppression is the right to protest.

Accepting this extreme commitment to the first amendment is neither easy, nor natural. It is a concept one must learn, and it barely survives the hard cases. There is much speech that comes close to action. Conspiratorial speech, inciting speech, fraudulent speech, obscene speech, and defamatory speech are examples of words that seem to emerge from human mouths as more than ideas. Examples might include a merchant's lies about the efficacy of a product, a gang leader's order to murder an enemy, sexual description broadcast to an audience of children, and threats of physical harm. The American doctrine recognizes a few limited categories of speech that take on qualities beyond expression. These areas are doctrinally distinct, and our commitment to the first amendment value requires the most vigilant scrutiny to avoid suppression of ideas under the guise of controlling conduct.

What the American position means in the area of race is that expressions of the ideas of racial inferiority or racial hatred are protected. Anyone who wants to say that African Americans and Jews are inferior and deserving of persecution is entitled to. However loathsome this idea may be, it is still political speech. The law becomes strong at its edges. If we can hold fast to freedom when it is most difficult to do so, we will avoid making the easy and disastrous mistakes.

The strongest argument against criminalization of racist speech is that it is content-based. It puts the state in the censorship business, with no means of assuring that the censor's hand will go lightly over "good" as opposed to "bad" speech. Critics cite the Canadian experience of words of protest and satire mistakenly challenged using race-hatred laws, or the British experience, where censorship of racism is accompanied by censorship of political dissidents. If we outlaw the Ku Klux Klan as an organization repugnant to democratic values, then we can outlaw the Communist Party for the same reasons. Admitting one exception will lead to another, and yet another, until those in power are free to stifle opposition in the name of protecting democratic ideals.

A related and less persuasive argument is the fresh air position. This position suggests that the most effective way to control the Klan is to allow it to broadcast its ideas. When people are exposed to the hatred propagated by the Klan, they will reject it and organize against it. Suppressing the Klan will only force it to choose more violent and clandestine means of obtaining its goals.

A corollary to the American position of protection of racist expression is that the government must take certain affirmative steps to preserve that right.

The state must make public facilities available on a nondiscriminatory basis to individuals and groups wishing to express their race hatred. It must provide police protection to preserve order and protect speakers who are threatened by counter-demonstrators. Since groups like the Klan typically draw angry opposition when they parade in public streets, this has meant that the Klan is entitled to publicly financed police escorts. Without this, the right of free speech is meaningless. Angry and intolerant majorities could prevent unpopular minorities from using public facilities, rendering the right of free speech illusory.

The strong first amendment position outlined above represents certain values that are part of the American structure of government and the American commitment to political and civil rights. The American position may be extreme, but it responds to American circumstances. It recalls the times when our commitment to freedom was tested—the Sedition Act, the McCarthy era, the movement for racial justice, the riots and protests of the Vietnam age. Our commitment to the position has been neither steadfast nor universal. Judges have sometimes failed to understand it, resulting in loose doctrinal ends. The basic principle, however, has survived, and the thrust of the cases and commentary supports first amendment primacy.

The purpose of stating the strongest possible case for the American position is not merely to set the groundwork for an attack. The basic values of freedom of expression, while not provable in any natural law sense, are accepted by the international community. That the American commitment to the ideology of freedom has contributed to social progress and the limitation of repression is a part of our history. The question presented here is whether the values of the first amendment are in irresolvable conflict with the international movement toward elimination of racist hate propaganda, and whether any attempt to move United States law toward the international standard is worthwhile.

As a starting point in understanding what is really going on in the law of freedom of expression, it is helpful to note where the edges are. There are several forms of speech that are not entitled to the same protection that existing doctrine would afford racist propaganda.

In the area of commerce and industrial relations, expression is frequently limited. False statements about products, suggestions that prices be fixed, opinions about the value of stock, and pro-employer propaganda during union elections, are all examples of expressions of ideas that are limited by the law. An instrumental analysis might be that smooth operation of the entities of commerce, and the need for a stable setting for the growth of capital, have overcome the commitment to civil liberties in these instances. A doctrinal first amendment explanation is that those are examples of hard cases, representing more than the expression of an idea. Some statements are noncommunicative acts, subject to legal restraint. Alternatively, some would argue that many existing exceptions are simply a mistake.

Speech and associational rights are limited in certain professional contexts. Government employees are forbidden from engaging in political activity to avoid problems of undue influence. Those charged with the public trust are asked to profess loyalty to the Constitution, and are asked to limit expression that will undermine their ability to do their job. The class of less-favored speakers has included, dubiously, children and prisoners. These exceptions suggest that internal security and the functioning of government are other policies that override the first amendment in specific cases, to the legitimate discomfort of committed civil libertarians.

The override occurs again in the area of privacy and defamation. Expressing intimate and private facts about a private individual is subject to civil damages, as is the spread of untruths damaging to both public and private figures. First amendment protections are worked into the law of defamation and privacy, but they are not allowed to supersede completely the reputational interest and personal integrity of the victims of certain forms of expression. When courts are called into private disputes about defamatory speech, they are really mediating between competing interests of constitutional dimension: the right of expression, and the implicit right to a measure of personal integrity, peace of mind, and personhood.

Speech infringing on public order is another classic unprotected area. Bomb threats, incitements to riot, "fighting words," and obscene phone calls are a few of the speech-crimes that slip through the first amendment's web of protection. These categories edge close to the category of racist speech. Under existing law, insults of such dimension that they bring men—this is a male-centered standard—to blows are subject to a first amendment exception. The problem is that racist speech is so common that it is seen as part of the ordinary jostling and conflict people are expected to tolerate, rather than as fighting words. Another problem is that the effect of dehumanizing racist language is often flight rather than fight. Targets choose to avoid racist encounters whenever possible, internalizing the harm rather than escalating the conflict. Lack of a fight and admirable self-restraint then defines the words as nonactionable. When racist leaflets threatening Representative Tyrone Brooks urged whites to band together to keep civil rights activists out of Rome, Georgia, state officials felt that the first amendment prevented arrest because the leaflet "didn't threaten to kill anyone."

While it is sometimes suggested that the first amendment is absolute, even strong civil libertarians are likely to admit that the absolutist view is unworkable. As Professor Frederick Schauer has pointed out, absolute protection of expression would render unconstitutional "all of contract law, most of antitrust law, and much of criminal law." The need to distinguish protected from unprotected speech is inevitable.

If there are important competing interests represented in the international position on elimination of racist hate messages, if these interests are only met by limiting speech, and if the speech represented in racist hate propaganda is not the kind of speech most needful of protection, then it may be possible to remain true to the first amendment without protecting racist hate propaganda.

The following section will suggest that an explicit and narrow definition of racist hate messages will allow restriction while respecting first amendment values.

VI. NARROW APPLICATION AND PROTECTION OF FIRST AMENDMENT VALUES

This article attempts to recognize and accommodate the civil libertarian position. The victim's perspective requires respect for the idea of rights, for it is those on the bottom who are most hurt by the absence of rights, and it is those on the bottom who have sustained the struggle for rights in American history. The image of book burnings should unnerve us and remind us to argue long and hard before selecting a class of speech to exclude from the public domain. I am uncomfortable in making the suggestions made in this section if others fall too easily into agreement.

In order to respect first amendment values, a narrow definition of actionable racist speech is required. Racist speech is best treated as a *sui generis* category, presenting an idea so historically untenable, so dangerous, and so tied to perpetuation of violence and degradation of the very classes of human beings who are least equipped to respond that it is properly treated as outside the realm of protected discourse. The courts in the *Skokie* case expressed doubt that principles were available to single out racist speech for public limitation. This section attempts to construct a doctrinal and evidentiary world in which we might begin to draw the lines the *Skokie* courts could not imagine.

The alternative to recognizing racist speech as qualitatively different because of its content is to continue to stretch existing first amendment exceptions, such as the "fighting words" doctrine and the "content/conduct" distinction. This stretching ultimately weakens the first amendment fabric, creating neutral holes that remove protection for many forms of speech. Setting aside the worst forms of racist speech for special treatment is a non-neutral, value-laden approach that will better preserve free speech.

In order to distinguish the worst, paradigm example of racist hate messages from other forms of racist and nonracist speech, three identifying characteristics are suggested here:

1. The message is of racial inferiority;
2. The message is directed against a historically oppressed group; and
3. The message is persecutorial, hateful, and degrading.

Making each element a prerequisite to prosecution prevents opening of the dreaded floodgates of censorship.

The first element is the primary identifier of racist speech: racist speech proclaims racial inferiority and denies the personhood of target group members. All members of the target group are at once considered alike and inferior.

The second element attempts to further define racism by recognizing the connection of racism to power and subordination. Racism is more than race hatred or prejudice. It is the structural subordination of a group based on an idea of racial inferiority. Racist speech is particularly harmful because it is a mechanism of subordination, reinforcing a historical vertical relationship.

The final element is related to the "fighting words" idea. The language used in the worst form of racist speech is language that is, and is intended as, persecutorial, hateful, and degrading.

* * *

How can one argue for censorship of racist hate messages without encouraging a revival of McCarthyism? There is an important difference that comes from human experience, our only source of collective knowledge. We know, from our collective historical knowledge, that slavery was wrong. We know the unspeakable horror of the holocaust was wrong. We know white minority rule in South Africa is wrong. This knowledge is reflected in the universal acceptance of the wrongness of the doctrine of racial supremacy. There is no nation left on this planet that submits as its national self-expression the view that Hitler was right. South Africa is alone in its official policy of apartheid, and even South Africa, in making its case to the world community, is careful to avoid an explicit ideology of racial supremacy, preferring instead the rhetoric of one-step-at-a-time. At the universities, at the centers of knowledge of the international community, the doctrines of racial supremacy and racial hatred are again uniformly rejected. At the United Nations the same is true. We have fought wars and spilled blood to establish the universal acceptance of this principle. The universality of the principle, in a world bereft of agreement on many things, is a mark of collective human progress. The victim's perspective, one mindful of the lessons of history, thus accepts racist speech as *sui generis* and universally condemned.

Marxist speech, on the other hand, is not universally condemned. Marxism presents a philosophy for political organization, distribution of wealth and power, ordering of values, and promotion of social change. By its very content it is political speech going to the core of ongoing political debate. Many nations adhere to Marxist ideology, and it is impossible to achieve world consensus either for or against this view. Marxists teach in universities. While Marxist ideas are rejected and abhorred by many, Marxist thought, like liberal thought, neoconservative economic theory, and other conflicting structures for understanding life and politics, is part of the ongoing efforts of human beings to understand their world and improve life in it.

What is argued here, then, is that we accept certain principles as the shared historical legacy of the world community. Racial supremacy is one of the ideas we have collectively and internationally considered and rejected. As an idea connected to continuing racism and degradation of minority groups, it causes real harm to its victims. We are not safe when these violent words are among us.

Treating racist speech as *sui generis* and universally condemned on the basis of its content and the harmful effect of its content is precisely the censorship that civil libertarians fear. I would argue, however, that explicit content-based rejection of narrowly defined racist speech is more protective of civil liberties than the competing-interests tests or the likely-to-incite-violence tests that can spill over to censor forms of political speech.

Looking again to the emerging outsider jurisprudence, I derive basic principles: the need to fight racism at all levels, the value of explicit formal rules, and a fear of tyranny. These principles suggest the wisdom of legal intervention with only a narrowly defined class of racist hate propaganda.

A range of legal interventions, including the use of tort law and criminal law principles, is appropriate to combat racist hate propaganda. While the value of free speech can guide the choice of procedure—including evidentiary rules and burdens of persuasion—it should not completely remove recourse to the institution of law to combat racist speech. Racism as an acquired set of behaviors can be dis-acquired, and law is the means by which the state typically provides incentives for changes in behavior.

*   *   *

COMPELLED SUBSIDIZATION OF SPEECH

JOHANNS v. LIVESTOCK MARKETING ASSOCIATION

Robert Post

In recent years the Supreme Court has decided a spate of cases about the compelled subsidization of speech. All have involved federal statutes creating industry boards empowered to tax producers of specific agricultural products in order to promote and stabilize the market in those products. Some of these statutes were enacted during the New Deal era, whereas others are quite recent. In the past decade these statutes have been challenged on the ground that they compel producers to subsidize objectionable commercial advertisements. The resulting cases have raised conceptually difficult and complex First Amendment questions, which the Court has proved unable to master.

At first, in *Glickman v Wileman Bros. & Elliott*,[1] the Court upheld a federal marketing program for California summer fruits that required private parties to subsidize an advertising campaign. Dismissing claims that this mandated subsidization amounted to compelled speech in violation of the First Amendment, the Court in a narrow five-to-four opinion held that "our compelled speech case law . . . is clearly inapplicable to the regulatory scheme at issue here." Four years later the Court reversed course, and in *United States v United Foods, Inc.*[2] struck down a program designed to promote and stabilize the market in fresh mushrooms. The opinion, joined by six Justices, announced

From *Supreme Court Review* 195 (2005). Reprinted with permission of the University of Chicago Press.

that "First Amendment concerns apply" whenever the state requires persons to "subsidize speech with which they disagree."

The Court's opinion in *United Foods* sparked a cascade of lower-court decisions that rapidly developed what may be called compelled subsidization of speech doctrine, which in the remainder of this article I shall refer to as "CSSD." *United Foods* set forth the basic premise of CSSD: First Amendment scrutiny is triggered whenever someone is forced to pay for speech that she finds objectionable. Because taxation involves the compelled subsidization of government speech, an obvious difficulty with this premise is that it seems to imply that constitutional scrutiny is required every time a taxpayer disagrees with government messages supported by her tax dollars. This is plainly an untenable position, yet the seemingly inexorable pressure of CSSD led the Eighth Circuit in [in a lower court case] to conclude that "a determination that the expression at issue is government speech does not preclude First Amendment scrutiny in the compelled speech context."

The Supreme Court acted swiftly to check this radical implication of its own doctrine. Last Term in *Johanns v Livestock Marketing Ass'n*[3] it reversed the Eighth Circuit to hold "that compelled funding of government speech does not alone raise First Amendment concerns." Although *Johanns* is quite definite that citizens "have no First Amendment right not to fund government speech," it never offers a theoretical account of why taxation is an exception to the basic premise of CSSD. *Johanns* instead stresses the practical point that "it seems inevitable that funds raised by the government will be spent for speech and other expression to advocate and defend its own policies." The exemption accorded by *Johanns* to government speech is thus a blunt *ipse dixit*; it does not prompt the Court to reconsider the basic framework of CSSD.

This is unfortunate, for CSSD's failure to explain why taxation should not prompt constitutional scrutiny is merely the surface manifestation of deep conceptual insufficiencies. Indeed, I shall argue in this article that the fundamental premise of CSSD is flawed, and that the premise has accordingly generated a dangerously unstable doctrinal structure which *Johanns* patched but did not repair. It is simply not true that First Amendment concerns are implicated whenever persons are required to subsidize speech with which they disagree. My thesis is that CSSD cannot be rebuilt along theoretically defensible lines until we have some better explanation of when First Amendment review should be triggered and when it should not. Without such an explanation, the Court stands at risk of the kind of untoward consequences and embarrassing pirouettes that have afflicted its recent forays into this area.

I. CSSD AFTER JOHANNS

In 1985 Congress enacted the Beef Promotion and Research Act, which announced that it was "in the public interest to authorize the establishment... of an orderly procedure for financing (through assessments on all cattle sold in the United States and on cattle, beef, and beef products imported into the United States) and [for] carrying out a coordinated program of promotion and research designed to strengthen the beef industry's position in the marketplace and to maintain and expand domestic and foreign markets and uses for beef and beef products." The Act directed the Secretary of Agriculture to establish a "Cattlemen's Beef Promotion and Research Board," whose members would "be cattle producers and importers appointed by the Secretary," and in particular to establish a Beef Promotion Operating Committee, which would be composed of ten Board members elected by the Board "and ten producers elected by a federation that includes as members the qualified State beef councils." The function of the Committee was to "develop plans or projects of promotion and advertising, research, consumer information, and industry information, which shall be paid for with assessments collected by the Board."

The Act provided that the promotional campaigns of the Committee and the Board were to be subject to the approval of the Secretary of Agriculture, and that they were to be supported by an excise tax, or "checkoff," on the sale or importation of cattle or on the importation of beef products. Since 1988, "more than $1 billion has been collected through the checkoff and a large fraction of that sum has been spent on promotional projects authorized by the Beef Act—many using the familiar trademarked slogan 'Beef. It's What's for Dinner.'"

Two associations whose members paid the checkoff and several individuals who raised and sold cattle brought suit objecting to various statutory and constitutional aspects of the promotional program sponsored by the Beef Board and its Operating Committee. While their suit was pending, the Supreme Court decided *United States v United Foods, Inc.*, in which the Court, over the dissenting votes of Justices O'Connor, Ginsburg, and Breyer, upheld a challenge to the Mushroom Promotion, Research, and Consumer Information Act. The Act authorized the Secretary of Agriculture to create a Mushroom Council empowered to impose mandatory assessments on handlers of fresh mushrooms in order to serve the statute's goals of advancing projects of mushroom promotion, research, consumer information, and industry information. The Court concluded that requiring mushroom growers to subsidize a mushroom promotional campaign with which they disagreed violated their First Amendment rights.

The cattlemen amended their complaint to allege First Amendment violations of a similar nature. The Eighth Circuit concluded that "'[t]he beef checkoff program is, in all material respects, identical to the mushroom checkoff' at issue in *United Foods*." Although the Court in *United Foods* had pretermitted the claim that "the advertising here is government speech, and so immune from the scrutiny we would otherwise apply," the Eighth Circuit held that even on the assumption that the promotional programs sponsored by the Beef Board were government speech, compelled subsidization of the programs could be justified only if "the governmental interest in the commercial advertising under the Beef Act is sufficiently substantial to justify the infringement upon appellees' First Amendment right not to be compelled to subsidize that commercial speech." Answering that inquiry in the negative, the Eighth Circuit ruled that the beef checkoff program established by the Beef Promotion and Research Act was unconstitutional on its face.

The Supreme Court reversed the Eighth Circuit in *Johanns v Livestock Marketing Ass'n*. The opinion for the Court was authored by Justice Scalia. It was joined by Chief Justice Rehnquist and by Justices O'Connor, Thomas, and Breyer. Scalia began his analysis by dividing "First Amendment challenges to allegedly compelled expression" into two categories. He distinguished "true 'compelled speech' cases, in which an individual is obliged personally to express a message he disagrees with, imposed by the government," from "'compelled subsidy' cases, in which an individual is required by the government to subsidize a message he disagrees with, expressed by a private entity."

Acknowledging that the Court in *United Foods* had struck down "an assessment very similar to the beef checkoff, imposed to fund mushroom advertising," Scalia noted that *United Foods* had nevertheless rested "on the assumption that the advertising was private speech, not government speech." This assumption was decisive, because *Johanns* announced the categorical rule that individuals "have no First Amendment right not to fund government speech." Scalia did not seek to explain this rule, except to observe that "[s]ome of our cases have justified compelled funding of government speech by pointing out that government speech is subject to democratic accountability." The debate in *Johanns* was whether the advertisements sponsored by the beef checkoff program were in fact government speech. In the years after *United Foods*, lower courts had more or less come to the conclusion that the First Amendment did not prohibit the compulsory funding of government speech, and they had articulated an intricate jurisprudence to distinguish government from private speech. This jurisprudence asked two questions. The first focused on whether "the government nominally controls the production of advertisements, but as a practical matter has delegated control over the speech to a particular group that represents only one segment of the population." The second focused on whether persons were compelled to fund government speech through general taxation or instead through "assessments levied on a particular group."

Johanns flatly rejects both these factors. Even though the promotional campaigns of the Beef Board and its Operating Committee were supported by assessments levied specifically on beef producers, *Johanns* holds that the "First Amendment does not confer a right to pay one's taxes into the general fund, because the injury of compelled funding (as opposed to the injury of compelled speech) does not stem from the Government's mode of accounting." And even though as a practical matter the Beef Board and its Operating Committee were deliberately designed to include the interests of the beef industry, *Johanns* holds that "[w]hen, as here, the government sets the overall message to be communicated and approves every word that is disseminated, it is not precluded from relying on the government-speech doctrine merely because it solicits assistance from nongovernmental sources in developing specific messages." *Johanns* also deems it irrelevant that the promotional campaign subsidized by the Beef Board and its Operating Committee never announced that it was sponsored by the government, and indeed that the campaign seemed to disguise that fact by producing advertisements which typically displayed "the attribution 'Funded by America's Beef Producers.'"

Johanns holds that a First Amendment claim of compelled speech, as distinct from compelled subsidization of speech, would lie if the Beef Board's advertisements "were attributed" to individual plaintiffs. But such a claim of compelled speech could not be used to attack the Beef Promotion and Research Act on its face. At most it could be used to invalidate those particular applications of the Act in which specific plaintiffs could produce credible evidence that Beef Board advertisements were actually attributed to them. The Court could see no such evidence in the record.

Justice Thomas joined Scalia's opinion for the Court, but he wrote separately to emphasize his continuing allegiance to what he regarded as the fundamental premise of *United Foods*, which was "that '[a]ny regulation that compels the funding of advertising must be subjected to the most stringent First Amendment scrutiny.'" Thomas, like Scalia, did not explain why this principle did not apply to compelled funding of government speech. He pointed only to the brute practicalities of the situation: "I recognize that this principle must be qualified where the regulation compels the funding of speech that is the government's own. It cannot be that all taxpayers have a First Amendment objection to taxpayer-funded government speech, even if the funded speech is not 'germane' to some broader regulatory program."

Justice Breyer also authored a separate opinion. He had dissented in *United Foods* on the grounds "that the challenged assessments involved a form of economic regulation, not speech." Breyer joined the opinion of the Court in *Johanns* "[w]ith the caveat that I continue to believe that my dissent in *United Foods* offers a preferable approach." Justice Ginsburg concurred in the judgment of the Court. Although she refused to credit that the advertisements funded by the checkoff program were "government speech," because they were not "attributed to the Government," she nevertheless continued to maintain, as she had in *United Foods*, that "the assessments in these cases…qualify as permissible economic regulation."

Justice Souter authored the principal dissent; he was joined by Stevens and Kennedy. He began with the premise that the facts of *Johanns* were "on all fours with *United Foods*," which had struck down the Mushroom Promotion, Research, and Consumer Information Act because it "violated the growers' First Amendment right to refuse to pay for expression when they object to its content." Souter agreed with the Court that there was a "need to recognize the legitimacy of government's power to speak despite objections by dissenters whose taxes or other exactions necessarily go in some measure to putting the offensive message forward to be heard." But he argued that on the facts of *Johanns* the advertisements of the Beef Board and its Operating Committee ought not to be considered government speech.

Souter's argument is complex and not entirely transparent, but its gist is that infringements of the "presumptive autonomy" protected by the First Amendment against compelled subsidization of speech must be evaluated not only in light of the state's interest in requiring subsidization, but also with an eye to the precise forms of subsidization exacted by the state and to the mechanisms that could potentially serve as "an effective political check on forced funding for speech." Souter contrasted government speech supported by revenues secured through general taxation with government speech supported by revenues secured through narrowly targeted assessments, like those at issue in *Johanns*:

> [W]hen government funds its speech with general tax revenue, as it usually does, no individual taxpayer or group of taxpayers can lay claim to a special, or even a particularly strong, connection to the money spent (and hence to the speech funded). Outrage is likely to be rare, and disagreement tends to stay temperate. But the relative palatability of a remote subsidy shared by every taxpayer is not to be found when the speech is funded with targeted taxes. For then, as here, the particular interests of those singled out to pay the tax are closely linked with the expression, and taxpayers who disagree with it suffer a more acute limitation on their presumptive autonomy as speakers to decide what to say and what to pay for others to say.

Souter's basic point is that the "autonomy" of persons to refuse to fund speech with which they disagree grows more compromised as the link between the subsidy and the speech becomes closer and more direct. Speech supported by "a targeted assessment...makes the First Amendment affront more galling." In such circumstances "greater care is required to assure that the political process can practically respond to limit the compulsion...."

*   *   *

The exact function of political accountability in Souter's dissent is obscure. Souter writes as if accountability were necessary to check government taxation from becoming too violently inconsistent with the First Amendment interests of those forced to subsidize government speech. But why political accountability would perform this function is never explained. It is true that we can expect voters to cancel messages that they dislike, but voters have no particular reason to cancel those messages that especially violate the autonomy of taxpayers. It may be that cattlemen deeply object to, and find especially galling, a message that is quite popular with voters. Public approval of a message does not seem a plausible candidate for a mechanism to prevent the abuse of the autonomy of targeted taxpayers.

Souter proposes that the First Amendment interest protected by CSSD is the "autonomy" not to be connected through the medium of money to speech to which one objects. Souter invokes the "commonsense notion" that this "connection" can be "closer" or less close, depending upon the directness of the relationship between the subsidy and the speech it funds. As the connection grows closer, the violation of First Amendment autonomy grows greater; as the connection becomes more distant, the violation diminishes in significance. That is why for Souter the doctrinal notion of "government speech" is at most a label used to express the outcome of a detailed process of constitutional analysis and balancing. Souter's dissent is in fact carefully written to avoid the implication that "government speech" is a categorical exception to CSSD. Souter asks only whether the interests served by a particular instance of "government speech" are "sufficient to justify enforcement of a targeted subsidy to broadcast it."

In contrast, Scalia's majority opinion conceives "government speech" as a distinct category of expression that obliterates whatever First Amendment interest persons may have in not being required to subsidize the speech of others. Although Scalia apparently agrees with Souter that the underlying constitutional interest at stake is one of "personal autonomy," he conceptualizes the "government speech" exception to CSSD as categorical and without qualifications of degree. A First Amendment question is presented if persons are compelled to support the speech of a private individual, but not if persons are taxed, whether by a general tax or by a targeted assessment, to support the speech of the government. Scalia's approach seems to advance a clear and forceful rule, but it actually renders quite mysterious the nature of the First Amendment interests that CSSD aspires to protect. Exactly what kind of interests would require stringent First Amendment scrutiny to prevent the compelled subsidization of the expression of private parties, but no scrutiny at all to prevent the compelled subsidization of government speech?

The strangely dichotomous character of the First Amendment interests presupposed by Scalia is especially puzzling because we know that the First Amendment interests of persons in what Scalia at the outset of his opinion calls "true 'compelled speech' cases" do not disappear when persons are compelled to express the message of the government. Scalia cites two compelled speech cases: *West Virginia Board of Education v Barnette*,[4] in which schoolchildren were required to recite the Pledge of Allegiance, the text of which was set out by state regulation, and *Wooley v Maynard*,[5] in which George Maynard, a Jehovah's witness, was required to display the state motto of New Hampshire on the prefabricated license plate of his automobile. In each case the relevant message was composed by the government. In each case the First Amendment was interpreted to protect a right "to refrain from speaking at all," and in each case it did not matter whether the message whose utterance was compelled was that of the government or that of a private party.

Johanns itself establishes that there is no "government speech" exception to claims of compelled speech, for it holds that plaintiffs' allegation of compelled speech can succeed if they are able to prove on remand that the Beef Board's advertisements were "attributed" to them individually. Because *Johanns* holds that these advertisements are government speech, the Court necessarily concludes that plaintiffs have First Amendment interests in not being compelled to express government speech. But surely it is puzzling that First Amendment interests in not being compelled to speak are indifferent to whether the compelled speech is governmental or private, whereas First Amendment interests in not being compelled to subsidize speech depend entirely upon this distinction. Why should this be so?

What renders the question particularly disturbing is that Scalia's distinction between compelled speech cases and compelled subsidy cases is itself highly uncertain. In *Wooley*, for example, nobody could plausibly have imagined that George Maynard was actually speaking through the prefabricated license plate he was forced to display. Indeed (then) Justice Rehnquist dissented in *Wooley*, asking why there was "any 'speech' or 'speaking' in the context of this case.... The issue, unconfronted by the Court, is whether appellees, in displaying, as they are required to do, state license tags, the format of which is known to all as having been prescribed by the State, would be considered to be advocating political or ideological views."

The Court could not respond to Rehnquist's challenge; it could only vaguely mutter that "compelling the affirmative act of a flag salute [in *Barnette*] involved a more serious infringement upon personal liberties than the passive act of carrying the state motto on a license plate, but the difference is essentially one of degree." *Wooley* tells us that:

> Here, as in *Barnette*, we are faced with a state measure which forces an individual, as part of his daily life indeed constantly while his automobile is in public view to be an instrument for fostering public adherence to an ideological point of view he finds unacceptable.... New Hampshire's statute in

effect requires that appellees use their private property as a "mobile bill-board" for the State's ideological message or suffer a penalty, as Maynard already has.

Having one's car transformed into a "mobile billboard" for state messages is not precisely the same as being forced to speak. It is more like being forced to allow one's car to be used as a platform for the state to speak. This suggests that *Wooley* is not so much about George Maynard's First Amendment interest in not being forced to speak as it is about his First Amendment interest in not having his property appropriated to subsidize government speech. But *Johanns* seems to hold that this interest does not exist.

Souter's dissenting opinion is by contrast free from such internal tensions. He begins with the premise that a First Amendment autonomy interest is compromised whenever persons are required to subsidize speech with which they disagree, and he applies this premise to the context of government speech. Souter postulates that government speech subsidized by general taxation so minimally affects this autonomy interest as to be beyond judicial protection. But he concludes that this interest remains vivid and enforceable in the context of government speech supported by targeted assessments. This logic is faithful to the structure of CSSD as set forth in *United Foods*. The difficulty, however, is that Souter's dissent is based upon a false premise.

II. THE THEORETICAL FOUNDATIONS OF CSSD

Consider the case of *Banning v Newdow*,[6] in which Michael Newdow, the same prickly pro se litigant who challenged the constitutionality of the Pledge of Allegiance, was involved in an "ongoing child custody proceeding." Newdow objected to an order "to pay a portion of the attorney's fees of the child's mother." He advanced the argument, which no doubt would be unthinkable to a trained lawyer, that the order was unconstitutional because of CSSD. Newdow contended that requiring him to pay the attorneys' fees of his opponent was to compel him directly to subsidize expression with which he disagreed. Because the speech of the opposing attorney was private, Newdow's argument is not affected by the holding of *Johanns*, which purports to leave in place the doctrinal structure of CSSD that was established in *United Foods*.

Newdow's innovative argument should make us pause, because, in a literal sense, all statutes awarding attorneys' fees force "certain individuals to pay subsidies for speech to which they object." Souter's dissent in *Johanns* postulates an intrinsic "autonomy" interest in not being forced to pay for the speech of another, and it conceptualizes the strength of this interest as dependent upon the closeness of the connection between the subsidy and the speech it supports. We should note, therefore, that in Newdow's case this connection is as close and as direct as it is possible to be. And of course Newdow vigorously disagrees with the speech that he is forced to subsidize, for it is the expression of his opponent in litigation.

The logic of CSSD would thus support Newdow's position. Although that logic does not establish whether any particular attorneys' fees statute is constitutional or unconstitutional, it does raise the question of whether all such statutes must be given careful First Amendment attention. Newdow's argument forces us to ask whether we should regard all attorneys' fees statutes as raising constitutional concerns that need to be adjudicated on a statute-by-statute basis.

The *Newdow* case is only the tip of the iceberg, for there are many ordinary situations in which government compels persons directly to pay for the speech of third parties. Consider, for example, the requirement that cars can be registered only if mechanics are paid to certify that they meet smog emission standards. Consider the requirement that children can be enrolled in public school only if physicians are paid to certify their immunization records. Or consider the requirement that publicly owned businesses pay for the financial reports of independent accountants. We must decide whether these everyday government regulations have all along posed deep, unrecognized First Amendment issues, or whether, like the government speech at issue in *Johanns*, they do not present any constitutional question at all.

These examples suggest that there are strong reasons to conclude that First Amendment concerns are not always triggered whenever persons are forced to subsidize the speech of a third party. This conclusion would render CSSD consistent with First Amendment jurisprudence generally, because First Amendment concerns are not automatically activated whenever expression is restricted.... Constitutional review is triggered only when communication is regulated in a manner that implicates specific First Amendment values. As I have argued elsewhere, these values most conspicuously include democratic self-governance and participation in the construction of public opinion.

Just as the First Amendment is not triggered by all restrictions on speech, so the First Amendment is not triggered by all government compulsions to speak. In fact we experience such compulsions all the time, and no one regards them as raising constitutional issues. Examples range from compulsory jury service, to compulsory testimony before courts and legislatures, to compulsory reporting of vehicle accidents, to compulsory reporting of potential public health risks like those involving child abuse, to the myriad of public disclosures required by securities regulation, to the labeling requirements routinely required on consumer products. The very Beef Promotion and Research Act considered by *Johanns* provides that marketers and importers of beef and cattle shall "maintain and make available for inspection such books and records as may be required by the order and file reports at the time, in the manner, and having the content prescribed by" a "beef promotion and research order" issued by the Secretary of Agriculture.

There are thus innumerable circumstances in which the state forces persons to speak without raising First Amendment concerns. If speech can be compelled without triggering constitutional scrutiny, *a fortiori* the subsidization of speech can be required without raising First Amendment concerns. The First Amendment interest in not being compelled to subsidize particular speech derives from the First Amendment interest in not being compelled to express that particular speech....

CSSD, however, focuses specifically on the subsidization of objectionable speech. *United Foods* asserts that "First Amendment concerns apply" whenever the state requires persons to "subsidize speech with which they disagree." The basic logic seems to be that because First Amendment scrutiny should be triggered whenever a person is forced to speak in ways that she finds objectionable, First Amendment review ought also to be triggered whenever a person is forced to subsidize speech she finds objectionable. But the premise of this reasoning is false. First Amendment concerns are not automatically aroused when persons are forced to speak in ways that they find objectionable. Persons may experience as personally "galling" their obligation to testify before a court or a legislature; they may wish to refuse to pronounce a verdict as a juror; they may object to their responsibility to report a traffic accident; or they may find it repulsive to report an incident of child abuse. But in all these situations we nevertheless compel persons to speak without ever raising a First Amendment eyebrow.

*   *   *

These examples suggest that compelling persons to subsidize speech with which they disagree does not *automatically* arouse First Amendment concerns....

*   *   *

In the remainder of this essay...I shall postulate two simple heuristic principles that may prove helpful in educating our instincts in the context of CSSD. The principles function to connect the opaque and exotic circumstances of CSSD to the more familiar issues posed by cases involving compelled speech and restrictions on the subsidization of speech. I call these two principles the Non-Endorsement Principle and the Symmetry Principle.

The Non-Endorsement Principle is activated whenever subsidizing objectionable speech puts an individual in the position of appearing to endorse that speech. If the Non-Endorsement Principle applies, claims of compelled subsidization of speech merge into claims of compelled speech. Whenever the Non-Endorsement Principle applies, therefore, claims of compelled subsidization of speech will trigger constitutional review if claims of compelled speech would trigger constitutional review.

Wooley is best understood as a case involving the Non-Endorsement Principle. Although it is implausible to imagine that George Maynard was compelled actually to speak, it is clear that he was compelled to subsidize state speech by displaying the New Hampshire motto on the license plate of his car. The Court's reference to a "mobile billboard" suggests that it interpreted existing social conventions as supporting the conclusion that those who display slogans on their automobiles endorse those slogans. The particular way in which New Hampshire forced Maynard to subsidize its motto, therefore, implicated the Non-Endorsement Principle, which converted Maynard's claim of compelled subsidization of speech into a claim of compelled speech.

Because strict constitutional scrutiny would have been triggered if New Hampshire had compelled Maynard to affirm its motto, so strict constitutional scrutiny was triggered when New Hampshire instead forced Maynard to subsidize the display of its motto in a manner that could be understood as constituting endorsement. By contrast, if New Hampshire had merely required Maynard to display a license plate with numbers, it is very doubtful that First Amendment concerns would arise, because in such circumstances a claim of compelled speech would not trigger constitutional scrutiny. From a constitutional point of view, it would be no different than the state requiring Maynard to retain and display a social security card or a draft card. The application of the Non-Endorsement Principle thus does not trigger strict constitutional scrutiny unless, in the relevant context, a claim of compelled speech would trigger such scrutiny.

Not every subsidization of objectionable speech implicates the Non-Endorsement Principle. In *Prune Yard Shopping Center v Robins*,[7] for example, the Court held that state constitutional provisions authorizing "individuals to exercise free speech and petition rights on the property of a privately owned shopping center to which the public is invited" did not raise First Amendment concerns, even though these provisions required owners of shopping centers to make their property available for the speech of others with whom they could be in deep disagreement. The Court distinguished *Wooley* on the ground that the state constitutional provisions failed to implicate the Non-Endorsement Principle, because the views of persons "passing out pamphlets or seeking signatures for a petition . . . will not likely be identified with those of the owner."

The distinction between compelled subsidizations of speech that implicate the Non-Endorsement Principle and those that do not is neatly captured in *Johanns'* ruling that the case should be remanded to determine if plaintiffs can establish that the advertisements of the Beef Board and its Operating Committee were actually attributable to them individually. If the advertisements are not so attributable, plaintiffs' allegations would not implicate the Non-Endorsement Principle and accordingly their claim of compelled subsidization of speech would not merge with a claim of compelled speech.

The Symmetry Principle has two prongs. The first holds that if state restrictions on the ability of persons to pay for the speech of another do not raise First Amendment questions, so also state compulsions to pay for the speech of another will not, in the absence of special circumstances like a violation of the Non-Endorsement Principle, raise First Amendment questions. Although there are of course important differences between prohibitions of action and affirmative duties to act, these differences do not typically include First Amendment interests. If restrictions on the subsidization of speech do not raise First Amendment concerns, these concerns are unlikely to be created by the mere fact of legal compulsion, which does not independently infuse First Amendment values into transactions where these values are not otherwise present.

*   *   *

The second prong of the Symmetry Principle holds that if state restrictions on the ability of persons to pay for the speech of another do raise First Amendment questions, state requirements that persons affirmatively provide such support will likely trigger First Amendment review. I say "likely" because sometimes First Amendment interests are understood to inhere in the right of an audience to hear, rather than in the right of a speaker to communicate, and in such cases First Amendment scrutiny would be appropriate to review government efforts to restrict communication but not necessarily government efforts to compel communication. In the ordinary case, however, in which First Amendment rights attach to a speaker's decision to communicate or not to communicate, the Symmetry Principle holds that if a state restriction on the ability of a person to pay for speech triggers First Amendment review, so also will a state requirement that a person pay for speech, even if the Non-Endorsement Principle is not violated.

In *Buckley v Valeo*,[8] for example, the Court famously held that campaign "contribution and expenditure limitations" triggered First Amendment review because such requirements were constitutionally equivalent to direct "restrictions on political communication and association by persons, groups, candidates, and political parties." The Symmetry Principle would suggest that *Buckley* gives us good ground to believe that compelling persons to contribute to specific political candidates would also raise First Amendment questions.

The Court in fact drew this implication in *Abood v Detroit Board of Education*,[9] which held that serious First Amendment questions were raised by a state law creating an agency shop in which all employees were required to pay to the union that was their collective bargaining agent a fee that was equal in amount to union dues. *Abood* invoked *Buckley* to justify the conclusion that "[t]o compel employees financially to support their collective-bargaining representative has an impact upon their First Amendment interests. An employee may very well have ideological objections to a wide variety of activities undertaken by the union in its role as exclusive representative."

*   *   *

United Foods cites *Abood*…for the broad-ranging proposition that "mandated support is contrary to…First Amendment principles.…" This proposition now forms the basic premise of CSSD. In his *Johanns* dissent, Souter explicitly affirms this premise and attributes it to *Abood*.... Nothing that Scalia says in his majority opinion in *Johanns* in any way limits or disavows this premise, which therefore remains the law in CSSD cases that do not involve government speech. But this premise rests on a misreading of *Abood* and [similar cases]. These decisions do not hold that the compelled subsidization of speech always raises First Amendment concerns. They instead stand for the Symmetry Principle. They hold that if restrictions on subsidies for speech raise First Amendment concerns, so likely will mandated support for such speech.

The Symmetry Principle is helpful primarily because we have well-developed (if untheorized) intuitions about when restrictions on the funding of speech will trigger constitutional scrutiny. We can use these intuitions to guide us in the newer and far less familiar context of compelled subsidization of speech. *Johanns* illustrates the utility of this approach. The Symmetry Principle suggests that if government limitations on direct contributions to the state would not raise First Amendment concerns, so also, in the absence of special considerations like a violation of the Non-Endorsement Principle, compelled contributions to the state would not trigger First Amendment scrutiny. Since I very much doubt that we would regard such limitations as triggering First Amendment scrutiny, the Symmetry Principle would predict that the use of compulsory taxes to support government speech ought not to trigger First Amendment review.

*   *   *

This suggests that the fundamental constitutional question posed by the government speech exception in *Johanns* is whether the Beef Board advertisements, generically considered, should be understood as "speaking for" the private and particular views of the beef industry, which represents the perspective of one group in the community, or instead as "speaking for" the official views of the state, which represents the outlook of the whole community. Cases like *Glickman, United Foods,* and *Johanns* are difficult because the industry programs created by Congress are ambiguous mixtures of public and private, so that it is hard to characterize the promotional material that they produce. It is unclear whether to classify this material for constitutional purposes as expressing the private perspectives of the cattle industry or instead as expressing the public views of the state. The formalism of Scalia's opinion may be as satisfactory a way as any to resolve this question, because, as he notes, if "the government sets the overall message to be communicated and approves every word that is disseminated," it is fair to conclude that the message speaks for the official views of the government, rather than for the particular views of private industry.

Neither Scalia nor Souter can accept this explanation of the government speech exception, however, because each postulates that the fundamental First Amendment interest at issue in CSSD is autonomy, rather than participation in public debate. The difficulty with regarding autonomy as a fundamental First Amendment interest is that it is omnipresent; every restriction and compulsion will to some degree compromise autonomy. It is precisely for this reason that autonomy is not usefully regarded as a foundational First Amendment interest. Autonomy cannot explain why First Amendment interests are sometimes triggered and sometimes not.

To understand the actual shape of First Amendment jurisprudence, we must postulate a constitutional interest that is implicated in some circumstances, but not in all circumstances. If the circumstances in which an interest is involved happen to correspond to the actual pattern of First Amendment cases, we have a good candidate for the First Amendment interest that is in fact driving judicial decision making. The interest of autonomy, which would be compromised by compulsory taxation as well as by the compelled payment of attorneys' fees at issue in *Newdow*, does not well explain the configuration of existing or desirable First Amendment jurisprudence. The interest of participation in public debate, by contrast, which is involved neither in compelled contributions to the state nor in compelled contributions to a private lawyer in a private case, does have considerable explanatory power in explaining the government speech exception, as well as the contours of CSSD generally.

III. CONCLUSION

Johanns is a welcome development, but it leaves in place the central premise of CSSD, which is that *every* compelled subsidization of objectionable speech requires First Amendment review. This premise derives from a misreading of *Abood*..., and it gives clear doctrinal expression to the idea, advanced by both Scalia and Souter, that autonomy is a fundamental First Amendment interest which is always at stake whenever the state forces persons to pay for the speech of others. This idea is demonstrably false unless the Court plans to constitutionalize many common legal requirements that no one presently regards as raising First Amendment issues.

So long as the central premise of CSSD remains unrevised, however, the holding of *Johanns* can serve as nothing more than a kind of *force majeur* necessary to foreclose potentially embarrassing applications of the compelled subsidization of speech doctrine. The lesson of *Newdow* is that in the future the Court will be required to announce other equally ad hoc decisions. The only hope of avoiding a string of precedents as self-evidently ragged as the *Glickman–United Foods–Johanns* trilogy is to repudiate the premise of CSSD and to rethink the fundamental question of when the compelled subsidization of speech does and does not raise First Amendment issues. This may in turn require reconceptualizing the nature of the fundamental interests which the First Amendment should be interpreted to protect in the context of compulsions to speak. This essay is meant to be a first small step in that direction.

NOTES

1. 521 U.S. 457 (1997).
2. 533 U.S. 405 (2001).
3. 544 U.S. 550 (2005).
4. 319 U.S. 624 (1943).
5. 430 U.S. 705 (1977).
6. 119 Cal. App. 4th 438 (2004).
7. 47 U.S. 74 (1980).
8. 424 U.S. 1 (1976).
9. 431 U.S. 209 (1977).

POLITICAL MONEY AND FREEDOM OF SPEECH

Kathleen M. Sullivan

INTRODUCTION

There is much talk about political money in the wake of the 1996 election. Some find the sheer volume of money spent impressive: an estimated $3 billion on all elections, $660 million on electing the Congress, and $1 billion on the presidential election. Others focus on the questions raised about alleged fund-raising activities that are forbidden by existing laws, such as contributions to political parties by foreign nationals. Still others focus on "loopholes" in the existing laws that allow their nullification as a practical matter. Nearly all focus on the presumed special influence of large contributors on political outcomes.

Against this backdrop has arisen a hue and cry for campaign finance reform. Senators McCain and Feingold have revived a proposed Senate campaign finance reform bill that withered under filibuster in the 104th Congress; Representatives Shays and Meehan have introduced comparable bipartisan legislation in the House. President Clinton has endorsed those bills. Newly retired Democratic Senator Bill Bradley has called the McCain-Feingold proposal timid and advocates more sweeping reforms; he favors a constitutional amendment to overrule *Buckley v. Valeo*,[1] the 1976 Supreme Court decision holding that some campaign finance limits violate the right of free speech. Other prominent advocates of the overrule of *Buckley* include twenty-six legal scholars led by Ronald Dworkin, and twenty-four state attorneys general who argue that political money threatens the integrity of elections that it is their job to defend. Countless newspaper editorial pages have opined that the time is ripe—while public outrage is high—to finally do something about campaign finance reform. Voters in states such as California and Oregon have adopted ballot measures imposing limits on the financing of state election campaigns.

In short, the view that political money should be limited has become mainstream orthodoxy. Against this formidable array of thoughtful opinion, I offer here a contrary view. This essay first lays out briefly the current law of political money and the current landscape of proposals for its reform. It then offers a critical guide to the reformers' arguments by examining the political theories that more or less explicitly underlie them. It concludes that the much belittled constitutional case against campaign finance limits is surprisingly strong, and that the better way to resolve the anomalies created by *Buckley v. Valeo* may well be not to impose new expenditure limits on political campaigns, but rather to eliminate contribution limits.

I. THE LAW OF POLITICAL MONEY

In our political system, political campaigns are generally funded with private money—the candidates' own resources plus contributions of individuals, political parties, and organized groups. The presidential campaign is an exception, funded publicly since the 1976 campaign. In our system, candidates also communicate primarily through entities that are privately owned—the print and electronic press that provide candidates free news coverage and opportunities for paid political advertisements. One could imagine alternate systems, such as public funding of parties and candidate elections or public ownership of the communications media, but such systems are not our own, nor likely to be our own any time soon.

In the 1976 *Buckley* decision, the Court held that restrictions on political spending implicate freedom of speech. Invalidating some portions of the post-Watergate amendments to the Federal Elections Campaign Act but upholding others, the Court held that contributions to a candidate could constitutionally be limited, but expenditures could not, except as a condition of receiving public funds. Thus, after *Buckley*, candidates may spend all they want, unless they are presidential candidates who have taken public money; so may political parties, individuals, and organized groups such as political action committees (PACs)—as long as they act independently of the candidate. But direct donations to a candidate's campaign may be limited in amount. Under current federal law, an individual is limited in each election to contributing one thousand dollars to a candidate, five thousand dollars to a PAC, and twenty thousand dollars to a national party, and must keep the grand total to twenty-five thousand dollars. PACs may give only five thousand dollars to a candidate, five thousand dollars to another PAC, and fifteen thousand dollars to a national party. Political parties, too, face spending limits when they contribute to the campaigns of their candidates, though these are higher than those for PACs.

The split regime of *Buckley* thus authorizes government to limit the *supply* of political money, but forbids it to limit *demand*. Why the distinction? *Contributions*, the Court said, implicate lesser speech interests; they merely facilitate or associate the contributor with speech. They also raise the specter of "corruption" or the appearance of corruption—that is, the danger of a quid pro quo. *Expenditures*, the Court said, are more directly expressive, and involve no corruption—a candidate cannot corrupt herself, and those who spend independently of the candidate's campaign cannot reasonably expect a pay-back. Nor, held the Court, could spending limits be justified by the alternative rationale of equalizing political speaking power, because that rationale, the Court said, is "wholly foreign to the First Amendment." Thus, the Court held, the only way government may bring about political expenditure limits is through a quid pro quo of its own: government may induce a candidate to accept expenditure limits in exchange for public subsidies.

Various cogent criticisms have been leveled at the contribution/expenditure distinction. First, both contributions and expenditures may equally express political opinions. As Justice Thomas wrote last summer [in *Colorado Republican Federal Campaign Comm. v. Federal Election Comm'n*][2]:

> Whether an individual donates money to a candidate or group who will use it to promote the candidate or whether the individual spends the money to promote the candidate himself, the individual seeks to engage in political

expression and to associate with likeminded persons. A contribution is simply an indirect expenditure.

This argues for protecting both expenditures and contributions alike. Second, an "independent" expenditure may inspire just as much gratitude by the candidate as a direct contribution. This argues for regulating them both alike. Finally, it has been objected, it is unclear why expenditure limits may be induced with carrots if they may not be compelled with sticks. This argues for precluding private expenditure limits even as a condition of public subsidies.

These inconsistencies arise from the *Buckley* Court's attempt to solve an analogical crisis by splitting the difference. *Buckley* involved nothing less than a choice between two of our most powerful traditions: equality in the realm of democratic polity, and liberty in the realm of political speech. The Court had to decide whether outlays of political money more resemble voting, on the one hand, or political debate, on the other. The norm in voting is equality: one person, one vote. The norm in political speech is negative liberty: freedom of exchange, against a backdrop of unequal distribution of resources (it has been said that freedom of the press belongs to those who own one). Faced with the question of which regime ought to govern regulation of political money, the Court in effect chose a little of both. It treated campaign contributions as more like voting, where individual efforts may be equalized, and campaign expenditures as more like speech, where they may not.

II. LEADING REFORM PROPOSALS

Currently on the table are three types of reform proposals to impose new restrictions on political money. One advocates further limiting campaign contributions. The second proposes more conditioning of benefits upon corresponding "voluntary" limits on private spending. The third would place outright restrictions on campaign expenditures. The first two seek to operate within the *Buckley* framework; the third would overrule *Buckley* in part.

The first type of reform proposal would "close loopholes" in the existing regulatory scheme by extending the reach of contribution limits. For example, there are currently no restrictions on contribution "bundling" by intermediaries. One political entrepreneur may collect several individual contributions of one thousand dollars each and turn over the entire sum to the candidate, PAC, or party—taking political credit for a much larger amount than she personally could have contributed. Some reform proposals, such as McCain-Feingold, would treat such "bundled" contributions as contributions by the intermediary, and therefore subject to the otherwise applicable contribution limits. In other words, no more bundling.

Other such proposals would impose contribution limits on so-called "soft money"—those sums that now may be given without limit by individuals, PACs, and even corporations and labor unions (who are forbidden to give directly to candidates) to political parties for purposes of grass-roots "party-building" activities. Since the 1988 campaign, use of soft money to finance de facto campaign advertisements has proliferated. Advertisements celebrating one's party, its stand on issues, or the accomplishments of its leadership, after all, do serve to build party loyalty; but to the untutored eye, they may be difficult to distinguish from campaign ads. The same is true of soft money ads attacking the other party. The amount of soft money raised by the two major parties combined has increased from $89 million in 1992 to $107 million in 1994 to roughly $250 million in 1996. Some reform proposals, again including McCain-Feingold, would limit soft money contributions. The Democratic National Committee has announced its intention to limit annual soft money contributions from an individual, corporation, or union to one hundred thousand dollars, and President Clinton said that the Democratic Party would stop taking any soft money if the Republicans would do the same.

*   *   *

The second category of reform proposal would find new means to use public funds or other public benefits to induce candidates to agree to "voluntary" spending limits—a practice that *Buckley* held constitutional, at least as to full public financing of presidential campaigns. Extending full public funding with attached spending limits from presidential to congressional campaigns would be the most obvious version of such reform, but is probably politically infeasible. Some proposals seek to offer smaller carrots, including ones that would not directly incur public expense. For example, the McCain-Feingold Senate bill would extract from broadcasters free and discounted broadcast time. The bill would in turn give the time, as well as postage discounts, to those Senate candidates who complied with specified spending limits. California's Proposition 208 would give free space in the ballot statement and allow higher contributions to candidates who adopted spending limits.

Such proposals, too, raise First Amendment questions despite the public funding ruling in *Buckley*. For example, while a private funding ban might reasonably further the goal of full public financing of an election—in order to level the playing field—it is hardly clear that private spending limits are equally justified by the relatively trivial communications subsidies proposed in these bills. And of course, the broadcasters might object to the extraction of "free" air time as an unconstitutional compulsion of speech.

The third, most dramatic type of proposal would overrule the expenditure holding in *Buckley* and permit spending limits outright. Since the current Court seems quite uninterested in overruling *Buckley*, the most plausible vehicle for such a reform would be some type of constitutional amendment. Most advocates of such a reform support an amendment authorizing Congress to reimpose expenditure limits as under the pre-*Buckley* status quo, while leaving the authority to impose contribution limits intact.

III. THE POLITICAL THEORY OF CAMPAIGN FINANCE REFORM, OR THE SUPPOSED SEVEN DEADLY SINS OF POLITICAL MONEY

What political theory supports arguments for campaign finance reform? Arguments for greater limits on political contributions and expenditures typically suggest that any claims for individual liberty to spend political money ought to yield to an overriding interest in a well-functioning democracy. But what is meant by democracy here? The answer is surprisingly complex; several distinct arguments that democracy requires campaign finance limits are often lumped together. I will try to disaggregate them and critically assess each one. The reformers might be said to have identified seven, separate, supposedly deadly sins of unregulated political money.

A. POLITICAL INEQUALITY IN VOTING

The first argument for campaign finance limits is that they further individual rights to political equality among voters in an election. This argument starts from the principle of formal equality of suffrage embodied in the one person, one vote rule that emerged from the reapportionment cases. Each citizen is entitled to an equal formal opportunity, ex ante, to influence the outcome of an election. Moreover, each person's vote is inalienable; it may not be traded to others for their use, nor delegated to agents. Literal vote-buying is regarded as a paradigm instance of undemocratic conduct. We no longer countenance gifts of turkeys or bottles of liquor to voters on election day, nor the counting of dead souls. These qualities of voting distinguish the electoral sphere from the marketplace, where goods and services, unlike votes, are fungible, commensurable, and tradeable.

Reformers often proceed from the premise of equal suffrage in elections to the conclusion that equalization of speaking power in electoral campaigns is similarly justifiable in furtherance of democracy. The most radical of such proposals would bar expenditures of private campaign funds altogether, and limit candidates to spending public funds allocated to each voter equally in the form of vouchers that could be used solely for election-related speech. The principle here would be one person, one vote, one dollar.

More commonly, however, the analogy to voting is meant to be suggestive, not literal; few go so far as to say that campaign finance limits are constitutionally compelled, as equipopulous districts are. Nor do most advocates of campaign finance reform argue for literal equality in electoral expenditures; the asserted right to equal political influence on the outcome of electoral campaigns is usually depicted as aspirational. But reformers argue that the goal of equal citizen participation in elections at least helps to justify campaign finance limits as constitutionally permissible. On this view, campaign finance amounts to a kind of shadow election, and unequal campaign outlays amount to a kind of metaphysical gerrymander by which some votes count more than others in that shadow election.

Such arguments from formal equality of the franchise to campaign finance restrictions, however, often fail to articulate a crucial intermediate step: that political finance sufficiently resembles voting as to be regulable by the equality norms that govern voting. There is an alternative possibility: that political finance more resembles political speech than voting. That is the analogy drawn by the *Buckley* Court, at least with respect to expenditures. The choice of analogy is crucial. In the formal realm of voting—like other formal governmental settings, such as legislative committee hearings and trials in court—speech may be constrained in the interest of the governmental function in question. For example, at a town meeting, Robert's Rules of Order govern to ensure that orderly discussion may take place; at a trial, witnesses testify not to all they know but to what they are asked about, subject to rules of evidence and the constraints of relevant rights of the parties. Likewise, one voter does not get ten votes merely because he feels passionately about a candidate or issue.

By contrast, in the informal realm of political speech—the kind that goes on continuously between elections as well as during them—conventional First Amendment principles generally preclude a norm of equality of influence. Political speakers generally have equal rights to be free of government censorship, but not to command the attention of other listeners. Under virtually any theory of the justification for free speech, legislative restrictions on political speech may not be predicated on the ground that the political speaker will have too great a communicative impact, or his competitor too little. Conventional First Amendment norms of individualism, relativism, and antipaternalism preclude any such affirmative equality of influence—not only as an end-state but even as an aspiration. Indeed, such equality of participation as speakers in political debate is foreign even under the more collectivist approach to political speech outlined by Alexander Meiklejohn, who famously noted that the First Amendment "does not require that, on every occasion, every citizen shall take part in public debate.... What is essential is not that everyone shall speak, but that everything worth saying shall be said."

A few perceptive reform advocates have noticed this problem and sought to fill in the missing step—the analogy between political finance and voting that would make equality norms relevant to both. For example, Ronald Dworkin, who largely accepts arguments for unfettered political speech in other contexts, rests his argument for campaign finance limits on the proposition that the right to equal participation as voters must be understood to entail a corollary right to equal participation as advocates in the electoral campaigns that precede and determine the vote:

> Citizens play two roles in a democracy. As voters they are, collectively, the final referees or judges of political contests. But they also participate, as individuals, in the contests they collectively judge: they are candidates, supporters, and political activists; they lobby and demonstrate for and against government measures, and they consult and argue about them with their fellow citizens....(W)hen wealth is unfairly distributed and money dominates politics,...though individual citizens may be equal in their vote and their freedom to hear the candidates they wish to hear, they are not equal in their own ability to command the attention of others for their own candidates, interests, and convictions.

In other words, formal equality of voting power implies a corollary right to equality in the opportunity to speak out in politics—at least in the particular subset of political speech that is made in connection with electoral campaigns.

But what are the boundaries of an electoral campaign? Dworkin does not suggest that equalization of speaking power is a satisfactory justification for limitations of political speech in other contexts. Yet his own examples belie any easy distinction between the formal realm of electoral discourse, which he would regulate, and the informal realm of ongoing political discourse, which he presumably would not. For example, he lists "lobbying" and "demonstrations" as examples of relevant forms of citizen participation. But lobbying and demonstrations could not, without great alteration in ordinary First Amendment understandings, be regulated on the ground that their leaders had amassed too many resources. Further, elections are seamlessly connected to the informal political debates that continue in the periods between them. The more electoral campaign speech is continuous with such ordinary informal political discourse, the less campaign finance resembles voting, and the more it partakes of a realm of inevitable inequality.

The reformers might answer that the equality principle could be confined to speech made expressly by candidates or their committees during formal electoral campaigns, defined by reference to some particular period in relation to elections. But now practical difficulties arise even as analytical difficulties subside. Such an approach would leave unregulated advocacy that redounds to the benefit of candidates by persons, parties, and organizations independent of them. To the extent such independent speech operates as a substitute for express candidate speech—even if an imperfect one—the principle of equality of voter participation advanced by the limits on formal campaign expenditures will be undermined.

An alternate response by reformers might be to question conventional First Amendment principles generally, and to assert political equality as a justification for regulating a wide range of informal political discourse. Such an approach raises large questions that go beyond the topic here. The key point for now is simply that, short of major revision of general First Amendment understandings, campaign finance reform may not be predicated on equality of citizen participation in elections unless electoral speech can be conceptually severed from informal political discourse. But formal campaign speech has so many informal political substitutes that this proposition is difficult to sustain.

B. Distortion

A second argument against unregulated private campaign finance is related to the first, but focuses less on individual rights than on collective consequences. This argument says that the unequal deployment of resources in electoral campaigns causes the wrong people to get elected, distorting the true preferences of voters. Good candidates who cannot surmount the high financial barriers to entry never get to run, and the choice among those who do is influenced by spending power that is not closely correlated to the popularity of the candidate's ideas. On this view, unequal funding leads both candidates and voters to misidentify the electorate's actual preferences and intensities of preference.

The Supreme Court has accepted such an argument as sufficient to justify some administrative burdens on the deployment of political money. In *Austin v. Michigan Chamber of Commerce*,[3] the Court upheld a state requirement that corporations (except nonprofit corporations organized solely for ideological purposes) make political expenditures solely from separate segregated political funds, not from their general treasuries. The Court reasoned that the government's interest in preventing the "distortion" of the apparent strength of political preferences justified such a segregation requirement. A corporation that spent, for political purposes, money raised for investment purposes, would make it appear that there was more enthusiasm for the ideas it backed than was warranted. Funds raised for expressly political purposes and segregated in a separate political fund or corporate PAC, by contrast, would represent a more accurate proxy for the popularity of the ideas they supported.

Campaign finance reformers would extend this antidistortion principle beyond the particular problems of the corporate form at issue in *Austin*. They suggest that the ability to amass political funds in general does not correlate closely with voter preferences. Rather, the unequal distribution of campaign resources leads to misrepresentation of constituents' actual preferences and intensities of preference. The wealthy (or those who are good at fund-raising) can spend more money on a candidate they care relatively little about than can the poor (or those who are inept at fundraising) on a candidate to whom they are passionately committed. To the extent such "distorted" campaign speech influences voting, candidates will be elected and platforms endorsed that differ from what voters would otherwise choose.

This argument has both practical and conceptual difficulties. First, a candidate's ability to attract funds is at least to some extent an indicator of popularity. Money may flow directly in response to the candidate's ideas or indirectly in response to the candidate's popularity with others as reflected in poll numbers and the like. To the extent that fundraising accurately reflects popularity, the reformers exaggerate the degree of distortion. Second, there are limits to how far private funding can permit a candidate to deviate from positions acceptable to the mass of noncontributing voters: the free press will to some extent correct information provided in the candidate's advertisements, and polls will discipline the candidate to respond to preferences other than those of his wealthiest backers.

A third and deeper problem is that the concept of "distortion" assumes a baseline of "undistorted" voter views and preferences. But whether any such thing exists exogenously to political campaigns is unclear. Popular attitudes about public policy do not exist in nature, but are formed largely in response to cues from political candidates and party leaders. Moreover, the institutional press—itself owned by large corporations commanding disproportionate power and resources—plays a large role in shaping public opinion. Any attempt to equalize campaign spending would still leave untouched any "distortion" from the role of the press.

C. CORRUPTION, OR POLITICAL INEQUALITY IN REPRESENTATION

A third argument for limiting political contributions and expenditures is often made under the heading of fighting political "corruption." This is a misnomer. Properly understood, this argument is a variation on the political inequality argument. But unlike the first argument above, it focuses not on the unequal influence of voters on elections, but on the elected legislators' unequal responsiveness to different citizens once in office. The charge against unregulated political money here is that it makes citizens unequal not in their ability to elect the candidates of their choice, but in their ability to affect legislative outcomes.

The Court in *Buckley* held contribution limits permissible to prevent "corruption" or the appearance of corruption of legislators by contributors of significant sums. Popular rhetoric about political money often employs similar metaphors: polls show substantial majorities who say that Congress is "owned" by special interests or "for sale" to the highest bidder. It is important to note, however, that the "corruption" charged here is not of the Tammany Hall variety. There is no issue of personal inurement; the money is not going into candidates' pockets but into television advertisements, the earnings of paid political consultants, and various other campaign expenses that increase the chances of election or reelection. This is true a fortiori for expenditures made independent of the candidate's campaign.

The claimed harm here is not, as the term "corruption" misleadingly suggests, the improper treatment of public office as an object for market exchange, but a deviation from appropriate norms of democratic representation. Officeholders who are disproportionately beholden to a minority of powerful contributors, advocates of finance limits say, will shirk their responsibilities to their other constituents, altering decisions they otherwise would have made in order to repay past contributions and guarantee them in the future. Thus, properly understood, the "corruption" argument is really a variant on the problem of political equality: unequal outlays of political money create inequality in political representation.

Again, the difficulties with the argument are both practical and conceptual. First, political money is not necessarily very effective in securing political results. The behavior of contributors provides some anecdotal support: Many corporate PACs, to borrow Judge Posner's phrase, are "political hermaphrodites"; they give large sums to both major parties. This hedging strategy suggests a weak level of confidence in their ability to obtain results from any particular beneficiary of their contributions.

President Clinton captured the same point at a press conference where he said that he gives major donors an opportunity for "a respectful hearing" but not a "guaranteed result." While this comment might elicit skepticism, the proposition that campaign donations are a relatively unreliable investment has empirical support. Various studies of congressional behavior suggest that contributions do not strongly affect congressional voting patterns, which are for the most part dominated by considerations of party and ideology. Of course, such evidence may be countered by noting that contributors may be repaid in many ways besides formal floor votes—for example, by relatively invisible actions in agenda-setting and drafting in committees. Furthermore, the few votes that are dominated by contributions may occur when there is the greatest divergence between contributors' and other constituents' interests. Still, the case that contributions divert representative responsiveness is at best empirically uncertain, and not a confident basis for limiting political speech.

A second and deeper problem with the "corruption" argument, once it is properly recast as an argument about democratic representation, is conceptual. The argument supposes that official action should respond to the interests of all constituents, or to a notion of the public good apart from the aggregation of interests, but, in any event, not to the interests of a few by virtue of their campaign outlays. But legislators respond disproportionately to the interests of some constituents all the time, depending, for example, on the degree of their organization, the intensity of their interest in particular issues, and their capacity to mobilize votes to punish the legislator who does not act in their interests. On one view of democratic representation, therefore, there is nothing wrong with private interest groups seeking to advance their own ends through electoral mobilization and lobbying, and for representatives to respond to these targeted efforts to win election and reelection. It is at least open to question why attempts to achieve the same ends through amassing campaign money are more suspect, at least in the absence of personal inurement.

But the question whether disproportionate responsiveness to contributors is ultimately consistent with democratic representation need not be answered to see the problem with the reformers' argument. That problem is that selecting one vision of good government is not generally an acceptable justification for limiting speech, as campaign finance limits do. Rather, what constitutes proper representation is itself the most essentially contested question protected by freedom of speech. The ban on seditious libel, the protection of subversive advocacy, and the general hostility to political viewpoint discrimination illustrate that free speech, under current conceptions, protects debates about what constitutes proper self-government from ultimate settlement by legislatures. To be sure, legislatures are often permitted or compelled to select among democratic theories, or to privilege one version of representation over its competitors in setting up the formal institutions of government. "One person, one vote," for example, privileges egalitarian conceptions over various alternatives—such as the inegalitarian representation provided by the United States Senate. But the right to speak—and, it might be added, to petition—includes the right to challenge any provisional settlement a legislature might make of the question of what constitutes appropriate democratic representation.

In other words, the "anticorruption" argument for campaign finance reform claims the superiority of a particular conception of democracy as a ground for limiting speech. As a result, it runs squarely up against the presumptive ban on political viewpoint discrimination. Campaign finance reformers necessarily reject pluralist assumptions about the operation of democracy and would restrict speech in the form of political money to foster either of two alternative political theories. First, they might be thought to favor a Burkean or civic republican view, in which responsiveness to raw constituent preferences of any kind undermines the representative's obligation to deliberate with some detachment about the public good. Alternatively, they might be thought to favor a populist view in which the representative ought to be as close as possible to a transparent vehicle for plebiscitary democracy, for the transmission of polling data into policy. Either way, they conceive democracy as something other than the aggregation of self-regarding interests, each of which is free to seek as much representation as possible. But surely the endorsement of civic republicanism or populism—or any other vision of democracy—may not normally serve as a valid justification for limiting speech. Legislators may enforce an official conception of proper self-government through a variety of means, but not by prohibiting nonconforming expression.

Campaign finance reformers might object that, after all, campaign finance limits in no way stop would-be pluralists from *advocating* pluralism, but only from practicing it. The utterances being silenced are performative, not argumentative. Such a response, however, is in considerable tension with a long tradition of First Amendment protection for symbolic and associative conduct. A further objection might be that this argument extends only to legislative campaign finance reform, and not to a constitutional amendment such as Senator Bradley and others have proposed. That is surely correct, as an amendment could obviously revise the existing First Amendment conceptions on which the argument rests. But, apart from general reasons to tread cautiously in amending the Constitution, it might well be thought especially risky to attempt by amendment to overrule a constitutional decision that is part of the general fabric of First Amendment law, as the anomaly created by the new amendment might well have unanticipated effects on other understandings of free speech.

D. CARPETBAGGING

A fourth strand of the reform argument is a variant of the third, with special reference to geography. Except in presidential elections, we vote in state or local constituencies. The fundamental unit of representation is geographic. But money travels freely across district and state lines. Thus, political money facilitates metaphysical carpetbagging. Contributions from or expenditures by nonconstituent individuals and groups divert a legislator's representation away from the constituents in his district and toward nonconstituents, whether they are foreign corporations or national lobbies. Various reform proposals seek to limit carpetbagging by localizing funding: McCain-Feingold, for example, would require candidates not only to limit expenditures but also to raise a minimum percentage of contributions from residents of their home state in order to receive public benefits, such as broadcast and postage discounts.

Again, this seeks to decide by legislation a question of what constitutes proper representation. To some, it might be legitimate for a legislator to consider the views of national lobbies. For example, those lobbies might share strong overlapping interests with her own constituents. Or the legislator might conceive her obligation as running to the nation as well as a particular district. For the reasons just given, a privileged theory of what constitutes proper political representation cannot serve as an adequate ground for limitation of speech, for free speech is itself the central vehicle for debating that very question.

E. Diversion of Legislative and Executive Energies

A fifth critique of the current role of political money, made often by politicians themselves and sometimes elaborated as an argument for campaign reform, is that fundraising takes too much of politicians' time. Many think that incumbents spend so much time fundraising that governance has become a part-time job.

This argument supposes a sharp divide between the public activity of governing and the private role of fundraising. But this distinction is hardly clear. The "marketing" involved in fundraising consists principally of conveying and testing response to information about past and future policy positions. How this differs from the standard material of all political campaigning is unclear, and it may well be continuous with governing. If the need for fundraising were eliminated, legislators would still have to nurture their constituencies in various ways between elections. Some might think that nurturing grass roots is a more wholesome activity than nurturing fat cats; but in that case, the diversion of energies problem simply collapses back into the problem of inequality in political representation discussed earlier. To the extent the candidate makes secret promises to PACs or wealthy individuals that would be unpopular with the mass of the electorate, there are strong practical limits to such strategies, such as the danger of press exposure and constituent retaliation.

However serious the problem of incursion on the candidate's time might be, one thing is clear: the split regime of *Buckley* exacerbates it. Contribution limits mean that a candidate has to spend more time chasing a larger number of contributors than she would have to do if contributions could be unlimited in amount. Concern about time, therefore, may involve a tradeoff with concern about disproportionate influence.

F. QUALITY OF DEBATE

A sixth critique of the unregulated outlay of political money arises on the demand side rather than the supply side. The problem, in a word, is television. Where does all this political money go? The biggest expense is the cost of purchasing advertising time on television (though increasingly, political consultants take a hefty share). The critics regard repetitious, sloganeering spot advertisements as inconsistent with the enlightened rational deliberation appropriate to an advanced democracy. It is not clear what golden age of highminded debate they hark back to; the antecedent of the spot ad is, after all, the bumper sticker. Nonetheless, these critics clearly aspire to something wiser and better. Ronald Dworkin's lament is representative: "The national political 'debate' is now directed by advertising executives and political consultants and conducted mainly through thirty-second, 'sound bite' television and radio commercials that are negative, witless, and condescending." Political expenditure limits, some suggest, would cut off the supply of oxygen to this spectacle and force candidates into less costly but more informative venues such as written materials and town hall debates.

To the extent this rationale for campaign finance reform is made explicit, it would appear flatly precluded by conventional First Amendment antipaternalism principles. Permitting limitations on speech because it is too vulgar or lowbrow would wipe out a good many pages of *U.S. Reports*. Surely a judgment that speech is too crass or appeals to base instincts is a far cry from Robert's Rules of Order or other principles of ordered liberty consistent with government neutrality toward the content of speech.

In any event, the indirect means of limiting expenditures may not do much to solve this problem. Why not directly ban political advertising on television outright? Then everyone could campaign on smaller budgets. British politicians, for example, are barred from taking out paid spots on the airwaves. But Britain has strong parties and small districts; we have neither. Banning television advertising in our political culture would impair politicians', especially challengers', ability to reach large masses of the electorate. Banning television advertisements might make us more republican, but it is hardly clear that it would make us more democratic. Moreover, the special First Amendment dispensation the Court has shown for broadcast regulation is increasingly tenuous, and has not been extended to other, increasingly competitive media. To be fully effective, a ban on television advertising might have to extend to cable and the Internet, where the constitutional plausibility of regulation is even more dubious.

G. LACK OF COMPETITIVENESS

Finally, a last argument would locate the key problem in current campaign finance practices in the advantage it confers on incumbents over challengers. Here the claim is that a healthy democracy depends on robust political competition and that campaign finance limits are needed to "level the playing field." The reformers contend that unfettered political money confers an anticompetitive advantage upon incumbents. This advantage arises because incumbents participate in current policymaking that affects contributors' interests. Thus, they enjoy considerable fundraising leverage while in office, and indeed, incumbents received on average four times as much in contributions than challengers in the 1996 congressional election. This incumbent advantage, reformers argue, limits turnover and makes challengers less effective at monitoring and checking incumbents' responsiveness. It is no accident that, for such reasons, some prominent supporters of campaign finance reform, such as Republican Senator Fred Thompson of Tennessee, a cosponsor of the McCain-Feingold bill, are also prominent supporters of term limits.

But there is some practical reason to think this argument gets the competitiveness point backwards. Campaign finance limits themselves may help to entrench incumbents in office. Incumbency confers enormous nonfinancial advantages: name recognition, opportunity to deliver benefits, publicity from the free press, and the franking privilege. To offset these advantages, challengers must amass substantial funds. Challengers' lack of prominence may make it more difficult for them to raise funds from large numbers of small donations. They may therefore depend more than incumbents on concentrated aid from parties, ideologically sympathetic PACs, or even wealthy individual private backers. Of course, once again, contribution limits under the split regime of *Buckley* exacerbate the problem, as incumbents are more likely to be able to raise a large number of capped contributions than challengers can.

The effect of regulation or nonregulation on the competitiveness of elections is a difficult empirical question. But any prediction that campaign regulation will increase electoral competitiveness and turnover is, by virtue of its very empirical uncertainty, at least a questionable ground for limiting political speech.

CONCLUSION

The discussion to this point has sought to disentangle the separate elements of the campaign finance reformers' arguments about the evils of unregulated political money and to suggest why the proposed cure for the seven deadly sins might be worse than the disease, even on the reformers' own assumptions. I have sought also to show why limits on political money are in deeper tension with current First Amendment conceptions than is often supposed. Buckley's declaration of the impermissibility of redistribution of speaking power has been widely criticized; the effort here has been to show alternative reasons why the justifications for campaign finance reform might trigger First Amendment skepticism. These reasons include the inseverability of campaign speech from ordinary political discourse and the viewpoint basis inherent in campaign finance reform's selection of one conception of democratic representation over its competitors as a basis for curtailing speech.

If these alternative reasons have any force, then it is easier to see why campaign finance reform is especially prone to following the law of unintended consequences: for example, limits on individual contributions helped to increase the number of PACs; limits on hard money contributions stimulated the proliferation of soft money contributions; and limits on contributions generally spurred the growth of independent expenditures. The reason is not just that the demand for political money is peculiarly inelastic and thus, like the demand for other addictive substances, likely to create black markets in the shadow of regulation. The reason is that grim efforts to close down every "loophole" in campaign finance laws will inevitably trench unacceptably far upon current conceptions of freedom of political speech. Even if formal campaign expenditures and contributions are limited, the reformers' justifications attenuate as the law reaches the informal political speech that serves as a partial substitute for formal campaign speech. Without altering conventional free speech norms about informal political discourse, there are outer limits on the ability of any reform to limit these substitution effects.

What scenario are we left with if both political expenditure and contribution limits are deemed unconstitutional? Will political money proliferate indefinitely, along with its accompanying harms? Not necessarily, provided that the identity of contributors is required to be vigorously and frequently disclosed. Arguments against compelled disclosure of identity, strong in contexts where disclosure risks retaliation, are weaker in the context of attempts to influence candidate elections, as the *Buckley* decision itself recognized in upholding the disclosure requirements of the 1974 FECA amendments. Weekly disclosure in the newspapers, or better, daily reporting on the Internet, would be a far cry from earlier failed sunshine laws. If the lists of names and figures seemed too boring to capture general attention, enterprising journalists could "follow the money" and report on any suspect connections between contributions and policymaking.

Under this regime—in which contributions and expenditures were unlimited, but the identities of contributors were made meaningfully public—there would be at least three reasons for modest optimism that the harms the reformers fear from unlimited political money would in fact be limited.

A. INCREASED SUPPLY

If contributions, like expenditures, could not be limited in amount, the total level of contributions might be expected to increase as there might be a net shift from expenditures to contributions. The supply of political money to candidates would be increased. This might be expected to lower the "price" to the candidate of a political contribution. With more quids on offer, a politician has less reason to commit to any particular quo. In this politicians' buyers' market, concerns about unequal political influence that arise under the misleading "corruption" heading would arguably attenuate, and contributors might curtail their outlays in response to their declining marginal returns.

B. Decreased Symbolic Costs from Subterfuge

If contributions could be made in unlimited amounts, would-be contributors would not have to resort to the devices of independent advertisements or party contributions as substitutes. Public perception of a campaign finance system gone out of control rests at least in part on the view that politicians, parties, and donors skirt existing laws by exploiting evasive "loopholes." To the extent that all functional contributions are made as explicit contributions, the symbolic costs of the current split regime of *Buckley* would decrease.

C. Voter Retaliation

With contributions fully disclosed and their effects on political outcomes subject to monitoring by the free press, voters would be empowered to penalize candidates whose responsiveness to large contributors they deemed excessive. Voters could do retail what campaign finance reform seeks to do wholesale: encourage diversification in the sources of campaign funding. Political challengers could capitalize on connections between political money and incumbents' official actions. A striking demonstration of this point arose in the 1996 presidential election, when the Dole campaign's attack on alleged Democratic fund-raising scandals drove President Clinton's poll numbers into a temporary freefall. Political money would itself be an election issue; a candidate would have to decide which was worth more to her—the money, or the bragging rights to say that she did not take it.

Of course, the harms of political money cannot be expected to be entirely self-limiting. The deregulation outlined here is only partial; compelled disclosure avoids a regime of absolute laissez-faire. Even this partial deregulation might have unintended consequences. Some of the reformers' goals are widely shared and might require market intervention. For example, achieving adequate competitiveness in elections might require some public subsidies for challengers who can demonstrate certain threshold levels of support—floors but not ceilings for political expenditures. But the possibilities outlined here at least suggest some hesitation before deciding which way the split regime of *Buckley* ought to be resolved.

NOTES

1. 424 U.S. 1 (1976).
2. 518 U.S. 604 (1996).
3. 494 U.S. 692 (1990).

FROM WATERGATE TO KEN STARR

POTTER STEWART'S "OR OF THE PRESS"
A QUARTER CENTURY LATER

Vikram David Amar

In just seven law review pages, Potter Stewart's classic "Or of the Press" essay[1] provokes a lot of thought. Writing in 1974, mere months after the Watergate impeachment proceedings and the resignation of President Richard Nixon, Justice Stewart makes two related assertions: (1) that the so-called Press Clause of the First Amendment was designed to serve a government-checking function, by facilitating systematic scrutiny and criticism of the three branches of government to uncover and prevent abuse of government power; and (2) that because of this checking function, the Press Clause ought to be understood as a "structural" provision of the Constitution that gives the "organized press—the daily newspapers and other established news media—" some rights that the rest of us do not necessarily enjoy under the Speech Clause of the First Amendment.

Much has happened in the realm of the First Amendment, as well as in constitutional law and politics more generally, in the 25 years since Justice Stewart wrote "Or of the Press." Today seems a particularly fitting time to take a close second look at Justice Stewart's ideas, given the recently concluded impeachment affair that sparked so many people to draw parallels to and distinctions from the Watergate affair that inspired Stewart's reflections.

From *Hastings Law Journal* 50 (1999): 711–15. Reprinted with permission.

And so, with memories of Bill Clinton, Ken Starr, and Monica Lewinsky still quite fresh, I shall try in the next few paragraphs to sketch my own (admittedly tentative) thoughts on the two big points Justice Stewart advanced a quarter century ago.

Constitutional developments of recent decades have borne out the correctness and centrality of Justice Stewart's first big point—that criticism of government is fully protected expression that lies at the heart of the First Amendment. Of course, the notion that the First Amendment was designed to promote speech in order to check government abuse had been suggested even before 1974 and had often been thought to be an unstated but powerful explanation for many Court holdings, but lately the Court has been quite explicit. For example, in *Texas v. Johnson*,[2] Justice Brennan writing for the Court affirmed his remarks in *New York Times Co. v. Sullivan*[3] a quarter century earlier that "[i]t is as much [a citizen's] duty to criticize as it is the official's duty to administer. As Madison said, 'the censorial power is in the people over the Government, and not in the Government over the people.'" He then applied this teaching to Gregory Johnson's expressive (though perhaps distasteful) conduct by remarking: "Johnson was not, we add, prosecuted for the expression of just any idea; he was prosecuted for his expression of dissatisfaction with the policies of this country, expression situated at the core of our First Amendment values."

In his essay, Justice Stewart speculates that our Republic might have been able to survive even without the checking function facilitated by the First Amendment. I am not so sure. In any event, I—like Justice Stewart—am very thankful the Founders built into the Constitution the structural protection for government scrutiny and criticism. Indeed, I would have placed more faith in the safeguards the Founders set up than we have in recent years. Had we truly understood the power of the checking function Justice Stewart describes, we would have relied on the system in place that led to a satisfactory resolution of Watergate—a strong First Amendment coupled with congressional oversight and impeachment authority—instead of enacting the monstrous Independent Counsel Act that has haunted us for over a decade. In fact, those of us who favor letting the Act die this Summer do so in large part because we trust that the checking function protected by the First Amendment will enable Congress to police presidential abuse such that the costs (of all kinds) of an Independent Counsel are simply unnecessary to bear.

Potter Stewart's identification of the checking function is thus a deep constitutional insight. If Justice Stewart is to be faulted—and this brings me to Stewart's second main assertion—it is for not extending his insight far enough. Justice Stewart identifies the "structural" checking function underlying the Press Clause, but sees no such function underlying the Speech Clause under which the rest of the world lives. Thus, for Stewart, the "organized press" has special First Amendment rights the rest of us do not enjoy.

Let me explain briefly why I am disinclined to follow Justice Stewart here. To begin with, I see the checking function as animating the Speech Clause as well as the Press Clause, so that the press is entitled to no "special" protection....

*   *   *

...I reject his argument for special press protection for another reason as well—how could anyone (including the Founders) have ever given a coherent and principled definition of "the Press" itself? Justice Stewart offers one definition—"the daily newspapers and other established news media"—but his definition is immediately problematic. Would pamphleteers in 1787 qualify under his definition? Even if they would, surely radio and TV stations would not, given that they were not "established news media" in the eighteenth century. And yet Justice Stewart, later in his essay, includes electronic media within the zone of his protection—as well he must, given TV's role in the Watergate episode on which Justice Stewart relies. If "established" does not mean established at the time of the First Amendment, what does it mean? How would Justice Stewart feel about CNBC or MSNBC, the upstart and self-styled *anti*-establishment TV stations so important in pursuing the Lewinsky perjury matter? And even if one were to stretch "established" to include them, what of Matt Drudge, and his Internet-based "Drudge Report"—the real moving force behind public mobilization in Monicagate? Surely the Internet is not "established news media"—or is it? First Amendment jurisprudence frowns on laws whose vagueness creates substantial uncertainty about whose expressive conduct will be protected and whose will not. I don't think we ought to interpret the First Amendment itself so as to raise the ultimate vagueness issue.

NOTES

1. The essay was written and delivered in the fall of 1974. See Potter Stewart, "Or of the Press," Address at the Yale Law School Sesquicentennial Convocation (November 2, 1974), in *Hastings Law Journal* 26 (1975): 631.

2. 491 U.S. 397 (1989).

3. 376 U.S. 254 (1964).

APPENDIXES

CONSTITUTION OF THE UNITED STATES OF AMERICA

We, the people of the United States, in order to form a more perfect union, establish justice, insure domestic tranquility, provide for the common defense, promote the general welfare, and secure the blessings of liberty to ourselves and our posterity, do ordain and establish this Constitution for the United States of America.

ARTICLE I

Section I

1. All legislative powers herein granted shall be vested in a Congress of the United States, which shall consist of a Senate and House of Representatives.

Section II

1. The House of Representatives shall be composed of members chosen every second year by the people of the several States; and the electors in each

State shall have the qualifications requisite for electors of the most numerous branch of the State Legislature.

2. No person shall be a Representative who shall not have attained to the age of twenty-five years, and been seven years a citizen of the United States, and who shall not, when elected, be an inhabitant of that State in which he shall be chosen.

3. Representatives and direct taxes shall be apportioned among the several States which may be included within this Union, according to their respective numbers, which shall be determined by adding to the whole number of free persons, including those bound to service for a term of years, and excluding Indians not taxed, three-fifths of all other persons. The actual enumeration shall be made within three years after the first meeting of the Congress of the United States, and within every subsequent term of ten years, in such manner as they shall by law direct. The number of Representatives shall not exceed one for every thirty thousand, but each State shall have at least one Representative; and until such enumeration shall be made, the State of New Hampshire shall be entitled to choose three; Massachusetts, eight; Rhode Island and Providence Plantations, one; Connecticut, five; New York, six; New Jersey, four; Pennsylvania, eight; Delaware, one; Maryland, six; Virginia, ten; North Carolina, five; South Carolina, five, and Georgia, three.

4. When vacancies happen in the representation from any State, the executive authority thereof shall issue writs of election to fill such vacancies.

5. The House of Representatives shall choose their speaker and other officers; and shall have the sole power of impeachment.

Section III

1. The Senate of the United States shall be composed of two Senators from each State, chosen by the Legislature thereof for six years; and each Senator shall have one vote.

2. Immediately after they shall be assembled in consequence of the first election, they shall be divided as equally as may be into three classes. The

seats of the Senators of the first class shall be vacated at the expiration of the second year, of the second class at the expiration of the fourth year, and of the third class at the expiration of the sixth year, so that one third may be chosen every second year; and if vacancies happen by resignation, or otherwise, during the recess of the Legislature of any State, the executive thereof may make temporary appointments until the next meeting of the Legislature, which shall then fill such vacancies.

3. No person shall be a Senator who shall not have attained to the age of thirty years, and been nine years a citizen of the United States, and who shall not, when elected, be an inhabitant of that State for which he shall be chosen.

4. The Vice-President of the United States shall be President of the Senate, but shall have no vote unless they be equally divided.

5. The Senate shall choose their other officers, and also a President pro tempore, in the absence of the Vice-President, or when he shall exercise the office of President of the United States.

6. The Senate shall have the sole power to try all impeachments. When sitting for that purpose, they shall all be on oath or affirmation. When the President of the United States is tried, the chief-justice shall preside: and no person shall be convicted without the concurrence of two thirds of the members present.

7. Judgment in cases of impeachment shall not extend further than to removal from office, and disqualification to hold and enjoy any office of honor, trust, or profit under the United States; but the party convicted shall nevertheless be liable and subject to indictment, trial, judgment, and punishment, according to law.

Section IV

1. The times, places and manner of holding elections for Senators and Representatives shall be prescribed in each State by the Legislature thereof; but the Congress may at any time by law make of alter such regulations, except as to the place of choosing Senators.

Section V

1. Each House shall be the judge of the election, returns, and qualifications of its own members, and a majority of each shall constitute a quorum to do business; but a smaller number may adjourn from day to day, and may be authorized to compel the attendance of absent members, in such manner and under such penalties as each House may provide.

2. Each House may determine the rule of its proceedings, punish its members for disorderly behavior, and, with the concurrence of two thirds, expel a member.

3. Each House shall keep a journal of its proceedings, and from time to time publish the same, excepting such parts as may in their judgment require secrecy; and the yeas and nays of the members of either House on any questions shall, at the desire of one fifth of those present, be entered on the journal.

4. Neither House, during the session of Congress, shall, without the consent of the other, adjourn for more than three days, nor to any other place than that in which the two houses shall be sitting.

Section VI

1. The Senators and Representatives shall receive a compensation for their services, to be ascertained by law, and paid out of the treasury of the United States. They shall, in all cases, except treason, felony, and breach of the peace, be privileged from arrest during their attendance at the sessions of their respective houses, and in going to and returning from same; and for any speech or debate in either house, they shall not be questioned in any other place.

2. No Senator or Representative shall, during the time for which he was elected, be appointed to any civil office under the authority of the United States which shall have been created, or the emoluments whereof shall have been increased during such time; and no person holding any office under the United States shall be a member of either House during his continuance in office.

Section VII

1. All bills for raising revenue shall originate in the House of Representatives, but the Senate may propose or concur with amendments, as on other bills.

2. Every bill which shall have passed the House of Representatives and the Senate shall, before it become a law, be presented to the President of the United States; if he approve, he shall sign it, but if not, he shall return it, with his objections, to that House in which it shall have originated, who shall enter the objections at large on their journal, and proceed to reconsider it. If after such reconsideration two thirds of that House shall agree to pass the bill, it shall be sent, together with the objections, to the other House, by which it shall likewise be reconsidered; and if approved by two thirds of that House it shall become a law. But in all such cases the votes of both Houses shall be determined by yeas and nays, and the names of the persons voting for and against the bill shall be entered on the journal of each House respectively. If any bill shall not be returned by the President within ten days (Sundays excepted) after it shall have been presented to him, the same shall be a law in like manner as if he had signed it, unless the Congress by their adjournment, prevent its return; in which case it shall not be a law.

3. Every order, resolution, or vote to which the concurrence of the Senate and House of Representatives may be necessary (except on a question of adjournment) shall be presented to the President of the United States; and before the same shall take effect shall be approved by him, or being disapproved by him, shall be repassed by two thirds of the Senate and the House of Representatives, according to the rules and limitations prescribed in the case of a bill.

Section VIII

1. The Congress shall have power to lay and collect taxes, duties, imposts, and excises, to pay the debts and provide for the common defense and general welfare of the United States; but all duties, imposts, and excises shall be uniform throughout the United States.

2. To borrow money on the credit of the United States.

3. To regulate commerce with foreign nations, and among the several States, and with the Indian tribes.

4. To establish an uniform rule of naturalization and uniform laws on the subject of bankruptcies throughout the United States.

5. To coin money, regulate the value thereof, and of foreign coin, and fix the standard of weights and measures.

6. To provide for the punishment of counterfeiting the securities and current coin of the United States.

7. To establish post offices and post roads.

8. To promote the progress of science and useful arts, by securing for limited times to authors and inventors the exclusive rights to their respective writings and discoveries.

9. To constitute tribunals inferior to the Supreme Court.

10. To define and punish piracies and felonies committed on the high seas, and offenses against the law of nations.

11. To declare war, grant letters of marque and reprisal, and make rules concerning captures on land and water.

12. To raise and support armies, but no appropriation of money to that use shall be for a longer term than two years.

13. To provide and maintain a navy.

14. To make rules for the government and regulation of the land and naval forces.

15. To provide for calling forth the militia to execute the laws of the Union, suppress insurrections, and repel invasions.

16. To provide for organizing, arming, and disciplining the militia, and for governing such part of them as may be employed in the service of the United States, reserving to the States respectively the appointment of the officers, and the authority of training the militia according to the discipline prescribed by Congress.

17. To exercise exclusive legislation in all cases whatsoever over such district (not exceeding ten miles square) as may, by cession of particular States and the acceptance of Congress, become the seat of Government of the United States, and to exercise like authority over all places purchased by the consent of the Legislature of the State in which the same shall be, for the erection of forts, magazines, arsenals, dry docks, and other needful buildings.

18. To make all laws which shall be necessary and proper for carrying into execution the foregoing powers, and all other powers vested by this Constitution in the Government of the United States, or in any department or officer thereof.

Section IX

1. The migration or importation of such persons as any of the States now existing shall think proper to admit shall not be prohibited by the Congress prior to the year one thousand eight hundred and eight, but a tax or duty may be imposed on such importation, not exceeding ten dollars for each person.

2. The privilege of the writ of habeas corpus shall not be suspended, unless when in cases of rebellion or invasion the public safety may require it.

3. No bill of attainder or ex post facto law shall be passed.

4. No capitation or other direct tax shall be laid, unless in proportion to the census or enumeration hereinbefore directed to be taken.

5. No tax or duty shall be laid on articles exported from any State.

6. No preference shall be given by any regulation of commerce or revenue to the ports of one State over those of another, nor shall vessels bound to or from one State be obliged to enter, clear, or pay duties in another.

7. No money shall be drawn from the Treasury but in consequence of appropriations made by law; and a regular statement and account of the receipts and expenditures of all public money shall be published from time to time.

8. No title of nobility shall be granted by the United States. And no person holding any office of profit or trust under them shall, without the consent of the Congress, accept of any present, emolument, office, or title of any kind whatever from any king, prince, or foreign state.

Section X

1. No state shall enter into any treaty, alliance, or confederation, grant letters of marque and reprisal, coin money, emit bills of credit, make anything but gold and silver coin a tender in payment of debts, pass any bill of attainder, ex post facto law, or law impairing the obligation of contracts, or grant any title of nobility.

2. No State shall, without the consent of the Congress, lay any impost or duties on imports or exports, except what may be absolutely necessary for executing its inspection laws, and the net produce of all duties and imposts, laid by any State on imports or exports, shall be for the use of the Treasury of the United States; and all such laws shall be subject to the revision and control of the Congress.

3. No State shall, without the consent of Congress, lay any duty of tonnage, keep troops or ships of war in time of peace, enter into any agreement or compact with another State, or with a foreign power, or engage in war, unless actually invaded, or in such imminent danger as will not admit of delay.

ARTICLE II

Section I

1. The Executive power shall be vested in a President of the United States of America. He shall hold his office during the term of four years, and, together with the Vice-President, chosen for the same term, be elected as follows:

2. Each State shall appoint, in such manner as the Legislature thereof may direct, a number of electors, equal to the whole number of Senators and Representatives to which the State may be entitled in the Congress; but no Senator or Representative or person holding an office of trust or profit under the United States shall be appointed an elector.

3. [The electors shall meet in their respective States and vote by ballot for two persons, of whom one at least shall not be an inhabitant of the same State with themselves. And they shall make a list of all the persons voted for, and of the number of votes for each, which list they shall sign and certify and transmit, sealed, to the seat of the government of the United States, directed to the President of the Senate. The President of the Senate shall, in the presence of the Senate and House of Representatives, open all the certificates, and the votes shall then be counted. The person having the greatest number of votes shall be the President, if such number be a majority of the whole number of electors appointed, and if there be more than one who have such majority, and have an equal number of votes, then the House of Representatives shall immediately choose by ballot one of them for President; and if no person have a majority, then from the five highest on the list the said House shall in like manner choose the President. But in choosing the President, the vote shall be taken by States, the representation from each State having one vote. A quorum, for this purpose, shall consist of a member or members from two thirds of the States, and a majority of all the States shall be necessary to a choice. In every case, after the choice of the President, the person having the greatest number of votes of the electors shall be the Vice-President. But if there should remain two or more who have equal votes, the Senate shall choose from them by ballot the Vice-President.]*

---

*This clause is superseded by Article XII.

4. The Congress may determine the time of choosing the electors and the day on which they shall give their votes, which day shall be the same throughout the United States.

5. No person except a natural born citizen, or a citizen of the United States at the time of the adoption of this Constitution, shall be eligible to the office of President; neither shall any person be eligible to that office who shall not have attained to the age of thirty-five years and been fourteen years a resident within the United States.

6. In case of the removal of the President from office, or of his death, resignation, or inability to discharge the powers and duties of the said office, the same shall devolve on the Vice-President, and the Congress may by law provide for the case of removal, death, resignation, or inability, both of the President and Vice-President, declaring what officer shall then act as President, and such officer shall act accordingly until the disability be removed or a President shall be elected.

7. The President shall, at stated times, receive for his services a compensation, which shall neither be increased nor diminished during the period for which he shall have been elected, and he shall not receive within that period any other emolument from the United States, or any of them.

8. Before he enter on the execution of his office he shall take the following oath or affirmation: "I do solemnly swear (or affirm) that I will faithfully execute the office of President of the United States, and will, to the best of my ability, preserve, protect, and defend the Constitution of the United States."

Section II

1. The President shall be Commander-in-Chief of the Army and Navy of the United States, and of the militia of the several States when called into the actual service of the United States; he may require the opinion, in writing, of the principal officer in each of the executive departments upon any subject relating to the duties of their respective offices, and he shall have power to grant reprieves and pardons for offenses against the United States except in cases of impeachment.

2. He shall have power, by and with the advice and consent of the Senate, to make treaties, provided two thirds of the Senators present concur; and he shall nominate, and by and with the advice and consent of the Senate shall appoint ambassadors, other public ministers and consuls, judges of the Supreme Court, and all other officers of the United States whose appointments are not herein otherwise provided for, and which shall be established by law; but the Congress may by law vest the appointment of such inferior officers as they think proper in the President alone, in the courts of law, or in the heads of departments.

3. The President shall have power to fill up all vacancies that may happen during the recess of the Senate by granting commissions, which shall expire at the end of their next session.

Section III

He shall from time to time give to the Congress information of the state of the Union, and recommend to their consideration such measure as he shall judge necessary and expedient; he may, on extraordinary occasions, convene both Houses, or either of them, and in case of disagreement between them with respect to the time of adjournment, he may adjourn them to such time as he shall think proper; he shall receive ambassadors and other public ministers; he shall take care that the laws be faithfully executed, and shall commission all the officers of the United States.

Section IV

The President, Vice-President, and all civil officers of the United States shall be removed from office on impeachment for and conviction of treason, bribery, or other high crimes and misdemeanors.

ARTICLE III

Section I

The judicial power of the United States shall be vested in one Supreme Court, and in such inferior courts as the Congress may from time to time ordain and establish. The judges, both of the Supreme and inferior courts, shall hold their offices during good behavior, and shall at stated times receive for their services a compensation which shall not be diminished during their continuance in office.

Section II

1. The judicial power shall extend to all cases in law and equity arising under this Constitution, the laws of the United States, and treaties made, or which shall be made, under their authority; to all cases affecting ambassadors, other public ministers, and consuls; to all cases of admiralty and maritime jurisdiction; to controversies to which the United States shall be a party; to controversies between two or more States, between a State and citizens of another State, between citizens of different States, between citizens of the same State claiming lands under grants of different States, and between a State, or the citizens thereof, and foreign States, citizens, or subjects.

2. In all cases affecting ambassadors, other public ministers, and consuls, and those in which a State shall be party, the Supreme Court shall have original jurisdiction. In all the other cases before mentioned the Supreme Court shall have appellate jurisdiction both as to law and fact, with such exceptions and under such regulations as the Congress shall make.

3. The trial of all crimes, except in cases of impeachment, shall be by jury, and such trial shall be held in the State where the said crimes shall have been committed; but when not committed within any State the trial shall be at such place or places as the Congress may by law have directed.

Section III

1. Treason against the United States shall consist only in levying war against them, or in adhering to their enemies, giving them aid and comfort. No person shall be convicted of treason unless on the testimony of two witnesses to the same overt act, or on confession in open court.

2. The Congress shall have power to declare the punishment of treason, but no attainder of treason shall work corruption of blood or forfeiture except during the life of the person attained.

Article IV

Section I

Full faith and credit shall be given in each State to the public acts, records, and judicial preceedings of every other State. And the Congress may by general laws prescribe the manner in which such acts, records and proceedings shall be proved, and the effect thereof.

Section II

1. The citizens of each State shall be entitled to all privileges and immunities of citizens in the several States.

2. A person charged in any State with treason, felony, or other crime, who shall flee from justice, and be found in another State, shall on demand of the Executive authority of the State from which he fled, be delivered up, to be removed to the State having jurisdiction of the crime.

3. No person held to service or labor in one State, under the laws thereof, escaping into another shall, in consequence of any law or regulation therein, be discharged from such service or labor, but shall be delivered up on claim of the party to whom such service or labor may be due.

Section III

1. New States may be admitted by the Congress into this Union; but no new State shall be formed or erected within the jurisdiction of any other State, nor any State be formed by the junction of two or more States, or parts of States, without the consent of the Legislatures of the States concerned, as well as of the Congress.

2. The Congress shall have power to dispose of and make all needful rules and regulations respecting the territory or other property belonging to the United States; and nothing in this Constitution shall be so construed as to prejudice any claims of the United States, or of any particular State.

Section IV

The United States shall guarantee to every State in this Union a republican form of government, and shall protect each of them against invasion, and, on application of the Legislature, or of the Executive (when the Legislature cannot be convened), against domestic violence.

ARTICLE V

The Congress, whenever two thirds of both Houses shall deem it necessary, shall propose amendments to this Constitution, or, on the application of the Legislatures of two thirds of the several States, shall call a convention for proposing amendments, which, in either case, shall be valid to all intents and purposes, as part of this Constitution, when ratified by the Legislatures of three fourths of the several States, or by conventions in three fourths thereof, as the one or the other mode of ratification may be proposed by the Congress; provided that no amendment which may be made prior to the year one thousand eight hundred and eight shall in any manner affect the first and fourth clauses in the Ninth Section of the First Article; and that no State, without its consent, shall be deprived of its equal suffrage in the Senate.

ARTICLE VI

1. All debts contracted and engagements entered into before the adoption of this Constitution shall be as valid against the United States under this Constitution as under the Confederation.

2. This Constitution and the laws of the United States which shall be made in pursuance thereof and all treaties made, or which shall be made, under the authority of the United States, shall be the supreme law of the land, and the judges in every State shall be bound thereby, anything in the Constitution of laws of any State to the contrary notwithstanding.

3. The Senators and Representatives before mentioned, and the members of the several State Legislatures, and all executive and judicial officers, both of the United States and of the several States, shall be bound by oath or affirmation to support this Constitution; but no religious test shall ever be

required as a qualification to any office or public trust under the United States.

ARTICLE VII

The ratification of the Conventions of nine States shall be sufficient for the establishment of this Constitution between the States so ratifying the same.

THE AMENDMENTS
TO THE CONSTITUTION*

The Conventions of a number of the States having, at the time of adopting the Constitution, expressed a desire, in order to prevent misconstruction or abuse of its powers, that further declaratory and restrictive clauses should be added, and as extending the ground of public confidence in the Government will best insure the beneficent ends of its institution;

Resolved, by the Senate and House of Representatives of the United States of America, in Congress assembled, two-thirds of both Houses concurring, that the following articles be proposed to the Legislatures of the several States, as amendments to the Constitution of the United States; all or any of which articles, when ratified by three-fourths of the said Legislatures, to be valid to all intents and purposes as part of the said Constitution, namely:

Amendment I

Congress shall make no law respecting an establishment of religion, or prohibiting the free exercise thereof; or abridging the freedom of speech, or of the press; or the right of the people peaceably to assemble, and to petition the Government for a redress of grievances.

---

*The Bill of Rights consists of the first ten amendments to the Constitution.

AMENDMENT II

A well regulated Militia, being necessary to the security of a free State, the right of the people to keep and bear Arms, shall not be infringed.

AMENDMENT III

No Soldier shall, in time of peace be quartered in any house, without the consent of the Owner, nor in time of war, but in a manner to be prescribed by law.

AMENDMENT IV

The right of the people to be secure in their persons, houses, papers, and effects, against unreasonable searches and seizures, shall not be violated, and no Warrants shall issue, but upon probable cause, supported by Oath or affirmation, and particularly describing the place to be searched, and the persons or things to be seized.

AMENDMENT V

No person shall be held to answer for a capital, or otherwise infamous crime, unless on a presentment or indictment of a Grand Jury, except in cases arising in the land or naval forces, or in the Militia, when in actual service in time of War or public danger; nor shall any person be subject for the same offense to be twice put in jeopardy of life or limb; nor shall be compelled in any criminal case to be a witness against himself, nor be deprived of life, liberty, or property, without due process of law; nor shall private property be taken for public use, without just compensation.

AMENDMENT VI

In all criminal prosecutions, the accused shall enjoy the right to a speedy and public trial, by an impartial jury of the State and district wherein the crime shall have been committed, which district shall have been previously ascertained by law, and to be informed of the nature and cause of the accusation; to be confronted with the witnesses against him; to have compulsory process for obtaining witnesses in his favor, and to have the Assistance of Counsel for his defence.

AMENDMENT VII

In Suits at common law, where the value in controversy shall exceed twenty dollars, the right of trial by jury shall be preserved, and no fact tried by a jury, shall be otherwise re-examined in any Court of the United States, than according to the rules of the common law.

AMENDMENT VIII

Excessive bail shall not be required, nor excessive fines imposed, nor cruel and unusual punishments inflicted.

AMENDMENT IX

The enumeration in the Constitution, of certain rights, shall not be construed to deny or disparage others retained by the people.

AMENDMENT X

The powers not delegated to the United States by the Constitution, nor prohibited by it to the States, are reserved to the States respectively, or to the people.

AMENDMENT XI

The Judicial power of the United States shall not be construed to extend to any suit in law or equity, commenced or prosecuted against one of the United States by Citizens of another State, or by Citizens or Subjects of any Foreign State.

AMENDMENT XII

The Electors shall meet in their respective states, and vote by ballot for President and Vice-President, one of whom, at least, shall not be an inhabitant of the same state with themselves; they shall name in their ballots the person voted for as President, and in distinct ballots the person voted for as Vice-President, and they shall make distinct lists of all persons voted for as President, and of all persons voted for as Vice-President and of the number of votes for each, which lists they shall sign and certify, and transmit sealed to the seat of the government of the United States, directed to the President of the Senate; The President of the Senate shall, in the presence of the Senate and House of Representatives, open all the certificates and the votes shall then be counted; The person having the greatest Number of votes for President, shall be the President, if such number be a majority of the whole number of Electors appointed; and if no person have such majority, then from the persons having the highest numbers not exceeding three on the list of those voted for as President, the House of Representatives shall choose immediately, by ballot, the President. But in choosing the President, the votes shall be taken by states, the representation from each state having one vote; a quorum for this purpose shall consist of a member or members from two-thirds of the states, and a majority of all the states shall be necessary to a choice. And if the House of Representatives shall not choose a President whenever the right of choice shall devolve upon them, before the fourth day of March next following, then the Vice-President shall act as President, as in the case of the death or other constitutional disability of the President. The person having the greatest number of votes as Vice-President, shall be the Vice-President, if such number be a majority of the whole number of Electors appointed, and if no person have a majority, then from the two highest numbers on the list, the Senate shall choose the Vice-President; a quorum for the purpose shall consist of two-thirds of the whole number of Senators, and a majority of the whole number shall be necessary to a choice. But no person constitutionally ineligible to the office of President shall be eligible to that of Vice-President of the United States.

Amendment XIII

1. Neither slavery nor involuntary servitude, except as a punishment for crime whereof the party shall have been duly convicted, shall exist within the United States, or any place subject to their jurisdiction.

2. Congress shall have power to enforce this article by appropriate legislation.

Amendment XIV

1. All persons born or naturalized in the United States, and subject to the jurisdiction thereof, are citizens of the United States and of the State wherein they reside. No State shall make or enforce any law which shall abridge the privileges or immunities of citizens of the United States; nor shall any State deprive any person of life, liberty, or property, without due process of law; nor deny to any person within its jurisdiction the equal protection of the laws.

2. Representatives shall be apportioned among the several States according to their respective numbers, counting the whole number of persons in each State, excluding Indians not taxed. But when the right to vote at any election for the choice of electors for President and Vice-President of the United States, Representatives in Congress, the Executive and Judicial officers of a State, or the members of the Legislature thereof, is denied to any of the male inhabitants of such State, being twenty-one years of age, and citizens of the United States, or in any way abridged, except for participation in rebellion, or other crime, the basis of representation therein shall be reduced in the proportion which the number of such male citizens shall bear to the whole number of male citizens twenty-one years of age in such State.

3. No person shall be a Senator or Representative in Congress, or elector of President and Vice-President, or hold any office, civil or military, under the United States, or under any State, who, having previously taken an oath, as a member of Congress, or as an officer of the United States, or as a member of any State legislature, or as an executive or judicial officer of any State, to support the Constitution of the United States, shall have engaged in insurrection or rebellion against the same, or given aid or comfort to the enemies thereof. But Congress may by a vote of two-thirds of each House, remove such disability.

4. The validity of the public debt of the United States, authorized by law, including debts incurred for payment of pensions and bounties for services in suppressing insurrection or rebellion, shall not be questioned. But neither the United States nor any State shall assume or pay any debt or obligation incurred in aid of insurrection or rebellion against the United States, or any claim for the loss or emancipation of any slave; but all such debts, obligations and claims shall be held illegal and void.

5. The Congress shall have power to enforce, by appropriate legislation, the provisions of this article.

AMENDMENT XV

1. The right of citizens of the United States to vote shall not be denied or abridged by the United States or by any State on account of race, color, or previous condition of servitude.

2. The Congress shall have power to enforce this article by appropriate legislation.

AMENDMENT XVI

The Congress shall have power to lay and collect taxes on incomes, from whatever source derived, without apportionment among the several States, and without regard to any census or enumeration.

AMENDMENT XVII

The Senate of the United States shall be composed of two Senators from each State, elected by the people thereof, for six years; and each Senator shall have one vote. The electors in each State shall have the qualifications requisite for electors of the most numerous branch of the State legislatures. When vacancies happen in the representation of any State in the Senate, the executive authority of such State shall issue writs of election to fill such vacancies: Provided, That the legislature of any State may empower the executive thereof to make temporary appointments until the people fill the vacancies by election as the legislature may direct. This amendment shall not be so construed as to affect the election or term of any Senator chosen before it becomes valid as part of the Constitution.

AMENDMENT XVIII

1. After one year from the ratification of this article the manufacture, sale, or transportation of intoxicating liquors within, the importation thereof into, or the exportation thereof from the United States and all territory subject to the jurisdiction thereof for beverage purposes is hereby prohibited.

2. The Congress and the several States shall have concurrent power to enforce this article by appropriate legislation.

3. This article shall be inoperative unless it shall have been ratified as an

amendment to the Constitution by the legislatures of the several States, as provided in the Constitution, within seven years from the date of the submission hereof to the States by the Congress.

AMENDMENT XIX

The right of citizens of the United States to vote shall not be denied or abridged by the United States or by any State on account of sex. Congress shall have power to enforce this article by appropriate legislation.

AMENDMENT XX

1. The terms of the President and Vice President shall end at noon on the 20th day of January, and the terms of Senators and Representatives at noon on the 3d day of January, of the years in which such terms would have ended if this article had not been ratified; and the terms of their successors shall then begin.

2. The Congress shall assemble at least once in every year, and such meeting shall begin at noon on the 3d day of January, unless they shall by law appoint a different day.

3. If, at the time fixed for the beginning of the term of the President, the President elect shall have died, the Vice President elect shall become President. If a President shall not have been chosen before the time fixed for the beginning of his term, or if the President elect shall have failed to qualify, then the Vice President elect shall act as President until a President shall have qualified; and the Congress may by law provide for the case wherein neither a President elect nor a Vice President elect shall have qualified, declaring who shall then act as President, or the manner in which one who is to act shall be selected, and such person shall act accordingly until a President or Vice President shall have qualified.

4. The Congress may by law provide for the case of the death of any of the persons from whom the House of Representatives may choose a President whenever the right of choice shall have devolved upon them, and for the case of the death of any of the persons from whom the Senate may choose a Vice President whenever the right of choice shall have devolved upon them.

5. Sections 1 and 2 shall take effect on the 15th day of October following the ratification of this article.

6. This article shall be inoperative unless it shall have been ratified as an amendment to the Constitution by the legislatures of three-fourths of the several States within seven years from the date of its submission.

AMENDMENT XXI

1. The eighteenth article of amendment to the Constitution of the United States is hereby repealed.

2. The transportation or importation into any State, Territory, or possession of the United States for delivery or use therein of intoxicating liquors, in violation of the laws thereof, is hereby prohibited.

3. The article shall be inoperative unless it shall have been ratified as an amendment to the Constitution by conventions in the several States, as provided in the Constitution, within seven years from the date of the submission hereof to the States by the Congress.

AMENDMENT XXII

1. No person shall be elected to the office of the President more than twice, and no person who has held the office of President, or acted as President, for more than two years of a term to which some other person was elected President shall be elected to the office of the President more than once. But this Article shall not apply to any person holding the office of President, when this Article was proposed by the Congress, and shall not prevent any person who may be holding the office of President, or acting as President, during the term within which this Article becomes operative from holding the office of President or acting as President during the remainder of such term.

2. This article shall be inoperative unless it shall have been ratified as an amendment to the Constitution by the legislatures of three-fourths of the several States within seven years from the date of its submission to the States by the Congress.

AMENDMENT XXIII

1. The District constituting the seat of Government of the United States shall appoint in such manner as the Congress may direct: A number of electors of President and Vice President equal to the whole number of Senators

and Representatives in Congress to which the District would be entitled if it were a State, but in no event more than the least populous State; they shall be in addition to those appointed by the States, but they shall be considered, for the purposes of the election of President and Vice President, to be electors appointed by a State; and they shall meet in the District and perform such duties as provided by the twelfth article of amendment.

2. The Congress shall have power to enforce this article by appropriate legislation.

AMENDMENT XXIV

1. The right of citizens of the United States to vote in any primary or other election for President or Vice President, for electors for President or Vice President, or for Senator or Representative in Congress, shall not be denied or abridged by the United States or any State by reason of failure to pay any poll tax or other tax.

2. The Congress shall have power to enforce this article by appropriate legislation.

AMENDMENT XXV

1. In case of the removal of the President from office or of his death or resignation, the Vice President shall become President.

2. Whenever there is a vacancy in the office of the Vice President, the President shall nominate a Vice President who shall take office upon confirmation by a majority vote of both Houses of Congress.

3. Whenever the President transmits to the President pro tempore of the Senate and the Speaker of the House of Representatives his written declaration that he is unable to discharge the powers and duties of his office, and until he transmits to them a written declaration to the contrary, such powers and duties shall be discharged by the Vice President as Acting President.

4. Whenever the Vice President and a majority of either the principal officers of the executive departments or of such other body as Congress may by law provide, transmit to the President pro tempore of the Senate and the Speaker of the House of Representatives their written declaration that the President is unable to discharge the powers and duties of his office, the Vice President shall immediately assume the powers and duties of the office as

Acting President. Thereafter, when the President transmits to the President pro tempore of the Senate and the Speaker of the House of Representatives his written declaration that no inability exists, he shall resume the powers and duties of his office unless the Vice President and a majority of either the principal officers of the executive department or of such other body as Congress may by law provide, transmit within four days to the President pro tempore of the Senate and the Speaker of the House of Representatives their written declaration that the President is unable to discharge the powers and duties of his office. Thereupon Congress shall decide the issue, assembling within forty eight hours for that purpose if not in session. If the Congress, within twenty one days after receipt of the latter written declaration, or, if Congress is not in session, within twenty one days after Congress is required to assemble, determines by two thirds vote of both Houses that the President is unable to discharge the powers and duties of his office, the Vice President shall continue to discharge the same as Acting President; otherwise, the President shall resume the powers and duties of his office.

AMENDMENT XXVI

1. The right of citizens of the United States, who are eighteen years of age or older, to vote shall not be denied or abridged by the United States or by any State on account of age.
2. The Congress shall have power to enforce this article by appropriate legislation.

AMENDMENT XXVII

No law, varying the compensation for the services of the Senators and Representatives, shall take effect, until an election of Representatives shall have intervened.